IT'S ALL THE RAGE

Other Books by Wendy Kaminer

I'm Dysfunctional, You're Dysfunctional
A Fearful Freedom
Women Volunteering

IT'S ALL THE RAGE

Crime and Culture

WENDY KAMINER

 Addison-Wesley Publishing Company

Reading, Massachusetts   Menlo Park, California   New York
Don Mills, Ontario   Wokingham, England   Amsterdam   Bonn
Sydney   Singapore   Tokyo   Madrid   San Juan
Paris   Seoul   Milan   Mexico City   Taipei

Author's Note

In general, I try to use gender neutral plurals or arbitrarily choose between the masculine and feminine pronouns, to avoid the clunkiness of "he or she." In this book, I occasionally used masculine pronouns (to the dismay of my copy editor), because the great majority of people arrested, prosecuted, and convicted for violent crimes, particularly capital crimes, are male.

Many of the designations used by manufacturers and sellers to distinguish their products are claimed as trademarks. Where those designations appear in this book and Addison-Wesley was aware of a trademark claim, the designations have been printed in initial capital letters.

Library of Congress Cataloging-in-Publication Data

Kaminer, Wendy.
    It's all the rage : crime and culture / Wendy Kaminer.
        p.   cm.
    Includes bibliographical references (p.   ) and index.
    ISBN 0-201-62274-2
    1. Violent crimes—United States—Public opinion.   2. Capital
punishment—United States—Public opinion.   3. Criminal
justice, Administration of—United States—Public opinion.   4.
Public opinion—United States.   I. Title.
HV6789.K36   1995
364.1'5'0973—dc20   94-23639
                                                                 CIP

Copyright © 1995 by Wendy Kaminer

Portions of this book appeared, in somewhat different form, in *The Atlantic Monthly* and *The San Francisco Examiner*.

Jacket design by David High
Text design by Diane Levy
Set in 10.5-point Meridien by Weimer Graphics, Inc.

1 2 3 4 5 6 7 8 9 10-DOH-9998979695
First printing, March 1995

To Fritz Gold

Contents

Acknowledgments

Radcliffe College continues to provide me with an office and a lot of good company, for which I continue to be grateful. I'm indebted as well to the Guggenheim Foundation for its financial support. Thanks to my editor, Nancy Miller, and my agent, Esther Newberg, for their patience and good sense and to Frank Hartmann at the Kennedy School of Government for including me in a stimulating series of discussions. Thanks to David Kennedy, Nancy Rosenblum, and Abbe Smith for helping me think things through (Abbe gets extra credit for coming up with the title to this book), and to my invaluable research assistant, Francisca Mok, for helping me get it together. Thanks to Katiti Kirondi and John Flitter for—whatever.

Introduction

When I was a senior in high school I fantasized about murdering my drivers ed teacher. He was a violent, sadistic man, a gym teacher known for humiliating boys in his classes who were clumsy, weak, or slow. He taught girls how to drive by bellowing at them until they broke down and cried. "Once you cry," my classmates assured me, "he'll leave you alone."

I never cried. When I got behind the wheel of the car and he started yelling at me, I'd turn into stone. I always obeyed him but never engaged. I never looked at him and never spoke to him unless he asked me a direct question. I never answered with any emotion. For four months, he battered at me, but I was a wall. It drove him nuts, which was worth my F in drivers ed. One day he said I was the "coldest, hardest bitch" he'd ever seen. He never knew my white-hot rage. When one of the boys was driving (I was the only girl in the car), I'd sit in the back seat and stare at his short, thick neck and imagine plunging a knife into it.

I never felt guilty about my fantasy. I felt entitled to it, precisely because it was only a fantasy, never a temptation. Murder wasn't part of high school life in 1967. Perhaps my fantasy might frighten me a little today; perhaps it might seem possible.

It's easy to imagine the headline: "Teacher Slain by Female Student." It's easy to imagine the story: "A 17-year-old high school senior shot and killed her drivers ed teacher, claiming he'd subjected her to relentless verbal abuse. Her attorney is expected to offer a defense of battered student syndrome."

How should we resolve a case like this? Is it a justifiable homicide, considering the "abuse and intimidation" suffered by the student? Should we declare her not guilty because she was traumatized? How do we determine whether or not her experience qualifies as traumatic? Must we decide whether she had good reason to be traumatized, just as we decide in self-defense cases whether a defendant had good reason to fear for her life (or, as we decide in sexual harassment cases, that a plaintiff had good reason to feel harassed)?

Do we posit different standards of reasonableness for males and females, assuming that females are naturally more easily traumatized and intimidated than males? Should the outcome of my hypothetical case differ if the shooter were a seventeen-year-old boy? In 1977, the Supreme Court in Washington state issued a landmark decision (*State v. Wanrow*) holding that in a self-defense case, the reasonableness of a woman's perception of imminent harm should be judged partly in the context of pervasive, historic discrimination against women. Should that decision be extended to cases involving racial or ethnic minorities or homosexuals? Should standards of reasonableness in criminal trials vary according to race, ethnicity, gender, and sexual orientation?

Or, should we dispense with objective standards or reasonableness and let subjectivity reign, allowing the standard in every case to be dictated by the defendant's state of mind? Should we say, "If a woman feels threatened, she is threatened. If a woman feels harassed, she is harassed"? Some feminists say, "If a woman feels raped, she's been raped." A woman's feelings are her reality, a therapist might point out. Should a defendant's feelings be reality under law and the facts of the case in a courtroom as well as a therapist's office?

Drawing the line between law and therapy is one of the philosophical challenges to criminal justice today. Whether or how popular notions of victimhood derived from the personal development tradition should affect assessments of guilt and innocence was one of the primary questions pondered in the wake of the Bobbitt and Menendez trials of 1993–94. My own view, in brief, is that in many cases excuses for criminal behavior should affect the sentence more than the verdict. Excuses often mitigate guilt but don't obliterate it. Yet, relatively little attention has been paid to this question of how a defendant's personal history of victimization should affect sentencing, once guilt has been determined, particularly in homicide cases. Who deserves to spend twenty-five years in prison, and who deserves a life sentence? Who deserves to die?

Who can be trusted to answer that last question? I've never felt competent or entitled to mete out death to anyone, in cold blood, regardless of the crime, although I can imagine sentencing someone to a lifelong prison term. I've always wondered at the relative ease with which societies assume the power to execute criminal offenders, and it was, in part, my sense of wonder at the death penalty that inspired this book.

I have always opposed the death penalty, because it is unnecessary (we can incapacitate people by incarcerating them), and because it is not fairly applied, in general, and never will be, given the vagaries of the criminal justice system as well as its inherent biases. My own brief tenure as a public defender in the Brooklyn criminal courts in the late 1970s only confirmed my suspicion that the system can't be trusted to prosecute larcenies sensibly, much less select people to die.

Skepticism about the system hardly puts me in the minority. Mistrust of the criminal courts is as pervasive as mistrust of government bureaucracies in general. There's a great deal of cognitive dissonance in public support for the death penalty. People don't trust the Postal Service to deliver the mail, or the IRS to enforce the tax code with fairness and good sense; they don't trust the Parking Violations Bureau to process traffic tickets or refrain from towing cars for no good reason. Yet, out of fear or fury or wishful thinking about deterrence, they trust the criminal justice system with the power to put people to death. What is perhaps most notable about the death penalty debate is its irrationality. It is a case study in demagoguery.

We ought to know better. So much ink has been spilled over the death penalty and so much airtime spent. Capital punishment has been the subject of more books, law review articles, radio and TV talk shows, op ed pieces, and dinner table debates than anyone can possibly enumerate. There is more information about the death penalty than anyone can possibly absorb. Social scientists, legal scholars, litigators, historians, human rights activists, journalists, and philosophers have collected enough data and formulated enough arguments and ideas about the theory, practice, and morality of capital punishment to rationalize our debates and occupy us intellectually for years.

I've felt challenged and sometimes intimidated by the wealth of research and commentary by people who've spent years studying the death penalty and litigating capital cases. Still, I found the nerve to write this book, which focuses partly on the death penalty, because knowledge about it is not widely shared.

Our knowledge about the death penalty is striking partly because its richness is matched by its irrelevance to popular opinion. More than three-quarters of all Americans are said to favor the death penalty, in the absence of a life without parole alternative, but relatively few know very much about it—how it is applied and to whom, what it costs and accomplishes. Public perceptions about the death penalty—that it is cheaper to execute people than imprison them for life, that appeals in capital cases are a great burden to the courts—are almost invariably wrong. What ought to be among our most informed policy debates is one of our most ignorant, driven not by knowledge but by anger, desperation, and fear.

I set out to write about the capital punishment debate as much as I set out to write about capital punishment. I wanted to focus on the resurgent demand for the death penalty and to explore underlying notions of individual accountability, self-control, moral agency, victimhood, and justice.

I was most struck by the contradictions between the lenient standards of personal responsibility that apply in the recovery movement (which teaches us that practically everyone is the hapless victim of a dysfunctional family) and the harsh standards applied to people on death row, whose histories of addiction and abuse might overwhelm even the talk shows. If you argue for leniency in a typical, uncelebrated criminal case, pointing out that the defendant suffered abuse in childhood or that the crime resulted from some post-traumatic stress disorder, you're likely to be dismissed as a bleeding heart liberal. "We're tired of Twinkie defenses. No one takes responsibility for himself anymore," people say. Meanwhile, millions of Americans are complaining about their own histories of addiction and abuse, refusing to take responsibility for their own bad behaviors. That the occasional high-profile defendant—Lorena Bobbitt, Erik or Lyle Menendez—manages to exploit the recovery movement's leniency for self-proclaimed victims, while the vast majority of people arrested evoke little sympathy and lots of demands for swift, strict sentencing only underscores our confusion about personal responsibility and people's capacity for redemption.

The more I studied the death penalty, the more I thought about notions of agency and accountability that underlie our ideas of criminal justice. A critique of the death penalty in America in the 1990s seemed incomplete without a critique of cultural and political responses to violent crime, which took on renewed urgency during the two years I worked on this book. Popular solutions to the crime problem, such as "three time loser" laws, imposing life sentences on three time felons, reflect the same volatile mix of fear, fury, and wishful thinking about simple solutions to violent crime that drives demands for the death penalty.

Criminal justice debates are strikingly irrational, as are many criminal justice policies. Congress and state legislatures enacted new mandatory minimum sentencing laws during the 1980s not because they were effective in controlling crime—perhaps their primary effect was to crowd prisons with nonviolent, low-level drug offenders—but because they were effective rhetorically. Like capital punishment, mandatory minimum sentencing became a symbol for toughness on crime. Meanwhile, standards of toughness became strikingly harsh and hard to satisfy with anything less than extremism. In 1994, the Democratic Congress and the President embraced the death penalty, three time loser laws, and other mandatory minimum sentencing schemes, and allocated substantial new funding for prisons and police, and still they weren't seen as tough enough. (In part, Republicans succeeded in focusing public attention on the Democrats' continued, if reduced, commitment to crime prevention, not their increased support for harsh punishment.) What will satisfy public fury over violent crime and the concomitant desire for authority? Corporal punishment, one time loser laws, and the mandatory mingling of thirteen-year-old offenders with adults, as well as the virtual elimination of prevention programs, have all been proposed.

But if capital punishment and long mandatory prison terms for a wide range of offenders are symbols of toughness on crime, the toughness itself is more symbolic than real. The public seems to judge politicians according to what they say about crime, not what they accomplish. The utter failure of the Reagan administration's antidrug policies and harsh sentencing laws to stem drug traffic and use in the inner cities and to prevent gun violence, particularly among juveniles, did not tarnish Reagan's image as a cynosure on law and order. It was almost as if the public suspected subliminally what seasoned law enforcement professionals, policymakers, and community activists know—that there are no sweeping solutions to the problem of violent crime. Any progress we make will be discrete and incremental; only the symbols have sweep.

Some people confront this frightening reality creatively, by fashioning small-scale solutions, engaging in grass-roots activity aimed at redeeming their neighborhoods, focusing on individualized, localized change or lobbying for particular programs and reforms. Others retreat to a fantasy world in which political posturing becomes a substitute for political action. Sometimes it seems that criminal justice debates involve a knowing suspension of disbelief. People deny their suspicions and skepticism about what politicians and the criminal justice bureaucracy can accomplish in order to take comfort in promises to accomplish the impossible—identify violent offenders pre-emptively and isolate them forever, make the streets safe soon.

I have no faith in metasolutions to crime or the crisis in

criminal justice and have not attempted to offer one (any-more than I've attempted to write a comprehensive book about crime, capital punishment, or justice). I simply offer one perspective. My own goal is not to solve problems but to help rationalize our discussion of them. I suspect that any discernible reductions in violence and disorder will be gradual and localized, as violence is localized. It is a national problem and a national responsibility, but it is a problem that affects some localities much more than others. Poor urban neighbor-hoods are considerably more dangerous than affluent sub-urbs. Nationwide, violent crime outside the home is more geographically concentrated than diffuse. And while the sta-tistics, the cumulative tallies of crime, are numbing, people are murdering and maiming each other one by one and they will have to make their peace one by one, not *en masse*.

This is not a plea for the assumption of personal responsi-bility instead of a commitment to social reform. What could be more obvious than the fact that progress requires and re-flects both individual and collective action? Of course, all people are shaped by the conditions of their lives over which they've had little control; and, of course, all people with min-imal mental competency must eventually assert control over their actions and assume responsibility. We will differ wildly over how to apply this general notion to particular cases, but the principle should be clear and not that controversial, al-though it does require a willingness to hold countervailing ideas simultaneously—not one of the hallmarks of our culture.

Indeed, one measure of the idiocy of our political debates is the belief that countervailing approaches to problems, like crime, are not complementary but mutually exclusive. Put very simply (and it usually is), liberals are supposed to focus on social change while conservatives demand change of indi-viduals—as if society changes with the weather, not through the efforts of individuals, as if individuals change in a vacuum. Liberals are supposed to address the root causes of crime, while conservatives address its consequences; liberals are supposed to focus on crime prevention, through social welfare programs, while conservatives focus on punishment, through enhanced law enforcement.

Meanwhile, sensible people of various political persuasions must know that we can't ignore either prevention or punishment, that we would not effectively eliminate crime by eliminating social or economic inequities nor would we effectively control crime simply through law enforcement, unless we were transformed into a virtual police state. Sensible people must doubt that we would solve the crime problem either by burning down prisons or by dismantling social programs, although we could alleviate the problem by improving both the prisons and the programs.

But, debates about crime control are rarely sensible. They're ruled by politics and fear and the mindless exchange of attitudes that dominates the worst talk shows, where people never exchange ideas. Rationality, in general, has been out of fashion in recent years. New Agers condemn it as left brain thinking, some feminists consider it male-identified, while some self-styled radical academics are apt to dismiss it as a pretense of objectivity; on the right, religiosity is a much more potent political force than reason. I expect that we'll proudly become even less rational as the millennium approaches: more people will report being visited by aliens or abused by Satanic cults in childhood or graced by their guardian angels. In my worst moments, I imagine that this book would be taken more seriously by a broader audience if I claimed to be channeling the spirit of a two-thousand-year-old shaman or an extraterrestrial with our interests at whatever passes for its heart. But God doesn't talk to me. This is not a book of revelation.

◀ 1 | Guilty Victims

In the parking lot of a suburban shopping mall, a sixteen-year-old boy points a gun at your head, takes your wallet and jewelry, and hijacks your car. Somehow, he is arrested and brought to trial. He admits having robbed you but pleads not guilty by reason of insanity. He has grown up in an anarchic community in which drugs and guns are common and few of his peers expect to grow old. He was badly abused in childhood, sustaining head injuries that contributed to his poor impulse control. He suffers from post-traumatic stress disorder and has occasional blackouts and flashbacks in which he relives his childhood abuse. He has testosterone poisoning. He was unable to resist the impulse to rob you. In fact, he barely remembers the attack, which he walked through in a trancelike state. Not guilty?

If Lorena Bobbitt was innocent of intentionally dismembering her husband, because she was in the grip of an irresistible impulse, then a large majority of people in prison should probably go free. Violent offenders often have trouble resisting their impulses—that's what makes them violent; they often have terrible histories of deprivation and abuse and were raised in environments in which violence was a primary form of self-expression. They have good reason to be crazy, at least temporarily, and many may have more credible insanity defenses than the one successfully raised by Lorena Bobbitt in 1994. If her story of marital rape was convincing, her claim about not remembering mutilating her husband was contradicted by admissions she made to police shortly after the attack: "He doesn't wait for me to have orgasm," she explained. "He's selfish. I don't think it's fair. So I pulled back the sheet and then I did it."[1]

But if the story of my fictitious mugger could easily be true, perhaps truer than Lorena Bobbitt's story, it's not likely that a jury would find it as persuasive. The mere suggestion of a diminished capacity defense in a case involving a typical, random street crime infuriates people who say that they're sick of crime and violence and a justice system that routinely sets criminals free. According to a 1994 *National Law Journal* poll, 59 percent of the public feels that claims of prior victimization by criminal defendants have "gotten out of hand."

Lamentations about the "abuse excuse" and our low standards of accountability abounded in the weeks following the Bobbitt verdict, which neatly coincided with the 1994 mistrials of Erik and Lyle Menendez, who, as Dominick Dunne wrote, "shot their mother's face off and their father's brains out."[2] The Menendez brothers claimed that they were abused as children ("adult children," they might have said), and had acted preemptively, in the belief that their parents were plotting to kill them. The mistrials came as a shock to a lot of people, given the facts of the case. The brothers were financially independent, young adults who were free to leave home but stayed and shot their parents instead; there was no evidence of an alleged plot by Kitty and Jose Menendez to kill their sons; Lyle and Erik admitted killing their parents to a psychiatrist, without mentioning a history of sexual abuse or any claim of self-defense.

Presented this way, the case against the Menendez brothers seems damning, but this recitation of the facts does not really tell the story of the case; it's only the starting point for different stories formulated by the prosecution and defense. In this case, while the prosecutors told a story about cold-blooded murder for money, the defense told an even more sensational story about incest, which enough members of each jury believed. Hazel Thorton, a member of Erik Menendez's jury, underscored her belief that he acted out of fear, not hatred or greed. The jury deadlocked partly over this question of motive, she said. Convinced that the brothers were motivated by fear, however unreasonable, Thorton stressed that they were guilty of manslaughter, not murder.[3]

None of us can know whether the claim of abuse in this case was true, but we can be fairly sure that it would not have succeeded thirty years earlier. Whether you consider the Menendez verdicts a sign of progress depends partly on whether you consider incest so common that most allegations of it are probably true, and whether you think defendants' histories of abuse should mitigate their guilt, if not absolve them completely. A majority of people surveyed by the *National Law Journal* in 1994 were displeased by the outcomes of both the Bobbitt and Menendez trials. Fifty-two percent of respondents said they would have convicted Lorena Bobbitt in the malicious wounding of her husband; 68 percent said they would have convicted the Menendez brothers of murder.

Some jurors in these cases respond that the people who say they would have decided the cases differently weren't in the courtroom and didn't hear the evidence. That's not quite true, given that both trials were televised to large and faithful audiences. The public had unprecedented exposure to the evidence and the arguments in each case. But, it is true that the responsibility of sitting on a jury leads many people to second guess opinions they might proclaim with certainty out of court. It's easy to hold opinions of no consequence. The TV audience was also not directly subjected to the manipulative powers of defense attorneys, which in the Menendez case were said to be considerable. (Anyone who protests this description of trial lawyers as manipulative should listen to them talk about how to handle jurors.)

In any case, whether people were dismayed or relieved by the outcome of these trials, they were compelled to discuss them relentlessly. For weeks, the talk show commentators (myself included; I have no shame), pondered the use of claims of abuse as defenses in criminal cases. The question of ice skater Tonya Harding's complicity in the attempt to cripple her rival Nancy Kerrigan was also front-page news at the time, along with tales of abuse Harding suffered in childhood and at the hands of her husband, which many speculated would constitute her defense, were she ever tried. (She pled guilty to obstructing justice.)

Suddenly, people started wondering whether expanding our definitions of abuse and restricting our notions of accountability were conducive to maintaining the law and order so many craved. Even Oprah Winfrey engaged in a little self-criticism, devoting an hour to the role of talk shows in "popularizing abuse." Have we "glorified victimhood," she asked, and "made it easy for weak people to come up with 101 excuses to explain when they can't take charge of their lives?"

Yes. Of course, talk shows have helped transform victimhood into a kind of status symbol. People have been parading their addictions and histories of abuse on these shows for years now. Worse yet, they've been parading the abuse they've inflicted on others. The talk shows don't simply promote victimhood; they promote shamelessness. On national

NB
battered women

TV, people regularly testify to cruelties, infidelities, and perversities—with apparent pride and pleasure in appearing on TV. At least, their confessions are rarely etched in shame, and we, in the audience, are not supposed to make them feel ashamed. We're supposed to make them feel affirmed. "To feel ashamed is bad," a woman on Oprah asserts. (Shame is, after all, a threat to self-esteem.) But, what if you murder somebody? Shouldn't you feel ashamed, or, at least—I don't know—maybe a little embarrassed?

In the jargon of recovery, shame is toxic. And, of course, you shouldn't feel ashamed of being victimized by family members or strangers, but surely you should feel ashamed of victimizing. The distinction between the shame that should attach to cruel or criminal behavior and the stigma that should not be imposed on its victims is lost on the talk shows, as well as gradations of innocence and guilt. What's lost too is the sense that shame is one source of civilization. If some people don't commit crimes because they fear the shame of being apprehended, then shame is an antidote for violent or dishonest impulses, not just a "toxin."

Still, neither the talk shows nor the therapeutic culture invented shamelessness or the tendency of defendants in criminal cases to shift the blame for their behaviors. Throughout much of our history, for example, popular culture and notions of criminal justice allowed men to blame sexual violence on women. A man could offer evidence of a woman's "provocative" dress or "promiscuous" past as a good excuse for raping her. No pundits clicked their tongues and said, "My, my, no one takes responsibility for himself anymore." But, when women started offering battered women's syndrome as an excuse for killing their husbands, we were said to have a crisis of accountability.

I point this out not to suggest that Lorena Bobbitt had good reason for dismembering her husband. Unlike many battered wives, she seemed motivated more by rage than fear. In some ways, she might have been a more sympathetic defendant had she killed him: killing may be an act of self-defense; sexual mutilation is an act of hatred or revenge. The concept of battered woman's syndrome was intended to redefine self-defense in a domestic violence case in which a woman had good reason to believe that her husband would kill her if she didn't kill him first. It is an acknowledgment that in a very limited category of cases, self-defense may include preemptive action. Lorena Bobbitt could hardly claim to have been protecting herself from her husband when she took a knife to him. Her actions were more likely to escalate conflict than resolve it. Cutting off a man's penis, as someone said, "tends to piss a guy off."

But putting aside the bizarre circumstances of the Bobbitt case, there's nothing new or particularly alarming about a defendant raising a claim of irresistible impulse or temporary insanity in a criminal case. The modern prototype for an insanity defense was formulated by a British judge in 1843. It has long been a basic principle of law that defendants are legally guilty only when they have some conscious understanding and control of their acts, when they are capable of forming the intent to commit the acts of which they are accused.

That principle, however, is now under attack. Shortly after the Bobbitt and Menendez trials, the Supreme Court upheld a Montana law abolishing the plea of not guilty by reason of insanity and replacing it with a plea of guilty, but insane.[4] This means that instead of mitigating guilt, evidence of a defendant's mental state mitigates sentence. This could have limited practical effect. Insanity defenses are rarely successful, and whether defendants are judged not guilty because they're insane, or guilty but insane, they may be institutionalized almost indefinitely.

But if symbolism matters, if the values reflected by law

have some attenuated effect on behavior, then the abolition of the insanity defense is an important statement about accountability, which some will applaud and others bemoan. You might argue that one measure of a civilized society is the compassion it shows to people who commit crimes out of madness, not badness. But you might also point out that the question of whether an offender is mad or bad sometimes seems academic. We are all the victims or beneficiaries of genes and environmental influences and circumstances of our childhoods; none of us is singly, absolutely responsible for our behavior, which is why criminal justice proceeds from notions of relative accountability. Courts are neither churches nor therapists' offices. Perhaps the mad must sometimes be punished along with the bad, especially in a post-Freudian age when madness threatens to subsume badness entirely.

Determinations of sanity and accountability have become quite complicated. Religion can lend more credence to free will than does psychoanalysis, which tends to blame bad behaviors on bad parenting and other childhood traumas or disease, instead of on bad character. Or, rather, bad character is apt to be presented as an inheritance rather than a conscious choice of evil. In the popular view, psychoanalysis has absolved people of responsibility for their crimes (although psychiatrists testify for the prosecution as well as the defense). But psychoanalysis hasn't been nearly as generous to defendants as the recovery movement, which has elevated shamelessness and greatly expanded the list of excuses available to the accused. According to recovery experts, practically everyone is addicted, everyone has been abused, and only practicing codependents try to resist their impulses by themselves. Self-control is not simply dismissed or ignored as a personal development goal; it is denigrated as a symptom of the disease of codependency.

It was the intrusion of this particular personal development ethos into the criminal courts that was dramatized by the Bobbitt and Menendez cases. That is partly why they generated so much debate. Of course, a great deal of attention was paid to these cases because they involved sex and violence, because the trials were televised, and people enjoyed them immensely. But interest in the Bobbitt and Menendez cases wasn't simply voyeuristic. Both trials occurred at a time when criticisms of "victimism" were common enough to be fashionable and concern about crime was intense.

The postwar therapeutic culture of vulnerable individualism has always been countered by an older, frontier tradition of rugged individualism. (Each of these American traditions is reflected respectively in the personas of Bill Clinton and Ronald Reagan.) In the past several years, calls for self-reliance began to catch up with exercises in self-pity encouraged by the recovery movement, and considering the responses to the Bobbitt and Menendez cases, a significant segment of the public seemed genuinely concerned about importing popular personal development ideals into the courtroom. What might seem merely silly on a talk show was unsettling in the courts.

No one should have been surprised that trials were beginning to reflect the talk shows and the culture of recovery. If juries comprise average Americans, then as cross sections of the community they include people who disapprove of the therapeutic culture and people who embrace it. They include people who watch talk shows and have been encouraged not to judge the self-proclaimed victims of addiction and abuse simply because they've engaged in bad behaviors. They include people who've been taught that incest is common, if not ubiquitous (as well as people who believe it is rare). They include people who are familiar with such terms as "posttraumatic stress disorder" (which allegedly afflicted Lorena Bobbitt), terms that might once have been dismissed as jargon but now are part of the vernacular.

If juries comprise average Americans who watch talk shows and read mass market self-help books, they include people who have been encouraged always to believe the victim. In the world of recovery, to question a claim of abuse is to perpetuate it. To question the relevance of abuse in the Menendez case, for example, is to condone it. Yet, this seemed to be one case in which the scenarios of both the prosecution and defense may be partly true: it may be that the Menendez brothers were somehow abused in childhood and that they grew into monsters who killed their parents out of anger, not fear, and for money.

We tend to forget that a claim of victimization is not a claim of innocence. Indeed, people find victimhood appealing because they believe it absolves them of their own misdeeds; it imbues them with a sense of righteousness. But victimization often brings out the worst in people, as the biographies of many violent offenders would show. We are aware of the destructive effect of abuse, although we like to forget it from time to time in ordinary criminal cases when we want to impose unmitigated blame. It is, after all, conventional wisdom, and probably true, that children who are victims of violence may well become violent adults. If the Menendez brothers are innocent because they were abused, so are many inmates on death row. Death row is filled with people who had worse childhoods than Erik and Lyle Menendez, in addition to worse lawyers.

There is, however, little patience with pleas for mercy for the condemned based on their histories of addiction and abuse. Erik and Lyle Menendez successfully portrayed themselves as the passive victims of their parents, trapped by circumstances they did not create. The less telegenic people on death row—poor, ill-groomed and often ill-coached by their lawyers, and, in many cases, mentally or emotionally disabled, with awful histories of abuse—are presumed to be unfettered moral agents with a capacity for self-control, masters of their fates.

It's true that we're experiencing a crisis of accountability, as the pundits say. But the crisis is not simply a matter of failing to hold people accountable. In assigning accountability, we seem to be drawn to extremes—conferring too much absolution on some people and too much guilt on others. To some extent, our inconsistencies reflect racial biases. The death penalty is imposed disproportionately in cases involving white victims, for example, which means that people who kill whites are more likely to be held accountable to the death than people who kill blacks. But racial bias can also be invoked in favor of black defendants, to support claims of diminished capacity. Damien Williams, a young black male, was acquitted of attempted murder, convicted of the lesser charge of felony mayhem in the near fatal beating of the white truck driver Reginald Denny in 1992 (following the acquittal of police officers who beat up Rodney King), because his lawyer successfully argued that during the attack, Williams was in thrall to the mob—incapable of forming a conscious intent to kill. Williams framed his indulgence in mob violence as a quasi-religious experience: "I was just caught up in the rapture," he said, as white men have, no doubt, been caught up in the "rapture" of lynching.[5]

Crimes are often motivated by a self-righteous sense of aggrievement, and trials often involve competing claims of victimization. Southern whites tortured and lynched scores of African American men in the decades following the Civil War partly because they felt victimized by Reconstruction and the emancipation of slaves. Damien Williams was the victim of institutionalized racism, some asserted (blaming his indictment on racial bias). In one view, Williams was not engaged in criminal activity when he joined the mob; he was conducting a political protest, participating in an uprising, not a riot.

"I did it but I had a good reason," or "I did it but circumstances left me bereft of my reason": these are traditional criminal defenses. Saints and sinners, from Martin Luther King to Oliver North, have broken laws for what they believed were good reasons (although King was willing to face the consequences). And a democratic society depends on a willingness to break laws as well as a willingness to obey them. Surely, Nazism made clear the dangers of abdicating your conscience to the state.

Deciding when a law is unjust is often the equivalent of deciding when a claim of victimization is true, and that is a formidable challenge today. It does seem that practically everyone feels victimized by some injustice or other: black or white racism, the sexism of men or women, homophobia, or the decline of traditional family values. Conservatives like to blame the "culture of victimhood" on liberals, framing feminism and the civil rights movement as exercises in victimology, not battles against injustice. But victimhood has appeal right and left. When former Vice President Dan Quayle complained about the cultural elite, he was rallying people who felt victimized by a television character—single mother Murphy Brown. The religious right relies on people who feel victimized by secularism—the absence of prayer in school and the teaching of evolution. In the 1994 midterm elections, Republicans played to feelings of victimization among angry, frightened white males.

Whose politics, whose sensibilities do we invoke when we evaluate claims of victimization? When do we blame ourselves for our troubles, when do we blame others, and when is there no one to blame? "When is a disaster a misfortune and when is it an injustice?" the late political theorist Judith Shklar asked.[6] The Los Angeles earthquake was a misfortune, we'd agree—nature has no moral agency (although, as Shklar pointed out, the failure of officials to respond with disaster

relief might be considered an injustice). But how do we characterize the violence in Los Angeles sparked by the acquittal
of white police officers who assaulted black motorist Rodney
King? Was it a riot or an uprising? Who was to blame? Was
the beating of Reginald Denny an act of injustice or a reaction
to injustice, a plea for equal justice, or was it simply a misfortune—the unintended consequence of a series of events, beginning with the King case, which no single agent controlled?
(Responsibility is spread so thinly through bureaucracies that
they sometimes seem as blameless as nature.) Was Denny a
victim of injustice or fate? We have to try to draw a line
between the two, Shklar wrote, but there are no simple rules
to guide us. Instead, we're guided by politics and ideology,
and our own willingness to intervene on behalf of victims.
When we are not inclined to help people or assign blame for
their suffering, we call it a misfortune.[7] We're also guided by
conscience, which is why it's so essential for society to reach
consensus on what constitutes ethical behavior, instilling it in
people early on.

Juries are supposed to be the conscience of the community.
That is a fiction, given the divisions within communities and
the "science" of jury selection. But it's a convenient fiction
that authorizes juries to determine guilt and innocence, so
that cases are not decided simply by state officials—police,
prosecutors, and judges. It may be, however, that some of the
arguments presented to juries today confuse questions of guilt
and questions of punishment.

If Erik and Lyle Menendez were molested by their parents,
they could still be guilty of murder (putting aside their tenuous
claim of self-defense), but their sentences should be mitigated
by their histories of abuse. If Lorena Bobbitt were repeatedly
raped by her husband, she could still be guilty of maiming him
(putting aside her tenuous claim of temporary insanity), but
her sentence should be mitigated as well. The widespread

sense that people are no longer being held to account for their crimes partly reflects the fact that in highly publicized cases, defendants who admit that they committed the acts of which they're accused manage to mitigate their guilt with evidence that should, instead, mitigate their sentences.

Criminal defendants have always offered explanations for their behavior, and it has always been the job of the criminal justice system to determine when an explanation is an excuse. Excuses may seem less like evasions of accountability if they're considered in passing sentence rather than in determining guilt. This would leave defendants more at the mercy of judges and less at the mercy of juries (since judges decide sentences), and it is impossible to say whether, in general, judges can be trusted with justice more or less than jurors. This would also present problems in the increasing numbers of cases in which judges have very limited sentencing discretion, because sentences are set by mandatory minimum sentencing laws or by guidelines. In these cases, if mitigating factors are not considered by juries when they determine guilt or innocence, they will not be considered at all. So, without reforming sentencing laws, we could not reform determinations of guilt.

Still, consider the possibilities. In 1924, Clarence Darrow offered explanations for the senseless murder of a young boy by two teenagers, Leopold and Loeb. He described them as victims of their environment and their genes: We are each "the sport of all that goes before (us) and is applied to (us)." Darrow was an unabashed bleeding heart, who believed that eliminating injustice would eliminate a great many criminals, except for a few, "like Rockefeller," who suffered from "some peculiar formation of their brain."[8] He did not believe in free will and so was not prepared to hold people accountable, existentially, for their acts; but Darrow was prepared to see them imprisoned, conceding society's right to self-defense. In the Leopold and Loeb case, however, Darrow was not arguing that his clients were innocent (they'd pled guilty); he was arguing for life imprisonment instead of death. He was arguing for modesty in assessing our own capacity to administer justice and for the recognition that there is ultimately no bright line between innocence and guilt.

Our notions of accountability are confused in part because we have immodest expectations of justice. We want it to be clear and final and true. We want people to be either victims or victimizers, without recognizing that many of us are both, without knowing when and how to punish guilty victims.

◥ | Existential confusion about holding victims to account is exacerbated by the politics of victimization and the exploitation of high-profile cases by activists whose causes are at stake. Some feminists, for example, made a poster girl out of Lorena Bobbitt in their campaign to end sexual violence (against women, that is). On *Larry King Live*, National Organization of Women (NOW) President Patricia Ireland welcomed the Bobbitt verdict and used it as an occasion for urging passage of the federal Violence Against Women Act. Others idealized Bobbitt's aggressiveness as an example of a new, grass-roots militancy. In *Time*, the usually sensible feminist critic Barbara Ehrenreich wrote approvingly that all over America, "retail clerks and homemakers," inspired by Lorena Bobbitt, were sharpening their knives; according to Ehrenreich, only an overly fastidious feminist elite, fearful of being called man-hating, disapproved of Bobbitt's act. This dubious assertion was belied by NOW's support for Bobbitt as well as a number of dumb Bobbitt jokes issuing from feminist intellectuals, like Ehrenreich, who encouraged other women to "disarm" their abusive mates. Ehrenreich likened Bobbitt to a "warrior woman" in the tradition of Thelma and Louise, two fictional working-class women played by two actually wealthy women in a movie adored by the middle class.[9]

No one seemed to notice that this view of Lorena Bobbitt as a woman who took control of her life did not exactly conform to her defense. Instead of claiming that she was finally in control when she attacked her husband, she claimed to have been entirely out of it, or "impaired by disease," as the jury found. But, once she was acquitted, Bobbitt too presented herself as a sort of freedom fighter: "She did once and will again seek her American dream when she is able," her spokesperson said after the trial, "and if all the publicity of her abuse can help one person find freedom, then all this is not in vain."[10]

The irony is that, despite the rhetoric, feminism probably had less to do with Lorena Bobbitt's acquittal than did a traditional antifeminist reluctance to intervene in domestic disputes. The view of marital violence as a private affair, reflected in laws that have made it difficult to prosecute marital rape and that helped acquit John Bobbitt of abusing Lorena, helped acquit her as well. Unlike a teenager who robs strangers at gunpoint, Lorena Bobbitt was not generally considered a threat to the public. She may have indulged in a spot of shoplifting, but her act of violence was confined to the "private sphere" and was recompense for a "private" wrong.

Lorena Bobbitt and the Menendez brothers may have been victims of private violence, but they were also perpetrators who benefited greatly from the distinctions we make between "private" and "public" offenders. Public sympathy for O.J. Simpson, evident from the time of his arrest, expressed, in part, a willingness to forgive putatively private crimes. Simpson was not accused of a crime in which strangers, like you and I, were put at risk. He wasn't accused of shooting anyone in a mall. His girlfriends may have been chilled by his arrest, but the public at large didn't fear him. Nicole Simpson's neighbors were probably relieved when he was arrested and not some homicidal maniac who just happened to be in the neighborhood.

Feminists have always excoriated the historic failure to prosecute domestic violence; and sexism, in one of its cruder forms, has surely contributed to dismissals of wife beating and marital rape as private matters between husband and wife. But it's likely that even in an enlightened world in which sexual equality reigned within and outside the home, we would still regard "private" and "public" offenders differently. Even to those who believed them guilty, Lorena Bobbitt, the Menendez brothers, and O.J. Simpson could be viewed as private, not public menaces. When asked how she felt about the Menendez brothers in the end, a woman on Erik's jury who believed he was guilty only of a lesser charge of manslaughter said, "He didn't scare me. I didn't think if I were in a room with him, he would do anything to me."[11]

To people who believed their incest stories, the Menendez brothers, like Lorena Bobbitt, were only "doing things" to others who had badly abused them. To people who believed their stories, these defendants were vigilantes—private law enforcers, victims fighting back, refusing to be victims any longer. Even Damien Williams, acquitted of all serious charges in the Reginald Denny beating, could be seen as a kind of vigilante, exacting payback for wrongs done to his community. (In his case, the initial wrong was public and so was the consequent crime.) None of the verdicts in these cases were popular, but neither were they universally condemned. The degree of support garnered by each defendant was remarkable, considering the strength of the cases against them. It revealed, in part, an utter lack of faith in the possibility of public justice.

Lorena Bobbitt had no recourse but self-help, her supporters claimed, because law enforcement officials don't care about marital rape; besides, she was an immigrant. The Menendez brothers allegedly felt compelled to kill their parents in order to save themselves. What help is there for victims of child abuse? (In a 1993 *Vanity Fair* interview, TV star Roseanne said that sexually abused children have a right to kill their parents.) Damien Williams and other rioters are described by some as political protesters who had no choice but violence in the fight against racial injustice. Williams's acquittal also provided some rough justice to a community outraged by the initial acquittal of the officers who assaulted Rodney King. So, while many people decry violence in general, they're apt to condone it in particular cases, as a way of fighting back.

Maybe it started with Bernhardt Goetz, the mild-mannered electronics engineer who shot four teenagers on a subway car in New York City in 1984 when they asked him for five dollars. Goetz paralyzed one of his victims, Darryl Cabey, whom he shot twice. According to his own videotaped confession, he shot Cabey once, looked at him and said, "You seem to be all right; here's another." In his confession, which the jury saw, Goetz also described the pleasure he took in this attack: "I know and God knows what was in my heart. It was sadistic and that was me. . . . It was attempted, cold-blooded murder. . . . My problem was I ran out of bullets."[12]

Goetz quickly became a folk hero anyway. Contradicting his confession, he claimed at trial that he had been acting in self-defense, reacting reasonably to a reasonable apprehension that he was about to be robbed. One of his victims, he said, was smirking at him and had a "shine in his eye." The jury apparently believed him or had reasonable doubts about disbelieving him (according to his attorney, Goetz's confession was a false recollection), and he was acquitted of attempted murder and assault, convicted only of illegally carrying a firearm.

There was little logic to this case except for the logic of racism and fear. Goetz was white, his victims were young black males. Much was made of the fact that three of them had criminal records, but Goetz hadn't seen their rap sheets before he shot them (although he did see the "shine" in their eyes). Much was made of the fact that they were carrying screwdrivers, but they didn't display them to Goetz. Little was made of one report that Goetz seated himself next to the apparently sinister young men, instead of sitting with the apparently law-abiding people at the other end of the car. Any seasoned New Yorker might readily have inferred from this that Goetz was looking for trouble. Armed illegally and angry at having been mugged previously, he may have purposefully sat next to four black youths who looked menacing, expecting or even hoping they would approach him, giving him an excuse to claim his payback. Perhaps this would not have seemed unreasonable to some of his supporters who saw him as a former victim, fighting back. A lot of people took a lot of vicarious pleasure in this case.

Since then, acts of "citizen justice" have either been increasing or the media has paid increasing attention to them. In a 1990 article in *New York* magazine, Eric Pooley cited ten cases in a six-month period "in which crime victims and 'Good Samaritan' bystanders have turned the tables on their attackers, meeting force with force. In five of the cases, the victims pulled out guns they didn't have permits for and blasted the thugs."[13]

Some ten years after Charles Bronson blew away bad guys in *Death Wish*, vigilantism was beginning to seem less like a fantasy than a quotidian aspect of urban life. These are among the cases Pooley chronicled: A knife-wielding man dubbed the Subway Samaritan attacks two men who are robbing another passenger, killing one of them (to popular acclaim). He flees and is never apprehended. A witness to a mugging catches one of the thieves while he is running away, takes him back to the victim for an identification, shoots him and disappears. A young woman takes out an unlicensed gun and shoots a man in the face when he allegedly tries to rob her; in what may have been a retaliatory act, her friend is killed by his accomplice. She spends four weekends in jail after pleading guilty to illegal possession of a gun.

From one perspective, these are relatively easy cases; the vigilante apparently acted in defense of self or others, or re-acted to a crime in progress, without injuring any innocent bystanders. The law-abiding public can identify with the vigilantes and not their victims. (Bernhardt Goetz's jurors proba-bly never imagined he'd turn his gun on them; to many people he was less frightening than the young men he shot.)

Taking action to stop a crime or preempt one that seems about to occur is exactly the kind of action that pro-gun forces applaud, arguing that in most cases only an armed citi-zen can stop a crime in progress. People cannot expect police to be present when most crimes occur, they point out. Police, like prosecutors, generally act after the fact. "You can pretty much bet your life (and you are) that they won't be there at the moment you actually need them," Jeffrey Snyder wrote in the *Public Interest* advocating widespread gun possession. Most people, he asserted, don't confront this reality (although polling data on public skepticism about police protection sug-gests that many do). "If, however, you understand that crime can occur anywhere at anytime, and if you understand that you can be maimed or mortally wounded in mere seconds, you may wish to consider whether you are willing to place the responsibility of safeguarding your life in the hands of others."[14]

For gun possession advocates, like Snyder and others who don't feel protected by the police, vigilantism is not a prescrip-tion for escalating violence but for controlling it. In Septem-ber 1990 (three months after *New York* magazine published Eric Pooley's article "Frontier Justice"), New York gubernatorial candidate Pierre Rinfret proposed creating a force of one hundred thousand volunteer vigilantes to patrol the streets. "What I really want," Rinfret explained, "is a vigilante system with people carrying guns, unknown to anybody."[15]

Rinfret's proposal was never officially implemented (a fringe candidate, he lost the election), but it's likely that the "system" he envisioned is already in place. There are probably millions of guns in circulation in New York, which is why the city feels so dangerous. Walking down the street or riding in the subway, you suspect that there are people nearby carrying guns who are, as Rinfret said, "unknown," as is the actual number of cases of vigilante justice. "For every publicized case," Eric Pooley noted, "there's probably another case that never makes the news."[16]

Cases that are publicized often generate considerable public support, even when the vigilante acts not to deter but to avenge a crime already committed. (Lorena Bobbitt, the Menendez brothers, and Damien Williams could all be seen as avengers.) In a 1984 Louisiana case, Gary Plauche shot and killed Jeffrey Doucet, who was accused of molesting Plauche's son. Plauche killed Doucet, on camera, while he was in custody, awaiting prosecution. (This was not a case in which the vigilante could complain that the system failed him; he never gave it a chance to work.) Plauche, who denies being a vigilante, seems unrepentant (he'd do it again, he said in an interview on TV), and his sense of righteousness was probably confirmed by the response of the community and the justice system to his crime. He was allowed to plead guilty to a lesser charge of manslaughter and received a sentence of probation coupled with community service.[17]

Perhaps the public is sympathetic to these vigilantes because they kill suspects presumed guilty. But there is also some support for vigilant citizens who kill the innocent, by mistake, as armed people who live in fear of crime are apt to do. In another widely reported Louisiana case of 1994, Rodney Peairs was acquitted of manslaughter after he shot and killed a Japanese exchange student who mistakenly rang his doorbell, looking for a Halloween party at another address. Peairs's wife was frightened by the stranger at the door and told her husband to get his gun. Without asking questions, he complied and killed the boy when he failed to "freeze" on command. The entire encounter took less than a minute. "There was no thinking involved," the wife testified. The jury acquitted after only three hours of deliberation. Some court-room spectators cheered.[18]

Never mind that the stranger who approached the Peairs house was utterly innocent. Peairs was fighting back against the army of strangers just waiting to invade your home and maybe even steal your children. As our sense of anarchy rises, along with our sense of danger, so will gun sales rise and incidents of vigilantism, or private, citizen justice. "You have the absolute right to answer your door with a gun," Rodney Peairs's lawyer argued.[19]

It's hard to condemn violence with a gun in your hand. Crime that seems to make potential victims of us all makes us all potential victimizers. Listening to the daily crime reports, we fantasize about blowing the bad guys away. It's only natural; we don't need to disown the fantasy, but neither should we celebrate it, much less consider it a plan of action. We don't need politicians or activists emulating the justice system of Dodge City or gun possession activists exaggerating the danger of crime in the suburbs. We don't need columnists in the national press exhorting women to dismember their abusive husbands or TV stars encouraging sexually abused children to murder their parents, anymore than we need putative civil rights leaders endorsing racial violence or self-proclaimed pro-lifers urging people to murder doctors who perform abortions.

Victimology politicizes violence and effectively condones it, in various forms—from Damien Williams's attack on Reginald Denny to Bernhardt Goetz's shooting spree to Lorena Bobbitt's maiming of her husband. We may deplore these cases when they frighten us, but we revel in them when they make us feel avenged. If we're sincere about decrying violence, we'd better stop displaying so much pleasure in it.

↘ 2 | Voyeurism and Vengeance

"Free the Juice." By the time this book is published, public response to the arrest of O.J. Simpson in the summer of 1994 will be old news. Still, the image of Simpson's fans, cheering his apparent flight from police, declaring their love and support for his cause, as if his alleged crimes were politically motivated, will linger long after his case is resolved. From the beginning, the Simpson case dramatized the contradictions between public attitudes toward violence and criminal justice in particular cases and attitudes toward violence and criminal justice in general.

At the time of Simpson's arrest, California was in the early stages of a gubernatorial campaign pitting tough-on-crime incumbent Pete Wilson against the less tough State Treasurer Kathleen Brown, handicapped, it seemed, by her opposition to the death penalty, which voters generally favored, as long as it wasn't applied to O.J. Simpson. (And, of course, the prosecution declined to seek it in his case.) With one of the nation's largest death rows, California had recently enacted a harsh "three strikes you're out" law (mandating life sentences for three time felons), following public outrage over the kidnapping and killing of twelve-year-old Polly Klaas in 1993. (The law was so harsh that even a judge well known for his conservatism refused to apply it; the law swept so broadly, applying to nonviolent offenders, that Polly Klaas's father lobbied to change it.)[1] Pete Wilson, however, called for even harsher sentences. "Not three strikes you're out," not two strikes you're out, "but one strike you're out," he declared, cheered by an exuberant crowd. Soon a different crowd, or maybe the same crowd, was cheering O.J. Simpson as he fled from police, demanding the immediate liberation of the prime suspect in a brutal double murder. It was easy to imagine a demonstrator holding a sign saying "Three strikes you're out" in one hand and "Free the Juice" in the other.

What was perhaps most striking about this dissonance was how rarely it was noticed. People took for granted public support for Simpson; columnists wrote about our need for heroes and role models, and some bemoaned our veneration of athletes. Maybe the dissonant attitudes toward justice for the Juice and justice for practically every other defendant in the state of California was ignored because it was so disconcerting. Or maybe the dissonance was accepted because the reasons for it were clear.

So many people liked Simpson. They "loved" him, the way they love Michael Jackson, Barbra Streisand, Oprah Winfrey, Katie Couric, and millions of other celebrities they've never met. "We love you man and we're gonna see you through this," one fan declared on the radio. His image of Simpson seemed indelible, as if it would not have been altered by proof that he'd slaughtered two people. "We don't care what happened man. We love you. We know you're hurtin'."

Sympathy and support for Simpson were hardly universal.

In the beginning, the case generated renewed expressions of concern about domestic violence, which was briefly rediscovered by politicians. The House Judiciary Committee held a hearing on the subject; the New York legislature passed a new domestic violence law. Reports of battering were said to increase. But, outside feminist circles, there seemed to be relatively little public anger directed toward Simpson.[2]

On the basis of scantier evidence, people generally exhibit more anger and less compassion toward the average thirteen-year-old charged with a street crime. Sympathy for Simpson and belief in his innocence were remarkable; they were especially strong among blacks, but even among whites, although a majority surveyed believed him guilty, a strong minority (42 percent) expressed sympathy for him. By mid-summer of 1994, despite relentless, practically unavoidable coverage of the case, 44 percent of Americans surveyed said they had not decided whether he was innocent or guilty.[3]

This hesitancy to pass judgment on a case before trial would have been admirable were it not so unique. In general, the concern the public showed for procedural rights in the Simpson case was in striking contrast to general disdain for "criminal's rights." Many people who normally rail against "legal technicalities" said to benefit the guilty seem to root for Simpson's defense team when it sought to suppress evidence seized from his home during a warrantless search. At least, they were transfixed by the story of constitutional rights. Larry King queried a California judge about the Fourth Amendment rules on search and seizure and the intricacies of California trial practice. Viewers phoned in with their questions.

This could have been an educational experience (and was billed as one), but it was clear that the lessons of this case would not be extended to the thousands of criminal cases that pass through the courts every day. It was clear that the public would continue showing little concern for the rights of most criminal suspects, who are likely to be labeled "animals." Certainly, in the wake of this case, there was no diminution of demand for tough anticrime measures, such as preventative detention based on a presumption of guilt, even as people were rightly insisting that Simpson enjoy his presumption of innocence. There was no hint of any public demand to rethink the new death penalties and harsh "three strikes you're out" law that Congress was in the process of adding to the federal penal code. The belief that O.J. Simpson might be innocent did not translate into a belief that other criminal defendants might be innocent too—or, at least, not beyond redemption.

Meanwhile, when the media wasn't purporting to educate us about criminal justice, it simply diverted us with trivia about O.J. (During a slow news week, the *Boston Globe* ran a front-page story about what he ate for breakfast.) The media covered the case the way it covers presidential campaigns, tracking the public mood, taking its pulse in daily or weekly polls. (41 percent of the public believed Simpson was guilty, *USA Today* reported on July 1, 1994, down from 50 percent on June 17.) Panels of legal pundits deconstructed every move by the prosecution and defense, just as political pundits deconstruct political campaigns. ("Who won the public relations contest this week?" an anchor woman on CNN asked me and two other commentators in the early days of the case.)

What's the point of predicting the outcome of an election, I always wonder. Why don't we just wait and see what happens in November? Usually, by early October, I've stopped reading the election news and watching *MacNeil-Lehrer Newshour,* and others seem tired of the spectacle too. But the public never seemed to tire of O.J. The fascination with his case was simply stunning. The criminal justice system had rarely been so compelling.

◤ | The only match for a televised trial, and a high-profile defendant, might be a televised execution. Today, with executions conducted privately, behind prison walls, they provide only vicarious entertainment to the relatively few people who meet outside the prison to cheer the execution, alongside abolitionists who come to mourn it.

In 1989, some 300 people gathered outside the state prison in Starke, Florida, to celebrate the execution of Ted Bundy, who murdered at least thirty women. The execution party aroused more public criticism and concern about the public taste for violence than the execution itself. "The sheer light-hearted boisterousness" of the event was "extraordinary," *Newsweek* lamented. Filled with college students, the execution vigil was like a "football rally," replete with beer, stupid T-shirts, and signs, which read "Roast in Peace" or "This Buzz Is for You." One law enforcement official complained that the crowd made "a sham of the criminal justice process."[4]

But the carnival was predictable. Bundy had always been a crowd pleaser. He was, perhaps, America's smartest, sexiest serial killer (Mark Harmon played him in the TV movie), and one of the most anomalous, except for a somewhat violent childhood. He had no history of drug or alcohol abuse, unlike many people on death row, he was not impoverished, nor did he show any sign of mental illness or brain damage. A young Republican law student with a 3.5 average, he was not lacking in academic or social skills, as were the proverbial serial killers Joel Rivkin, who lived with his mother and murdered prostitutes, and weird David Berkowitz, the Son of Sam.

Bundy did, however, finally offer an excuse for his behavior: he went to his death blaming his proclivity for rape and murder on pornography. Antipornography feminists, who might otherwise put little faith in the rationalizations of a serial killer who preyed on young women, now sometimes point to Bundy's assertions about pornography's influence on him as evidence of its harm. Bundy did have a gaggle of female admirers who stayed loyal through his trials. Perhaps antiporn feminists would have supported him too, had he raised a "pornography made me do it" defense.

Soon enough, however, people accused of violent crimes may be blaming their bad behavior on the media, claiming they were addicted to action movies or TV cop shows or movies of the week about incest and other forms of family violence, just as people in support groups claim that they're addicted to pornography. Although they will generate new rounds of discussions about failures of responsibility, some jurors will, no doubt, find these defenses persuasive. Concern about violence in the media has been intensifying, since the late 1980s, along with concern about violent crime. It's likely that relatively few Americans would agree with antiporn crusader Catharine MacKinnon's assertion that there is virtually no difference between a violent image and an act of violence. (Surely most women would rather be assaulted by a magazine than by a man.) But, according to a 1994 *National Law Journal* survey, majorities of men and women believe that pornography encourages violence. Concern about the relationship between television and violence is even stronger.

Seventy-two percent of Americans believe that television entertainment programs are excessively violent, according to a 1993 Times Mirror Poll. (Gallup found that 80 percent of Americans shared this belief.) To a lesser extent, TV news disturbs people as well: 52 percent of people surveyed by Times Mirror found the news too violent; 43 percent of people surveyed by Gallup in 1993 said that local news reports encourage crime. There are gender and generation gaps on the subject of media violence: more women are troubled by it than men, and the old are troubled by it in greater numbers than the young, who are generally exposed to more of it. The Times Mirror Poll described a "video violence generation gap.

Those under 30 are far more likely to be heavy consumers of violent programming and movies." They are "far less bothered by violence on television, less likely to feel the news is too full of violence, and less likely to feel violence is harmful to society, than are older Americans." Still, overall, there is a strong consensus among adults about too much violence on TV, and a striking 80 percent of people surveyed by Times Mirror said that TV was harmful to society.

Do an equally strong majority of Americans want the government to save them from themselves? It's unclear how concern about media violence might translate into support for government regulation of it. The *National Law Journal* poll showed that by a "slight majority" Americans "reject government interference" with TV violence. A mere 12 percent surveyed said they would agree to restrictive legislation. But these results seem anomalous. According to Gallup, over half of all Americans want the government to "do more to regulate" TV violence. Even more telling is the finding that 75 percent believe TV contributes to the crime rate. A 1994 Harris Poll found that about 60 percent of people surveyed believe that television and movies "contribute a lot" to violence. Times Mirror found that about three-quarters of respondents identified TV violence as a cause of crime.

It is virtually axiomatic that a strong consensus about the existence of a national problem is likely to generate a strong demand for the government to solve it. (This is not only an axiom for liberals: conservatives who protest excessive reliance on government meddling in daily life would probably not oppose a federal education law providing incentives for prayer in school.) Given the widely shared belief that media violence causes crime, it seems possible, at least, to garner majority support for restrictive legislation. People may support a voluntary ratings system as a first step, but, according to Gallup, 61 percent believe that warnings do not "go far enough."

Public concern about TV violence has hardly been lost on Washington, which occasionally consummates its historic flirtation with censorship. Since the first federal obscenity law was passed in 1873, Congress has dipped in and out of the business of policing popular entertainments and "obscene" information (notably sex education and information about birth control, which were once proscribed by federal law). From the beginning, Congress has been alert to the alleged dangers of TV. In 1954, Republican Senator Robert Hendrickson proposed appointing a "TV czar" to monitor programs that might encourage juvenile delinquency.[5] Historically, the American tradition of free speech has had to co-exist, somehow, with a tradition of moral reform.

The conflict has usually pitted liberals against conservatives, but the recent focus on TV violence has been bipartisan. When Attorney General Janet Reno and Senator Paul Simon began calling for self-restraint by media executives, threatening them with regulation of violent programming in the alternative, it was clear that liberals were serious about staking out the family values territory long monopolized by conservatives. (At the same time, liberal rhetoric about welfare reform was becoming increasingly moralistic, focusing on the sins of single mothers.) Liberals and conservatives who could not agree about how best to address violence in real life could at least come together over the issue of violence in the media.

Apart from genuine concern about violence in the media, there were obvious political reasons for congressional action. Many more Americans are exposed to violent media than violent crime, which tends to be concentrated in low-income urban neighborhoods. In New York City, for example, in 1993, the overall homicide rate declined but the percentage of homicides occurring in depressed areas of the South Bronx, upper Manhattan, and Brooklyn, increased. Nearly half of the city's reported homicides took place in 16 percent of its precincts.[6] Violence in the media is much more equitably distributed and affects many more middle-class suburbanites than gang wars and drive-by shootings.

So, if violence in the media is a less compelling problem than violence in the streets, it's more widespread and at the same time less intractable. Actual violence is more likely to generate despair and nihilism than TV violence, which often leads to activism, because TV violence seems amenable to control. In Colombia, where the murder rate is eight times higher than in the United States, politicians and business people have crusaded against violence in the media.

"It's a catharsis," one Colombian sociologist explained to a *Wall Street Journal* reporter, commenting on the campaign against media violence.[7] If the Colombian government can't stop drug violence and won't attack domestic violence, it can prohibit imaginary violence. Pursuant to a court ruling, the government established family viewing hours on TV, until 10 P.M. and screened TV programs before they were shown to the public.

In this country, Congress can't summon all the violent felons or potentially violent felons in the nation to hearings on the effect of their antisocial behavior, but it can summon TV and movie executives to hearings on violence in the media and threaten them with regulation. And felons may be immune to social pressure, social critics, and consumer boycotts, but media moguls—public relations masters and slaves—are not. In fact, as the moguls always point out, they're in the business of giving the public what it wants. Action movies are produced because they're profitable. That studio executives don't spawn the desire for violence doesn't excuse them from so enthusiastically satisfying it. Still, they are no more than collaborators.

More worrisome than the public demand for violent feature films and action fantasies is the taste for sensational true crime stories, which have become primary sources of "information" about criminal justice. People who are spared first-hand experience with the system learn about it from docudramas about Amy Fisher (the Long Island teenager who shot her lover's wife), "reality-based" TV cop shows and crime stories, and talk show palaver about sensational cases. The most attention is paid to the least typical cases.

But at the same time that people draw misleading lessons about criminal justice in general from these cases assuming that they're educational, they also find them entertaining. That's what's most disturbing. People loved the Amy Fisher, Erik and Lyle Menendez, and O.J. Simpson cases, gorging themselves on TV movies, tabloids, and hours of boring televised courtroom proceedings, as if the victims in these cases were characters in B movies, not sentient human beings. If action movies desensitize people to violence, as critics charge, at least the violence they depict is fictional. We tend to forget or deny the difference between watching Clint Eastwood shoot blanks into an actor playing a character who never lived or died and watching a stand-in for Lyle Menendez shoot blanks into a stand-in for his mother.

This confusion about fact and fiction also distorts perceptions of the actual cases people follow. That was one of the lessons of the sympathetic response to murder suspect O.J. Simpson. Racial tensions, the pervasive fascination with celebrity, and the willingness to tolerate domestic crimes all contributed to the willingness to believe he was innocent. But it also reflected the influence of popular entertainments.

Televised, starring an established celebrity, the Simpson case seemed like popular genre fiction. He seemed less like a real life defendant than a hero in a Scott Turow or John Grisham novel slated for the screen; and on screen the defendant, especially when played by a star, is usually an innocent man, "caught in a web of circumstance," if he hasn't been framed. The story of an innocent man on the run—Robert Donat in *The Thirty-Nine Steps* or Harrison Ford in *The Fugitive*—has been a Hollywood staple for years. The Simpson case seemed just another installment. It was as if people presumed Simpson's innocence not out of respect for his constitutional rights but in anticipation of a last-minute plot twist.

If people sometimes mistake real courtroom dramas for entertainments, they may also relate to entertainment as if it were real life. (My grandmother seemed genuinely concerned about the characters on her favorite soaps.) Preschool children are particularly prone to confuse imaginary and actual violence, critics of TV charge. "In the minds of such young children, television is a source of entirely factual information regarding how the world works," Brandon Centerwall wrote, in a 1992 article in the *Journal of the American Medical Association*. They grow out of this confusion, but it can have a lasting impact on behavior, Centerwall asserted. "Serious violence is most likely to erupt at moments of severe stress—and it is precisely at such moments that adolescents and adults are most likely to revert to their earliest, most visceral sense of what violence is and what its role is in society."[8]

This merger of fact and fantasy is particularly acute for children who live in violent homes and neighborhoods, Sissela Bok has observed. These children are "especially likely to conclude that television violence reflects real life." For them, "the violence that they witness around them reinforces the realism they attribute to the violence they see enacted on the screen; and their view of the world is in turn strongly influenced by what they see on television."[9]

Children are instinctively imitative creatures, critics assert. Television teaches them how to behave. This argument has particular resonance in a culture that has become sensitized to child abuse. It is generally acknowledged that children who grow up in violent homes are at high risk of becoming violent partly in reaction to their own mistreatment and partly because they mirror the behavior of adults around them. If children do not distinguish between fact and fantasy, between entertainment and information, it follows that they may adopt the behavior they see on TV, as they adopt the behavior they see in the world. In other words, critics argue, children don't just watch TV, they experience it, the way they experience a day at school.

Statements about the effect of television violence on children are sometimes made with an air of discovery, but few of them are new. Since the early days of film and video, advocates for children, as well as moral reformers, have focused on the effects of screen violence. And intensified concern about media violence naturally accompanies intensified concern about crime. The first congressional hearings on TV violence took place in the early 1950s, when television was just beginning to take hold of American culture and youth crime was increasing, which in one view was no coincidence.

In 1954, a Senate Judiciary Committee convened a series of hearings on the effect of TV on "the shocking rise in our national delinquency rate." Television was characterized as "the most powerful force man has yet devised for planting and spreading ideas." The Senate took particular interest in "ideas that spring into the living room for the entertainment of the youth of America, which have to do with crime and horror, sadism, and sex."[10]

Television was "mental poisoning," according to Clara Logan, president of the National Association for Better Radio and Television. Toxic shows included *Roy Rogers, The Lone Ranger,* and *Captain Midnight.* Logan asserted that 40 percent of all children's programming focused on crime and violence, and she worried that TV might directly induce some young viewers to commit crimes. But, like many media critics today, Logan was most concerned about the indirect, brutalizing effect of TV violence. "How can a youngster see so many human beings killed each week without acquiring an indifference toward violent death?" she asked. "How can a child who sees countless incidents of sadism and meaningless violence keep from becoming callous and unconcerned toward human misery and suffering?"[11]

James Bennett, director of the Federal Bureau of Prisons, suggested at the Senate hearings that TV violence was most harmful to troubled, unstable children, and Harvard psychologist Eleanor Maccoby essentially agreed. Her experiments indicated that the effects of TV on children varied with their moods and personalities ("a TV program can have one function for one child and an entirely different function for another."). In this view, media violence doesn't cause aggression but may exacerbate aggressive tendencies. The causes of delinquency were more difficult to quantify than the shootings and fistfights on TV, Bennett observed. They included "lack of affection, feelings of rejection in the home, hostilities and anxieties." Bennett was also skeptical of anecdotal evidence of copycat crimes. He had conducted interviews of delinquents convicted of committing crimes that had been dramatized in the media. "It was not unusual for a boy to claim that he had gotten the idea for the offense out of some comic book or out of the radio. But there is a tendency for those people to rationalize their offense, to blame it on something else or not accept the responsibility for it themselves."[12]

Opinion was divided on the effect of TV crime shows: NBC Vice President Joseph Heffernan cited J. Edgar Hoover's support for "anti-crime programs" that showed criminals "playing a losing game." Indeed, NBC programming standards decreed that "criminals are always punished . . . crime is not condoned . . . law enforcement is upheld and portrayed with respect and dignity."[13]

Violence and villainy on TV could have positive effects on

children, Captain Video (aka actor Al Hodge) pointed out. "We have to have violence. Otherwise, there is no excuse for a heroic character existing. He has to go after somebody." Hodge stressed, however, that when Captain Video "went after" a bad guy in his TV show, he was armed only with a stungun. "This gun merely immobilizes an adversary to the point where we can take whatever lethal weapon he may have away from him, even to the point where we can say that this action of being stunned is not painful." Hodge also noted that Captain Video did not indulge in the violence of capital punishment. Villains were never hung: "We never have a line in the program which says, 'You had better do what we say or you will swing.' We do what we think will happen in the future. We confine our criminals in what we call a rehabilitation center. Actually it is a penal center on a planet of Ganymede, if you are familiar with your science fiction."[14]

Captain Video's hopeful vision of enlightened criminal justice in the future seems about as quaint today as this colloquy between the Senate subcommittee's Chief Counsel Herbert Beaser and NBC Vice President Joseph Heffernan, over a scene of cowboy Hopalong Cassidy bleeding to death:

Heffernan:	I would doubt [it showed] Hopalong Cassidy bleeding to death because the man never dies.
Beaser:	It looked like he was bleeding to death.
Heffernan:	It may have looked like he was bleeding.
Beaser:	He was bleeding.[15]

To contemporary audiences concerned with carnage in the media, Hopalong Cassidy with a spot of ketchup on his shirt is an image of the good old days. But, perhaps forty years from now, today's media violence will seem tame. The capacity of violent imagery to shock or damage or titillate people is relative. The westerns and crime shows that the Senate pondered in the early 1950s were the action movies of their day, appealing to a similar desire for order, justice, or vengeance, or pleasure in celluloid mayhem.

Still, if our enjoyment of violence isn't new, opportunities for indulging in it have been greatly expanded by technology, along with possibilities for portraying it. The evolution of special effects has been stunning. Video games and music videos, cable TV and Hollywood movies serve as more "powerful sources for promoting and spreading ideas" than the Senate of 1954 could ever have imagined. A large body of social science studies suggest that the media provides much more than harmless entertainment.

Since the advent of television, numerous studies have considered the link between violent TV and violent behavior. Critics of TV often claim that there have been 3,000 studies of television violence; but, in an enlightening critique of the social science data, American Civil Liberties Union attorney Marjorie Heins points out that many of the 3,000 studies cited are secondary reviews of primary studies of TV violence, which number about 100, and many of the oft-cited studies focus expansively on television, in general, not just television violence.[16] Studies that are said to prove that media violence causes actual violence also tend to rely on laboratory experiments, which cannot duplicate conditions in real life. Yet, the studies provide media critics with a lot of ammunition, because they are widely cited by critics (uncritically) and rarely read by the public at large. Most of us lack the patience to decipher dense academic studies or the training and skills to critique them. Many of us take on faith the proposition "studies show . . . " (as advertisers know). Nowadays, the proposition that violent media cause violent behavior is hardly considered open to question.

Are there reasonable doubts about the effect of TV violence and the compelling need to regulate it? A well-publicized study by the American Psychological Association reports that "the accumulated research clearly demonstrates a correlation between viewing violence and aggressive behavior—that is heavy viewers behave more aggressively than light viewers."[17] If you read that statement quickly on the front page of your local newspaper, it seems conclusive. But even if the statement is true, it doesn't justify regulating violence in the media, given the strong, practically irrefutable proof of harm (and causation) required to regulate speech. Television may correlate to rising violence without directly causing it. The popularity of TV may itself reflect other political and social changes that retard children's moral and emotional development. What if excessive, uncritical TV watching correlates to the dearth of decent day care or a decline in public education?

Defenders of TV violence also claim that it mirrors reality. That's not quite true. In reality, people hurled through plate glass windows do not get up, grimace, and walk away. Even TV news does not present a realistic view of the crime problem, considering the disproportionate coverage of violent crime, particularly random, stranger-to-stranger crime. (In general, you're less likely to be attacked by a stranger than by someone you know.) Indeed, when media moguls are not defending screen violence as realistic, they dismiss it as mere fantasy—harmless entertainment. But some evidence suggests that the demographic groups most attracted to violence in the media include people for whom it may seem most realistic, given the violence in their communities. According to the 1993 Times Mirror poll, reality-based TV crime and emergency shows "have their strongest following among the less educated, racial minorities, the young and the poor." Viewing of violent programming in general is highest among males, people under thirty, blacks, and urbanites.

Still, even if you believe that media violence contributes to violent behavior or exacerbates violent tendencies, particularly among children and adolescents (and I am willing to believe that it might), you may find the singular effect of the media virtually impossible to isolate and quantify (as James Bennett observed in his Senate testimony in the mid-1950s). How do we parse the environments of violent teenagers, putting aside questions about their physical and mental health? How do we separate on-screen violence from the actual violence a teenage boy may experience at home and in the streets and from cultural stereotypes of masculinity that long predate the movies?

The fact that the media is, at most, only one of many factors contributing to violence is not an excuse for ignoring it, Sissela Bok has pointed out. Consider our approach to heart disease, she argues. "Few critics maintain, that just because a number of risk factors such as smoking or heredity contribute to the prevalence of the disease, there is reason not to focus on risk of any one of them."[18] But there is also no reason to focus on any one risk factor exclusively. The trouble with campaigns against TV violence is that they tend to exaggerate its importance and distract us from other, more complicated and controversial causes of violence. Media violence seems cheaper and easier to address than, say, the deplorable state of many public schools or the social conditions that make television such an important presence in children's lives.

Television is watched most frequently by children in the inner cities, who are said to be most susceptible to its brutalizing effects because of the brutality that surrounds them. (According to the American Psychological Association, the average American child watches twenty-seven hours of television per week; inner city children watch as much as eleven hours per day.)[19] If watching TV is making these kids more prone to violence, watching TV is also one of the safest things they can do, Sissela Bok observes. The streets are dangerous, community programs are sparse; they are hiding out with their TVs because there are no safe places to play. What if, instead of focusing on making television shows less violent, politicians focused on making TV watching less necessary, by funding after-school programs for kids?

There are obvious political and fiscal answers to this question. A Senate hearing on the need for after-school programs in the inner cities would not be front-page news, nor would it garner as much bipartisan support as a hearing on media violence, nor would its proposed solutions be cost-free. Politicians and the public at large are attracted to the problem of TV violence partly because what is in everyone's living room is hard to ignore but also because we can easily envision simple, reactive solutions to it, such as a ratings system or restrictions on material that may be shown to minors. Addressing TV violence doesn't seem to require much affirmative action from government, such as the establishment of new social programs; it doesn't seem to require us to rethink social policy.

The irony is that media violence is a social problem, not a legal one—at least, it's not amenable to legal solutions as long as we value free speech. The primary mistake we make in regard to media violence is not ignoring it (we pay a great deal of attention to it, as the polls show). The mistake we make is approaching it legalistically.

The list of nonlegalistic, public and private approaches to media violence is easy to devise (without a Senate hearing), although it isn't terribly dramatic. Let consumers who are concerned about violence apply pressure to the industry. (Some civil libertarians argue that consumer pressure groups threaten the First Amendment, and in a way, that may be true but also irrelevant. Consumer-imposed censorship is our natural state, given the role consumer preferences play in determining which books are published and which movies produced.) Let gratuitously violent films and videos become as socially unacceptable as smoking or drunk driving (which can't be eliminated by social pressure, but can be reduced). Let parents monitor their kid's TV habits, but let us also recognize that the children who watch the most TV and are most vulnerable to TV violence may enjoy the least parental supervision. Let schools teach children how to watch television critically. And, let media consumers confront their own predilections for violence.

One of the most remarkable findings of the 1993 Times Mirror poll was that a majority of people who are considered heavy viewers of violent entertainment believe that TV violence is harmful to society (37 percent believe it is "very harmful"; 34 percent label it "somewhat harmful"). Nearly half of people surveyed who watch a lot of violent entertainment say that they are "bothered by" violence on TV. Sometimes the media seems like Dr. Frankenstein's monster; sometimes it seems like the stock market. We created it; we sustain it; yet the media controls us.

Like Ted Bundy we tend to blame the media for increasing violence in order to absolve ourselves. And we look to the law to save us. Despite all the commentary about America's historical romance with violence, we rarely confront the contradictions between our own violent impulses and our expectations that laws—penal codes and censorship—will quell the violence that surrounds us. Many of the same people who drive with their car doors locked, keep guns by their beds, and demand death sentences or "three time loser" laws or government regulation of whatever they consider harmful speech also revel in such spectacles as the Simpson or Menendez trials or a Diane Sawyer sweeps week interview with Charles Manson.

◀ | Of course, there's nothing new about public appetite for violent media, or concern about its effects. In sixteenth- and seventeenth-century England, newsbooks described grisly crimes in graphic detail. Consider the "Butcher of Mr. Trat" (cited by Mitchell Stephens in *A History of News*): "These butchers, with their hands already smoking in his blood, did cut up his carcass, unbowel and quarter it; then did they burn his head and privy members, parboil his flesh and salt it up. . . . His arms, legs, thighs, and bowels were powdered up into two earthen steens or pots . . . the bulk of his carcass was placed in a vat or tub."[20] In the Victorian era, English readers could feast on newspaper accounts of Jack the Ripper. On the American frontier, the press regaled readers with stories of outlaws, valorizing the James Gang or Billy the Kid.

Sensationalism has always been part of news, Stephens observes. Sensationalism is, in a way, a synonym for newsworthy; it encompasses reports of the supernatural as well as violent crime. In the sixteenth and seventeenth century, newsbooks and pamphlets kept the public informed about witches and monsters,[21] as supermarket tabloids keep tabs on two-headed babies and UFOs today, while popular personal development books and TV specials keep us up to date on angels.

In addition to monsters and murders, executions were staples for the early presses. Eighteenth-century broadsheets circulated the scaffold speeches of the condemned. Stories of executions, like executions themselves, were supposed to be instructive as well as entertaining; ballads purportedly memorializing the confessions of notorious criminals were presented as moral tales about the perils and costs of crime. The tradition of gallows literature continued in nineteenth-century America. Indeed, public reports of executions gained new importance as public executions were replaced by private, invitation-only procedures within prison walls. In the 1830s and 1840s the new penny presses offered descriptions of executions and reports on the last moments of the condemned, allowing readers to imagine what they were no longer permitted to see.[22]

Prurient interest in violence deters the televising of executions. The ratings would be unseemly, like the party occasioned by Ted Bundy's execution, as a majority of Americans may acknowledge. Seventy-four percent of people surveyed by Times Mirror in 1993 opposed televised executions. Sixty-three percent of respondents to the 1994 *National Law Journal* poll feared they would devolve into entertainment, "just like wrestling." Today, the public has little chance to revel in executions; most are barely even publicized. Thirty-eight people were executed in 1993, mainly in obscurity. Most Americans probably can't name them or their victims, whom they probably didn't read about in their local papers. Occasionally a high-profile case, usually involving a strong claim of innocence, is highlighted by the national press, but in the average, uncelebrated case, an execution rates, at most, a paragraph or two buried deep in the *New York Times*.

Violence in the media is so much more newsworthy and apparently more troublesome to the public than the violence of executions. On June 30, 1993, the *New York Times* consigned brief reports of two executions to the middle of the metropolitan section. On the same day, the lead story in the *Times* was a report on an agreement by the networks to label violent programming on TV.

In the 1970s and early 1980s, when they were still novelties, executions were front-page news. Gary Gilmore's successful 1976 campaign to be executed by the state of Utah (he opposed appeals of his sentence) helped launch the then newly sensationalized version of the *New York Post* (which had recently been acquired by Rupert Murdoch). Gilmore, who gratuitously shot and killed two men during a robbery spree, was the first person executed after the Supreme Court reinstated the death penalty in 1976 (effectively reversing a 1972 holding that the death penalty was unconstitutional). Handsome, smart, and suicidal, as well as merciless, Gilmore was the subject of a riveting bestseller by Norman Mailer and a TV movie (he was played by Tommy Lee Jones). Like Ted Bundy, Gilmore was made for media.

Since Gilmore's execution about 250 people have been executed and, to date, nearly 3,000 people occupy death rows, nationwide. The statistics have little capacity to shock. With some 25,000 people killed every year by private citizens, its likely that relatively few people would be disconcerted even by 50 or more annual executions by the state.

Whatever purposes these unheralded executions might serve—retribution, vengeance, incapacitation of the condemned—it's unlikely that they have much deterrent effect on murder. Few people will be deterred by executions that few people notice. Does this mean we should publicize or even televise executions, after all? Should we increase their number to, say, 25,000 a year, so that there's a rough equivalence between the number of murders and executions? We come full circle. If executions were televised, they'd probably be censored.

The history of public executions is instructive. It does not testify to the nobility or compassion of the human spirit or to the tendency of capital punishment to limit violence. In previous centuries, in colonial America and Western Europe, executions were public and relatively common. The death penalty was applied to a range of property offenses, as well as crimes of violence, and until the eighteenth century, it was apt to be accompanied by torture. The history of capital punishment is, in part, a history of moderation. Today, with the exception of wartime offenses and extraordinary acts of treason or terrorism, the Western democracies (except the United States) have generally abolished the death penalty. In the

United States the class of capital crimes has narrowed (it is no longer constitutional to execute someone for rape). There have been attempts to make executions less painful, beginning with the introduction of the electric chair (which turned out to be relatively gruesome) and the use of lethal injections. And, in order to make them seem more civilized, executions were moved indoors.[23]

It's impossible to know whether public executions had any deterrent effect historically, but it's clear that they had less than a sobering effect on the crowds that attended them. Historical accounts of capital punishment invariably focus on the perverse behavior of spectators. Michel Foucault speculated that the public execution ritual failed as an instrument of terror partly because it fostered solidarity among petty offenders and turned the condemned into antiheroes. The tradition of gallows speeches and gallows literature lent them nobility.[24] In general, descriptions of public executions suggest that they were public theaters of the absurd, more festive than somber.

In nineteenth-century Paris, executions became "a major social event," Daniel Gerould writes in his history of the guillotine. But they were the kind of social events associated less with community than anomie. The more chilling accounts of public execution scenes, by Dickens and Turgenev (both of whom are cited by Gerould), stress the essential indifference of the crowds to the taking of life, the absence of any identifiable emotion among the spectators, despite their celebratory air. After witnessing a beheading in Rome, in 1845, Dickens wrote, "Nobody cared or was at all affected. There were no manifestations of disgust, or pity, or indignation, or sorrow. My empty pockets were tried several times in the crowd immediately below the scaffold, as the corpse was being put in its coffin." The crowd seemed to regard the execution as a kind of sporting event: people placed bets on the flow of blood from the head.[25]

Turgenev described the mob that attended the execution of a notorious criminal as a mindless, primal force, generating "an enormous, rumbling noise," like the sea. "And what, I could not help asking myself, did this noise signify? Impatience, joy, malice? No! It did not serve as an echo of any separate, human feeling," Turgenev wrote. "A whole stream of human beings, men, women, and children, rolled past us in disorderly and untidy waves. . . . And what drunken, glum sleepy faces! What an expression of boredom, fatigue, dissatisfaction, disappointment, dull, purposeless disappointment!" For all appearances, though, the crowd was exuberant—drinking, laughing, "overjoyed" at the appearance of the condemned before the scaffold.[26] Public executions fell out of favor during the nineteenth century and were eventually abolished, partly because people enjoyed them too much.

The irony is that mass indulgence in the passion of revenge, which partly accounts for execution carnivals in nineteenth-century Paris or twentieth-century Florida, was precisely what public executions were supposed to prevent. One primary purpose of the criminal justice system is to replace untamed, private vendettas with more measured, less emotional acts of public retribution. The disruptive, self-destructive power of revenge is a recurrent theme in Western literature—consider the *Iliad, Medea, Hamlet,* or *Moby Dick*—and it is a subtext to the most ordinary criminal prosecutions.[27] Today, prosecutors are likely to consult the crime victim or the victim's family, efforts to provide victim assistance have greatly increased in the past twenty years, and victims are now often allowed to make statements to the court regarding sentencing. But defendants are still prosecuted in the name of the state.

Revenge is an "expensive way of doing justice," Richard Posner remarks in his insightful review of revenge literature.[28] Revenge is, by nature, excessive and sometimes insatiable, driven by self-righteous rage. Revenge, as Posner observes, places inordinate value on honor and a willingness to seek redress for every slight. It breeds bravado and encourages tribalism, since it fuels and feeds upon familial and small group loyalties, and it often leads to the slaughter of innocents. Sometimes, you hurt people most effectively by hurting the people they love: on stage Medea kills her children to get back at her husband. In the real world of the Bronx, a seven-year-old girl is murdered to punish her mother for not paying back a forty dollar loan.[29]

Today, the ravages of revenge-based justice are dramatized most clearly by urban youth culture. It's marked by fierce loyalty to gangs that supersedes any claims of the larger community. It reflects a fragile, highly valued sense of honor, exaggerated sensitivity to slights, and no sense of proportion. Murder has become the punishment for giving offense, as well as a rite of passage. "We have situations today where kids say, almost as a dare, 'I'm going to commit a violent crime, then take my friends to see the body,' " criminologists James Fox and Glen Pierce observe. Murder proves manhood and earns honor. What seems to concern these kids more than life, Fox and Pierce remark, is "the impression of their peers."[30]

The stories are appalling but so common that they no longer surprise. A sixteen-year-old boy is shot at close range and killed by his classmates, while pleading for his life, after an argument over a jacket. A fifteen-year-old boy is fatally stabbed by a classmate in a feud over a pair of sunglasses. One fourteen-year-old boy is fatally stabbed by another because of a "childhood rivalry." A seventeen-year-old boy is stabbed to death on a basketball court by another teenager who was hit by an errant ball.[31]

I could go on. For nearly a year, I collected clippings on revenge murders like these, until I ran out of space to keep them. "Argument Ends in Death on Subway," "15-Year-Old Fatally Stabbed in School," "Revenge Is Motive in 7 Slayings," the headlines proclaim. It may be that what looks like an increase in random violence is actually an increase in revenge attacks for trivial and unwitting routine encounters that might once have been resolved with a fistfight, if not a shouting match, or maybe even an "excuse me."

The violence may be concentrated in the inner cities, but it's not limited to them. Pathological sensitivity, poor impulse control, and a readiness to seek revenge contribute to violence throughout society. Domestic violence is often motivated by revenge, and not just in cases of infidelity. Men kill or beat their wives to get back at them for leaving. Revenge in one of its pettiest forms also takes its toll on highways. The great majority of traffic disputes don't end in homicide or attempted homicide, but an increasing number do. A thirty-two-year-old woman is shot in the head while riding in a car with her husband who may have cut off her assailant. A twenty-four-year-old man is stabbed to death by a nineteen-year-old whose car he passed.[32] The social contract is increasingly fragile (which is why there's so much nostalgia for community). Seeking disconnectedness instead of connectedness with strangers on the street is a survival skill. Once, I was slapped across the face by a woman in a subway station after I inadvertently looked her in the eye. The perceived volatility or potential volatility of the middle class contributes to fear of crime. (Hollywood captured that fear in *Falling Down*, in which Michael Douglas plays a downwardly mobile white-collar worker who goes on a killing rampage after being stuck on the freeway.)

Revenge is also implicated in violence in the workplace. Murder is now the second leading cause of death on the job nationwide.[33] More than three-quarters of all workplace homicides occur during robberies, but in occasional, high-profile cases, disgruntled employees, clients, or members of the public are seeking vengeance in the workplace.[34] These cases are still uncommon, but they generate fear in disproportion to their numbers. Reading headline cases, you may conclude that firing or disciplining an incompetent employee is a high-risk activity, like cutting someone off in traffic. The U.S. Postal Service has been plagued by a series of on-the-job killings by angry employees. The killings have been attributed partly to working conditions and poor management, which may well be contributing factors but are hardly excuses.

Serving the public in a blue-collar or white-collar job may seem as scary as firing someone. Probate courts that handle domestic disputes saw seven people killed and thirteen people wounded in 1992. The *Boston Globe* called this a "deadly rampage," which exaggerates the danger;[35] twenty people represent a tiny percentage of court personnel and litigants, but like public schools and hospitals, which are also subject to increasing violence, courts are supposed to be safe havens. Social workers, particularly those who handle child welfare cases, are increasingly at risk, threatened or attacked when they visit their clients' homes and in social service offices. In Massachusetts, workers for the Department of Social Services report about ten incidents of threats or actual violence each month.[36] Utility workers fear being attacked when they shut off someone's service because of unpaid bills.[37] In Texas, a man repossessing a car for a finance company was shot and killed, no questions asked, by the would-be owner, who received considerable support from his community. The district attorney was reluctant to indict, in the apparent belief that a man has a right to open fire on someone who ventures onto his property.[38] Law-abiding citizens, after all, are feeling under siege and particularly aggrieved by crime.

Revenge also follows from the glorification of individual grievances. American culture in 1990 seemed poised to embrace revenge because it had already embraced victimhood. The pervasive sense of victimhood, which has been the subject of so much debate, is, after all, a sense of aggrievement. For many people who feel that they've been wronged by their families or society, vindictiveness as well as extreme sensitivity to slights may readily become personality traits. Some are bound to feel justified in seeking revenge for new setbacks they suffer, or at least they take vicarious pleasure in the vengeful acts of others, fictive or real; they cheer the nerdy Bernhardt Goetz or action hero avenger Steve Seagal.

Some may even feel sympathy for Colin Ferguson, who opened fire on a crowded Long Island commuter train in December 1993, killing six people and wounding nineteen. Ferguson was apparently motivated by racial hatred of whites, Asians, and "Uncle Tom Negroes," just as Goetz may have been motivated by hatred of blacks. Like the German neo-Nazis who attack immigrants because they feel threatened by them, Ferguson may have felt that he too was fighting back, and others who shared his hostilities may have believed that the morality of his actions was debatable. As Jim Sleeper reported in the *New Republic*, defense attorney Colin Moore, briefly involved in the case, remarked that some people in the black community wanted Ferguson to have proper representation, "whether they agree or disagree with what [he] did," as if reasonable people might differ about the morality of mass murder.[39]

It's not likely that a great many sane people "agreed" with Ferguson, but in the months following this attack, a surprising number expressed sympathy for his proposed "black rage" defense, according to the 1994 *National Law Journal* poll. Forty-nine percent of respondents said that "fury as a result of long term institutionalized racism that causes an individual to snap" was a compelling excuse for a crime. (68 percent of blacks and 45 percent of whites found this defense compelling.) Even attorney William Kuntsler, who dreamed up the defense of black rage, expressed surprise at its widespread acceptance among blacks and whites.

Given the pervasive mistrust of the criminal justice system among African Americans and their own personal experiences with racism, some degree of sympathy for Ferguson was predictable. Still Colin Ferguson indulged in the kind of random, unprovoked violence that people of every color fear most—the kind of violence from which there is no protection. Unlike Bernhardt Goetz, Ferguson didn't wait to be approached by his victims and he didn't choose victims who could be considered menacing. It's difficult to understand public sympathy for his defense. (Perhaps the poll was simply wrong; perhaps people who found black rage a compelling defense for crime were thinking of crime generically, not this particular random slaughter.) If the poll results are accurate, the public is at odds with itself; while 49 percent of respondents to the *National Law Journal* poll expressed support for Ferguson's proposed defense, 59 percent said that the portrayal of criminal defendants as victims was "out of hand."

The consequences of regarding violent offenders as the victims of their own rage, making rage a defense for violent behavior, are particularly worrisome. Should we make male rage a defense to rape or white trash rage a defense for skinhead assaults on African Americans or immigrants? Virtually all hate crimes and most violent crime, in general, are bound to be at least partly motivated by rage. Accepting rage as a defense would effectively decriminalize violent crime.

That a public so intent on increasing the prison population with three time loser laws (and decreasing it with executions) should be willing to excuse precisely the kind of behavior that criminal laws were designed to control is evidence of public confusion that borders on the pathological. Or maybe it simply reflects a failure to think things through. The *National Law Journal* suggested that sympathy for the black rage defense reflected a traditional American concern for injustice: "Sympathy for those who act against their perceived oppressors apparently runs deep in the American psyche."

I hope not. The key word here is "perceived." Colin Ferguson was not taking action against actual oppressors. He had no reasonable perception of being oppressed by the people he shot. Indeed, the unreasonableness of his actions was crucial to his initial proposed defense. He was insane, according to his former attorneys (whom he fired). Black rage made him crazy, distorted his perceptions, rendered him not accountable for his act.

If perceived oppression is an excuse for commiting violent crime then none of us is safe from each other. Disgruntled employees are free to shoot their "oppressive" bosses. Husbands are free to shoot their wives and wives in turn may shoot their husbands. Students may kill their teachers and racial and ethnic groups with histories of hostilities are free to kill each other. The list of people who feel oppressed goes on. A perceived sense of oppression, after all, is just a political term for a grudge.

You can condemn the desire for redress as a thirst for revenge or a search for justice, depending on whether you believe the underlying grievance is true. If African Americans hadn't felt aggrieved by segregation and the effective denial of voting rights, there would have been no civil rights movement. But if southern whites hadn't felt aggrieved by Reconstruction, there would have been no Ku Klux Klan. If women hadn't felt aggrieved by laws and customs consigning them to the home and refusing them the right to vote, there would have been no feminist movement. But if men didn't feel aggrieved by women who challenge their authority, there might be less sexual violence.

You can't generalize about the inherent value of grievances anymore than you can generalize about the value of the revolutions they inspire. It's likely that the majority of Americans who would express at least qualified support for the civil rights movement or feminism would express disapproval of heavily armed survivalist tax protesters. But without denying that people who focus on their own victimhood may be taking steps toward justice as well as toward mayhem or revenge, you might worry about a society in which people derive their identity from feeling victimized and demanding retribution for every grievance, great and small. That is a society prone to violence, a society that might define justice as the preservation of honor, even to the death.

Consider the history of the American South. Traditionally it has been one of the nation's most violent regions. In addition to the violence they visited upon slaves, southern whites inflicted considerable violence upon each other, promiscuously indulging in fistfights, feuds, and duels. Southern historians ascribe this violent history partly to the premium the culture placed on honor and what Sheldon Hackney called the "sense of grievance that is at the heart of the southern identity," a world view that "supports the denial of responsibility."[40] (He might have been talking about postrecovery America.) Bertram Wyatt-Brown describes the elevation of tribal loyalty—kinship and local community ties—which led to intergenerational feuds (and contributed to the Civil War), and he underscores the importance of violence in maintaining honor.[41]

A culture that values honor even above life is a culture that most fears shame. The South was largely a shame-based culture, Wyatt-Brown stresses. Losing your reputation and standing in the community was a little like losing your soul; at least, it entailed a loss of identity. Virtuousness was located in the community, not the individual; in other words, you knew your own virtue only to the extent that it was recognized. Honor stood in the place of conscience, Wyatt-Brown notes; shame stood in the place of guilt.

It's worth noting that unlike antebellum southern culture, our own grievance-based culture tends to pathologize shame, which implicitly pathologizes honor. With its relentless palaver about self-esteem, the recovery movement might seem to be invoking a notion of inner virtue divorced from reputation. But recovery experts also denigrate guilt. (Guilt, like shame, "makes everything harder," one best-selling guru has proclaimed.)[42] The popular therapeutic notion of virtue is flexible and forgiving. It includes practically everyone who claims to have been victimized and gets with the program. In some ways, virtue is merely the state of being in recovery. Recovering persons are taught to feel good about themselves, regardless of their sins, so long as they confess and start recovering. If, in the slave-holding South, you derived virtue from the good opinion of others, in the contemporary culture of recovery, you derive virtue from your own good opinions of yourself.

For all its preaching against shame, popular therapeutic culture imbues shame with inordinate power and fears it as much as the honor-bound culture of the South. Both cultures view shame as intolerable, whether it's portrayed as a primary form of abuse and cause of codependency (which experts agree can be fatal) or as a metaphoric exile from the community. Both cultures perpetuate shallow, self-destructive views of self-esteem, equating it with shamelessness. (Self-esteem isn't the absence of shame but the strength to accept it.) Lack of self-esteem is often cited as one of the many explanations for youth violence, particularly among minorities. And it's true that self-esteem, defined not as mindless self-affection but a sturdy, stable ego, might indeed make some minor disputes less volatile today, just as self-esteem, meaning less reliance on reputation for identity, might have led to fewer duels and feuds in the southern states 150 years ago.

Tribal loyalty, bravado, excessive concern for social standing, the impulse to retaliate for the slightest hint of disrespect—these are characteristics that twentieth-century inner city youth share with nineteenth-century southern planters. When historians describe the killings among southern whites occasioned by the most trivial affronts—calling someone a liar or otherwise impugning his virility—they might as well be describing killings over basketballs in Brooklyn. It is one of the ironies of history that the culture destroying so many young, African American men has some striking similarities to the culture that enslaved their ancestors.

◖ | How do people respond to this culture and the cyclical violence ordained by revenge? Some try to stop it, with community action groups or campaigns for violence prevention programs. Others demand still more revenge. Vigilantism becomes more, not less, popular during periods of increased lawlessness, and as private justice becomes increasingly respectable, public justice becomes increasingly harsh.

Demands for tougher and tougher sentencing and even corporal punishment emerge. The caning of teenager Michael Fay, convicted of vandalism in Singapore in 1994, was apparently supported by a significant segment of the American public, who seemed unmoved by the characterization of the flogging as torture (its purpose is to inflict intense pain). A *Wall Street Journal* editorial lauded Singapore's tough criminal code, conceding only in passing that flogging might have been a bit harsh in this case.[43] On *Cross Fire*, Pat Buchanan fondly recalled the beatings he'd received from his father. One congressman protesting the floggings reported receiving letters from his constituents supporting it. As one man told a *New York Times* reporter, "If you've ever had your antennae ripped off your car, you can sympathize with the government of Singapore. Lash him. Vandalism is a cowardly and insubordinate act."[44] The caning of Michael Fay was used to exemplify the deterrent value of harsh, swift punishment, invoked in defense of the death penalty. "How many teenagers are going to Singapore to spraypaint cars?" one Massachusetts legislator asked rhetorically, arguing in favor of a death penalty bill, as if before the Michael Fay case Singapore was regularly invaded by armies of American teenagers bearing paint cans.[45]

It's difficult to reconcile this endorsement of flogging with a popular obsession with child abuse. Indeed, the sense of grievance contributing to demands for revenge was itself generated in part by a widely shared concern that most of us are victims of abuse. But revenge is not empathetic: it's self-centered; it represents the vindication of the self at any cost. People who feel aggrieved and compelled to strike back don't generally consider the damage they do or the grievances of others. They think only of themselves, and the ethic of revenge takes hold.

3 The Right Victims and Victims Rights

In a classroom at Indiana University, a young man, Mike, whose sixteen-year-old brother was murdered, is explaining his opposition to the death penalty: "When someone in your family is killed, you have this great rage. But you have to stop and ask yourself—do you want to be responsible for an execution? I did not want to have someone killed in my brother's name."

Mike is a member of Murder Victims' Families for Reconciliation, a modest, grass-roots organization, composed of people who have lost family members to murder, dedicated to abolishing the death penalty. It is June 1993, and MVFR is conducting a "Journey of Hope," a grueling two-week pilgrimage through cities and towns in the Midwest. Camping out in state parks on very tight budgets, MVFR members travel long distances for rallies and marches and discussions in schools and churches and on local radio shows. There is some subliminal tension in the group; people are tired and emotionally drained and feel at least a little at risk. The day I leave them, they are expecting a confrontation with the Ku

Klux Klan. (It doesn't materialize.) The night before, at an organizing meeting on the camp grounds, one of the group's organizers warns people not to walk alone in the park at night. "We're not the only ones who know our itinerary," he reminds them.

People who are organizing against the death penalty because people they loved were murdered have to fear being murdered because they are organizing against the death penalty. I leave the campsite alone, not because I am brave but because the risk seems slight and because I am too embarrassed about staying in the nearby lodge instead of in a shelter to ask anyone to walk me back. I run into a teenage boy and his girlfriend on their way to the lodge to use the phone. They are MVFR veterans (he is the son of one of the organizers). They invite me to join them; the girl, who looks about fifteen, says matter of factly, "You shouldn't be walking alone. There are hate groups out here."

Given the premium placed on personal experience by the talk show culture, in which the authority of experience almost always trumps the authority of disinterested reflection, just as emotional appeals trump intellectual analyses, you'd expect the families of murder victims to be sanctified, immune to further violence. You'd surely expect them to present a most persuasive case against the death penalty; at least no one can tell them they don't know the pain that murder inflicts. And members of MVFR are met with sympathy and respect by many people who support the death penalty. (I don't want to sensationalize their opposition.) But they also encounter indifference and hostility, not just from the occasional hate group.

Sometimes people who believe fervently in the death penalty greatly resent victims who speak out against it. They can't effectively challenge the authority of experience granted to MVFR members (that would be practically impossible to do in this culture), so they challenge the experience itself, questioning the connection to the person who was murdered. Marie Deans, who founded MVFR after the murder of her mother-in-law, says that people sometimes rationalize her opposition to the death penalty by pointing out that she did not lose a blood relative; she "only" lost her mother-in-law. People who have lost a member of the immediate family—a child, parent, grandparent, or sibling—are accused more cruelly of not loving their slain relative enough. "You lost your daughter, you'd better prove that you loved her," one woman explains, as if the desire for vengeance were the measure of love.

The members of MVFR often talk about love and "healing," instead of vengeance, invoking a Christian ethic of forgiveness (there is much religiosity in this movement); and on occasion I wished they were more judgmental; I found myself longing for less love and a little brimstone. If proponents of capital punishment sometimes demonize the people on death row, abolitionists tend to romanticize them, which makes it easy to dismiss the abolition movement as naive. One woman on the Journey of Hope who ministers to death row inmates describes them as "men who are just like you and I. They just happened to get caught." She urges us to remember that they are not just human beings but "warm, tender human beings with families who are good citizens."

I don't think so. Putting aside the people on death row who may be innocent (and estimates of their number vary widely), many are guilty of horrific crimes. They may have lost the capacity for "warmth and tenderness," if it ever had a chance to develop in them, and they've surely experienced lapses of empathy. That they are human beings and not animals is no compliment to the human race but proof of its incivility. To the extent that we are "warm and tender," they are not just like you and I; but when we are cruel and vicious, you and I are just like them.

You can oppose capital punishment misanthropically, in the belief that human nature is, at heart, unspeakable and people who behave badly are simply less inhibited than those who behave well. But if misanthropy is generated by moral outrage over the evils men and women do, it quickly devolves into nihilism. The compassion of abolitionists is at least an antidote to that. Usually, the compassion is not naive or easily won. Members of MVFR have struggled with their faith, with "God working in [their] hearts" in order to forgive the murderers of people they loved. Bill Pelke, whose grandmother was stabbed to death by four teenage girls during a robbery in her home, found "love and compassion" for her murderers through prayer, a conversion experience, and the recollection of his grandmother's own strong Christian faith. "She spent her life trying to help girls like this. I felt she would have wanted someone in our family to have love and compassion" for her murderers. Pelke began writing to Paula Cooper, a young woman who had been sentenced to death in the killing (she was fifteen years old at the time), and he was instrumental in obtaining the commutation of her sentence to sixty years in prison.

Pelke believes that Cooper should serve a long prison term. "My grandmother was stabbed thirty-three times," he says. If she serves, say, twenty-five years, "that's less than one year per stab wound." But he does not regard Cooper as subhuman. "We need to call murderers animals because we can't accept that their actions are human." His insistence on her humanity, his penchant for forgiveness, and his involvement in the abolition movement do infuriate some people, Pelke notes. In the steel mill where he works, "people would try and intimidate me about the death penalty. They'd get in my face, yelling and screaming, and I just talked about love and forgiveness."

For people who most adamantly support the death penalty,

the opposition of people like Bill Pelke must be especially galling. Capital punishment is often invoked in the name of the victims' families, justified, in part, as retribution for their loss. And while executions do distress some survivors, like the members of MVFR, they comfort others. Families of murder victims also organize in support of the death penalty and lobby to expedite executions. Politicians routinely exploit sympathy for the victims' families (families that favor the death penalty, that is), holding press conferences on anticrime bills with mothers of murdered children at their sides. A mother's grief aborts debate. ("I know how easy it is to talk about mothers when you want to do something cruel," Clarence Darrow said.)[1]

"I wouldn't know how to put into words the heartache and loneliness of burying a child," Anne Schiavina testifies before the Massachusetts legislature. It is July 1, 1994, and the Committee on Criminal Justice is conducting a public hearing on a death penalty bill introduced by Governor William Weld (which will soon be voted down by the legislature). The governor and lieutenant governor lead off the hearing with testimony in favor of the death penalty. A phalanx of police officers in full regalia line the back of the room signaling their support for the governor's bill. Much of the morning is taken up with testimony by politicians on either side of the debate and by testimony against the death penalty by men who had been wrongly convicted of murder. In the afternoon it is the turn of people like Anne Schiavina who lost their children to murder and vehemently support the death penalty. Schiavina's son was a police officer, killed in the line of duty, at age nineteen:

> I'm not an old woman looking for revenge, but I do believe in justice, and my Michael believed in justice. Michael firmly believed in the death penalty. He felt it was a deterrent when he

wore a badge. He felt you could use it as a bargaining chip if you were ever looking down the barrel of a gun. You could tell them, in a few months down the line, they'd be facing the same punishment.

Schiavina stresses that "every police officer in the United States favors the death penalty." Of course, that's not true, but who would dare contradict her? Facts are less persuasive than the moral authority of grief. "The feelings of every police officer from here to Hawaii," she says, is that death row ought to be like "the old time barber shop—two chairs, no waiting." Schiavina's testimony is not an argument for more efficient appeals and swifter, surer punishment, and it cannot be answered with arguments. Her testimony is no more and no less than a raw indictment of her loss. How could she focus on ensuring the fair treatment of people accused of homicide? She is tormented by the dreadful unfairness that befell her son:

> All I've listened to all morning [is people saying] "What if an innocent man is executed?" Wasn't my son innocent? What was he guilty of? Why did he have to die? . . . I'd like to know where all the do-gooders were and all you people against the death penalty, where were you when my son was killed?

For Anne Schiavina, it seems, every show of compassion for offenders (and their families), every effort to humanize prison life, is an insult to the victims of crime and their families. "There's a bus taking all the prisoners' parents to visit them in jails on holidays. What did we get? The prisoners and their families get together every weekend to celebrate every birthday and every holiday. What do you give the victims? You give them less. You give them nothing."

What is the difference between the grief of a mother who loses her son to murder and the grief of a mother who loses her son to a murder conviction and an execution or twenty-five years in prison, or life without parole? How do we rate their sorrows and relative claims to compassion?

"A son she loved would be pursued, captured, tried, and imprisoned by the forces of law and order," John Edgar Wideman wrote in *Brothers and Keepers*, describing his mother's predicament when her son, his younger brother, Robbie, murdered a man during a robbery. How does she balance the demands of love and justice?

> On one side were the stark facts of his crime: robbery, murder, flight. . . . On the other side were the guardians of society, responsible for punishing her son's transgression. . . . [She] tried to situate herself somewhere in between, acknowledging the evil of her son's crime while simultaneously holding on to the fact that he'd existed as a human being before, after, and during the crime he'd committed. . . . He was her son, but he was also a man who had committed a robbery in which another woman's son had been killed.[2]

In the ideal world envisioned by some victims' families, who oppose the death penalty, mothers of victims and mothers of offenders would be allied by their losses. They'd help each other heal. (And MVFR does include families of the condemned.) In the real world evidenced by Anne Schiavina's testimony, there is no possibility of empathy and reconciliation and little hope of healing (at least there is no talk of it); there is only the grim comfort of retribution.

"My wife died of a broken heart because these guys [who killed her son] someday will walk free," George Hanna says, concluding his testimony before the Massachusetts legislature on July 1, 1994. The murderers of his son, a state trooper killed in the line of duty, were sentenced to life without parole, but Hanna expresses certainty that they will eventually be released. Even if they did remain in prison until they died, he would probably not be satisfied. In his view, "true justice" demands their execution. He describes, in some detail, what they did to his son:

> I'd like to take you back to that day he was brutally murdered and put you in my place. I was sitting at home with my family. The phone rang and they said my son had been shot. He was in critical condition. . . . When I finally arrived at the hospital and walked down that corridor and saw all those police officers there and peered into a room and saw my son lying on a slab-like cot with a priest and two doctors bending over, and to see the form soaking with blood with 7 bullets in his body, and he looked at me and tried to say something and he reached for my hand and I held his hand and he held my hand. Not only were 7 bullets in him, his whole face was mashed, where the killers got down and scratched his face with their boots. That's what you call premeditation with atrocity and that's what's going on in this Commonwealth today.

How do legislators opposed to the death penalty respond to testimony like this? Not with a discussion about the high costs of capital punishment, or its uselessness as a deterrent, or the difficulty of enforcing the death penalty fairly. Only another survivor, one who opposes the death penalty, can respond, with an equally dreadful story and a plea not to be embittered by a lifelong desire for revenge.

What role should either story play in policy debates? How should either story affect a legislative vote? It is wrenching to hear that Hanna's wife died of a broken heart, but is it relevant? Would she have lived longer if her son's killers had been executed? Would she have died with some measure of peace? Is ensuring her peace of mind at the expense of another life the business of law? These are hard questions to ask—our instinct in the face of grief is respectful silence—and they are questions beyond the ken of many legislators.

But it is partly the job of legislators to answer the general question: What role should victims and their families play in shaping criminal laws? If a nationwide survey showed that families of murder victims tended to favor life without parole with restitution, instead of executions, should we abolish capital punishment tomorrow? If the polls showed that family members believed that capital punishment should be applied more broadly to cases in which no one was killed, should we extend the death penalty to kidnappings, rapes, and grisly assaults that leave their victims maimed? Of course, crime victims and their families are part of every legislator's constituency (too large a part, some might point out). Of course, they should be heard. But should we pay them special heed because they have been victimized?

These are rhetorical questions. The answers are obvious, although difficult to offer in the aftermath of a victim's testimony. We do not authorize crime victims to write criminal laws, anymore than we authorize them to prosecute cases, because for at least two hundred years we have regarded crimes as public, not private concerns. Murder is not only an offense against an individual; it's an offense against the social order. Although in colonial America, victims had the power and responsibility to prosecute crimes against them, a system of public prosecutions took shape during the eighteenth century and was in place by the time of the Revolution. England maintained a private prosecution system until the mid-nineteenth century, when a public prosecutor's office was established in response to reformist concerns about the inconsistencies of a private system and the tendency to use it vindictively.[3]

The state, then, has long been responsible for prosecuting cases, as well as defining criminal behavior and prescribing sentence. Victims would hardly want it to abdicate this power; they wouldn't want to bear the burden of prosecution, and most probably couldn't afford it. Still, crime victims do want the state to prosecute on their behalf, not simply on behalf of the public. Some tend to regard the prosecuting attorney as their lawyer, as if they were plaintiffs in a private, civil action. To a victim, the notion that crimes are committed against society, making the community the injured party, can seem both bizarre and insulting; it can make them feel invisible, unavenged and unprotected. So, while we don't delegate to victims the power to formulate and enforce criminal justice policy, we should and often do take their experiences into account in designing the trial process and resolving individual cases.

That, however, is merely a general statement of principle. What should its practice entail? We can reach a theoretical consensus on the need to treat victims with compassion and respect, recognizing that crimes are also committed against individuals, but consensus breaks down over detail and the clash between the victim's needs and the defendant's constitutional rights.

Since the 1970s, victims rights has nearly displaced "law and order" as a rallying cry for people who believe that crime is largely the consequence of an excessively lenient criminal justice system, shaped by landmark Warren Court decisions of the 1960s. The exclusionary rule, announced in *Mapp v. Ohio*, prohibiting the prosecution from introducing evidence obtained in violation of a defendant's Fourth Amendment rights and the *Miranda* and *Escobedo* decisions, prohibiting the use of confessions obtained in violation of the right to remain silent and consult a lawyer, are perhaps the most famous and widely vilified Supreme Court decisions expanding defendants rights.[4] Numerous other decisions imposed significant reforms on state criminal justice systems, particularly with regard to prosecutions of poor people. *Gideon v. Wainwright* held that the states must provide indigent defendants with trial counsel.[5] *Douglas v. California* held that indigents must be provided with appellate counsel as well (in 1955, the Court had given indigent defendants the right to free trial transcripts for appeal).[6] In *Brady v. Maryland*, the Court established the defendant's right to obtain exculpatory evidence from the prosecution.[7] *Duncan v. Louisiana* confirmed a defendant's right to a jury trial in a criminal case.[8] The Warren Court federalized much criminal procedure, requiring the states to respect rights guaranteed to criminal defendants by the Fourth, Fifth, and Sixth Amendments of the federal Constitution (including protections against search and seizure and self-incrimination, and rights to fair trial and assistance of counsel).

These are the rights that are popularly condemned for contributing to a rise in crime and a decline in punishment. Public safety demands the repeal of "legal technicalities" that "allow the guilty to go free," state Representative Donna Cuomo suggested at the 1994 Massachusetts public hearing on the death penalty. Defense attorney Bryan Stevenson patiently explained that technicalities such as the Fourth, Fifth, and Sixth Amendments have also resulted in the release of several innocent men from death row, one of whom had just testified before Representative Cuomo. She seemed pleased that an innocent man had been spared but puzzled by the necessity of extending rights to the guilty as well—as if guilt were always self-evident. The system of rights and rules governing police and prosecutorial conduct is aimed, in large part, at distinguishing the guilty from the innocent.

The connection between "legal technicalities" and determinations of guilt is what's lost in public discussion of criminal justice. The notion that the Warren Court's "coddling" of criminals has caused a breakdown in criminal justice is, for many, an article of faith, like the belief that the abolition of prayer in school has contributed to the moral breakdown that causes crime (among other deviant behaviors).

All of these beliefs are politically potent but difficult to substantiate. The notion that guilty people routinely go free because police violate procedural technicalities in conducting arrests and searches is apocryphal, criminologist Elliot Currie has suggested, noting that it's contradicted by data about the disposition of cases. One study by the Vera Institute of Justice found that cases in New York City are more likely to be dismissed because the victim and suspect know each other and the victim declines to assist the state in prosecution.[9] It is even less likely that the *Miranda* rule, requiring police to inform suspects of their rights, impairs effective law enforcement. New York City Police Commissioner William Bratton scoffs at the notion that the *Miranda* rule ought to be repealed; it's so easy to obey. Police have successfully adapted the *Miranda* decision, he observes; they routinely recite the rights to remain silent and consult an attorney—rights that millions of TV-watching Americans already know by heart.

But anger over the Warren Court decisions isn't based on evidence demonstrating their deleterious effects on law enforcement and won't be dispelled by facts showing that their effects have been minimal. This is largely an ideological debate, not an empirical one. Anger over liberal criminal justice reforms dating back to the 1960s reflects a belief that defendants ought not to have so many rights and a perception that liberal judges (whose numbers have waned considerably) care more about the defendant's rights than those of the victim, and, in a way, they do.

Victims have moral claims to be treated fairly, with sympathy and respect, but they don't have rights, exactly, because they're not being prosecuted: the state isn't threatening their liberty. That probably seems academic to victims who feel they've already lost their liberty to crime and to others who feel imprisoned by the fear of it. But a trial is supposed to be a principled process, governed by a set of rules devised to implement a set of ideas about justice and the relationship between individuals and the state.

The first rule in a criminal case, of course, is the presumption of innocence conferred upon all defendants. It does not reflect a naive belief that most or even many defendants are innocent, or a cavalier attitude toward crime. It reflects mistrust of the state. Requiring the state to prove guilt is a way of saying, "We won't take your word for it." Rules about a defendant's Fourth, Fifth, or Sixth Amendment rights are, in part, efforts to prevent police brutality and corruption. (One way to ensure that police don't beat confessions out of people is to declare confessions obtained by force inadmissible.) But many of these Fourth, Fifth, and Sixth Amendment rules also follow inexorably from the presumption of innocence. Coerced confessions are inherently unreliable, as the Court suggested in *Miranda*: cases based on independent investigations are generally stronger than cases based on confessions. Trials in which the accused is not represented by competent counsel are unreliable as well. A host of rules in criminal cases, regarding admissibility of evidence or qualifications of jurors, for example, are designed to ensure what the advocacy system idealizes: a reasonably objective, trustworthy fact-finding process. It is a central paradox of this system that the search for facts requires respect for a fundamental fiction—that all defendants are innocent when charged.

If you fear crime more than you fear the state, that fiction becomes intolerable. Today, law-abiding Americans are likely to fear crime more, and so they find it increasingly difficult to accept a constitution written by men who feared the state. That's partly why the National Rifle Association's insistence that private citizens have a right to own firearms to prevent stormtroopers from invading their homes has less resonance with the public than the argument that private citizens have a right to own firearms to prevent invasions of burglars. The same fear of crime also increases public tolerance of minor intrusions of liberty, such as weapons detectors in public places, which some propose to extend to the street. Criminologist James Q. Wilson, for example, has advocated expanding police authority to conduct warrantless searches for guns.[10]

Americans express support for individual rights without much appreciation of what those rights entail, as Herbert McClosky and Alida Brill observed in *Dimensions of Tolerance*. Despite professions of support for rights in the abstract, there is considerable hostility for the exercise of rights in particular cases. The overwhelming majority of Americans strongly endorse rights of free speech, "the general right of individuals to think and speak as they choose," but less than half (49 percent) believe that the majority should not be able to ban the expression of an unpopular opinion. Only a small minority (18 percent) believe that an atheist should be allowed to speak against religious belief in a civic auditorium.[11]

Support for rights that can't withstand fear of atheism can hardly stand up to fear of crime. The desire for law and order is much stronger and more pervasive than concern about the rights of criminal suspects (unless they're famous former football players accused of killing their wives). How many politicians feel compelled to proclaim themselves tough on violations of constitutional rights?

There are, however, racial divides on the subject of crime and rights. There's likely to be stronger concern about the rights of the accused in the African American community, where mistrust of police and the courts is relatively high. The 1993 Gallup Poll on crime found that blacks were less supportive than whites of restricting the rights of both suspects and convicted offenders: 46 percent of blacks, compared to 61 percent of whites strongly favored restricting bail; 23 percent of blacks and 38 percent of whites strongly favored restricting appeals, and 53 percent of blacks as opposed to 68 percent of whites strongly favored making parole more difficult to obtain. Similar percentages of blacks and whites strongly favored tougher sentences and putting more police on the streets, while a significantly higher percentage of blacks favored tougher gun laws. What you may infer from this poll is that a majority of Americans, black and white, want more protection from each other; but black Americans also want more protection from the state.

That a majority of Americans, overall, don't seem terribly concerned about the rights of criminal defendants is hardly surprising. It's likely that a majority of Americans haven't experienced police brutality, FBI surveillance, or IRS audits (or if they have been the subject of surveillance and other intrusions, they may not know about them). They may regard the government derisively, assuming its incompetence or venality, but they tend not to fear it. They're more afraid of each other.

At its most extreme, that is the fear on which a police state thrives. For many Americans that fear is mediated by a strong sense of entitlement to their own privacy and freedom from the state. (When self-interest is aroused, Americans can generally be depended upon to defend individual rights.) Of course, it is mere hyperbole to compare America to a police state (a bit like comparing verbal abuse to rape). But as significant public support for the caning of Michael Fay demonstrated, there is a strong desire for a more authoritarian criminal justice system. The public evinced relatively little concern that Fay enjoyed no presumption of innocence upon his arrest in Singapore. Support for his punishment seemed matched by indifference to questions about his guilt, as the *New York Times* reported. The public debate about the caning assumed Fay's guilt, despite credible claims that he was terrorized by the Singaporan police (not known for their attention to human rights), detained for nine days with very little sleep or contact with his parents or American Embassy officials, and coerced into signing a confession. "I had no idea what I was truly admitting to," Fay said. "But they became nice to me from that stage on."[12]

Perhaps people who favor easing constitutional restrictions on law enforcement, so that American police can act more like Singaporans, believe that the police can be trusted to brutalize only the guilty. Perhaps they believe that the sacrifice of an occasional innocent is an acceptable price to pay for law and order. In any case, the apprehensive view of the state that shaped the Bill of Rights has been considerably undermined by the demands for more effective state control of crime.

In this context the rationale for protecting a defendant's rights is not terribly persuasive. In the popular view, a criminal trial does not pit the defendant against the state; it pits the defendant against the victim. In the popular view, if defendants have rights, then victims should have them too. Americans use the language of rights loosely, not just to describe formal legal relationships, governed by constitution, statute, or contract but to formalize personal preferences and feelings of entitlement. "I have a right not to be insulted," we say, meaning "I prefer to be treated with respect." Or, "I have a right to sing the blues."

Phrases like these seem harmless enough, as long as we don't take them literally. People who believe they have a right not to be insulted are apt to clog the courts with petty harassment or libel claims or, on college campuses, they demand speech codes that make every casual conversation subject to quasi-judicial review. American culture has been fertile ground for victimism partly because of our reliance on rights. Rights are primary vehicles for fulfilling desires, so we learn quickly to turn our desires into rights, by turning ourselves into victims. Along with a sense of aggrievement comes a sense of entitlement to recompense or, in other words, a right. "I prefer to be treated with respect" becomes "I have a right not to be insulted—because insults oppress me. They perpetuate my secondary status in society."

We have, however, relatively little consensus on who is oppressed in America and how badly, which is partly why claims of discrimination are so divisive. In contrast, there is little disagreement over claims of victimization raised by people who have been mugged, burglarized, assaulted, or defrauded: they are, we agree, crime victims. Perhaps only in rape cases is there much dispute about what constitutes victimization, because the feminist analysis of rape, which has helped shape the prosecution of rape cases, partly rests on a view of women as an oppressed class—a view that is not exactly universally accepted. It also rests on a challenge to traditional notions of natural sexual behavior, which idealize masculine aggressiveness and foster a belief in feminine coyness: boys will be boys and women will say no when they mean yes. Debates about rape cases, particularly those involving date rape, illustrate our confusion about victimism, which is the subject of so much criticism, and victims rights, which generate so much support. In our discussions of rape, disagreement about discrimination—gender bias and gender roles—converges with agreement about the scourge of violent crime.

The current fascination with victimhood, in general, is rooted both in recent civil rights movements—including disputes about who's oppressing whom—and pervasive fear of crime. Lately it does seem, however, that more people fear being victimized by crime than by racial or sexual oppression (though it is not always possible to distinguish between the two, as in the cases of lynching and rape). The virtual sanctification of victimhood, therefore, may owe even less to controversial demands for civil rights than to unassailable demands for sympathy and support raised by crime victims. It's worth noting that the term "victims rights" originated in campaigns to reform criminal justice, not in efforts to end discrimination.

In part, demands for victims rights have been demands for victims services, which local prosecutors began providing in the 1960s. The first Victim Assistance Program was initiated in California in 1965. Today VAPS are common in localities throughout the country; they provide support services, such as day care, transportation to and from court, assistance in obtaining compensation and in retrieving stolen property, and counseling. Reforms like these were relatively uncontroversial; they humanized the system for victims and helped ease the ordeal of testifying in a criminal prosecution without infringing on a defendant's rights. The victims rights movement has helped improve the prosecution's treatment of crime victims, which is supposed to enhance conviction rates. Victims who feel supported and relatively safe are more likely to assist in prosecutions than victims who feel slighted and scared.[13]

Campaigns for victims rights are, however, not aimed merely at improving support services; they're aimed at acquiring rights conceived as counterparts to defendants rights. In 1982, a federal Task Force on Victims of Crime, established by President Reagan, proposed amending the Constitution by adding to the Sixth Amendment guarantees of the accused's fair trial rights, a victim's right to be present and heard at all critical stages of a criminal proceeding. Since then, the movement has focused on constitutionalizing victims rights at the state level, and fourteen states have enacted constitutional amendments ensuring victims rights. Most states have enacted guidelines governing the treatment of victims in criminal cases; often these take the form of a victim's Bill of Rights.[14] These "rights" may be simple recitations of the services provided to victims; in Massachusetts, for example, the Victim's Bill of Rights includes a right to "expedited return of property" and the right to a "secure waiting area." They also include notification rights—the right to be informed about the progress and disposition of a case or the release of the offender from custody. Whether or not notification requirements are framed as rights, they are, in effect, important services that help protect the victim at no cost to the defendant's rights. But victims rights advocates seek more than humane, considerate treatment and some measure of security. They seek the power to help determine the disposition of cases, which raises questions about equal, public justice. How do we balance the victim's need to influence prosecution and sentencing with the defendant's right to an objective trial and a presumption of innocence unaffected by the reputation or emotional appeal of a particular victim?

The correct political answer to this is clear: public opinion favors the victim's needs over the defendant's rights. Victims' advocates stress the terrible effects of victimization—posttraumatic stress disorder, depression, and other emotional illnesses, drug and alcohol problems, a range of stress-related diseases, divorce, and unemployment. From the victims' perspective, the trial is, in part, a therapeutic process. They seek "healing" in the resolution of the case, which seems appropriate to the citizenry of a therapeutic culture. Indeed, the victims rights movement partakes of the popular confusion of law and therapy and the substitution of feelings for facts. But if feelings are facts in a therapist's office, where subjective realities reign, feelings are prejudices in a court of law, which strives for relatively objective decision making. Justice is not a form of therapy, meaning that what is helpful to a particular victim, or defendant, is not necessarily just and what is just may not be therapeutic.

In general, putting high-profile cases aside, the public doesn't have much trouble distinguishing between the demands of law and therapy when the defendant's fate is at issue. Just try to imagine politicians bragging about allocating funds to build more psychiatric hospitals instead of prisons. But, considering the plight of victims, people tend naturally to be drawn to the therapeutic. How could we not want to help them?

One consequence of this desire to heal victims has been the widespread use of victim impact statements to help determine sentences. Almost all states allow victims to testify about the suffering inflicted on them by the defendant, describing the physical and emotional effects of the crime. To deny victims the opportunity to make these statements seems cruel; but to provide it is often inflammatory. Judges and juries swayed by particularly appealing, articulate victims may impose disproportionately harsh sentences on the defendants who wrong them. Offenders who have the dumb luck to choose especially resilient victims may be treated more leniently than defendants whose victims are easily traumatized. Victim impact statements can be prescriptions for unequal justice; they discriminate against victims as well as defendants. Does an unappealing, inarticulate victim or a victim of low social status deserve less retribution, less of an opportunity to heal?

The dangers of victim impact statements are particularly clear in capital cases in which prejudices about the victim's worthiness have long played a role. The death penalty has been applied disproportionately in cases involving white victims, clearly implying that the lives of whites are valued more highly than the lives of racial minorities. In 1987, the Supreme Court prohibited the use of victim impact statements during the sentencing phase of a capital trial, when the jury is called upon to decide whether the defendant deserves to live or die.[15] In 1989, the Court also prohibited prosecutors from making statements about the victim's character in arguing for the death penalty.[16] The Court stressed in these cases that evidence about the victim's character or the loss suffered by the victim's family was not relevant to determining a defendant's "personal responsibility and guilt." Except in cases involving self-defense or provocation, the defendant's character is at issue, not the character of the victim. A defendant's guilt shouldn't be aggravated by a victim's happy family life and good character any more than it should be mitigated by a victim's bad character and lack of familial ties.

In 1991, however, the Supreme Court reversed itself on this issue (a 5 to 4 majority opposed to victim impact statements became a 5 to 4 majority in favor of them). In *Payne v. Tennessee* the Court held that victim impact evidence was relevant in determining whether or not to execute the defendant.[17] *Payne* was a horrible case, involving multiple stabbings of a twenty-eight-year-old mother, her three-year-old daughter and two-year-old son. Only the son survived, and at trial, the grandmother testified to the murder's effect on him. The prosecutor exhorted the jury to consider his loss and his need for retribution, as well as the loss suffered by his grandparents. Writing for the majority, Chief Justice William Rehnquist noted the injustice of allowing the defense attorney to introduce evidence of the defendant's character while prohibiting the prosecutor from introducing analogous evidence about the victim.

To a layperson, that argument makes sense; in general the public tends to assume that criminal cases are, like civil cases, contests between victims and defendants, with the prosecutor serving as attorney for the victim, not just the state. Judges, even first-year law students, however, should know better. Criminal and civil cases are not alike; the state doesn't prosecute civil cases, which are private, not public disputes. And victims are not on trial in criminal cases, although defense attorneys sometimes endeavor to try them, maligning victims in order to absolve defendants, to the dismay of victims rights advocates. Indeed, supporters of victim impact evidence, who believe that the good character of the victim is relevant, are apt to express outrage at defense lawyers who try to introduce evidence of a victim's bad character.

Consider the history of rape cases. Until the formulation of rape shield laws in the 1970s, it was customary for the defense to interrogate victims about their sexual histories in order to paint them as promiscuous and discredit their testimony. This tradition of trying the victim in rape cases helped fuel the victims rights movement. Victims rights advocates ought to recognize that focusing on the victim, instead of the defendant, leads to victim blaming as well as victim praising, both of which are irrelevant. The defendant's blameworthiness is what must be determined. It is not a lesser crime to rape a prostitute or to murder someone who might be considered a lesser person.

The Supreme Court, however, was not swayed by this argument. In *Payne*, the Court addressed the danger of prejudicial sentencing by denying it. Victim impact evidence is not designed to encourage judgments about a victim's worthiness, the Court observed; it was "designed to show instead each victim's 'uniqueness as a human being.'" True, but victim impact statements weren't challenged because they were believed to be intentionally prejudicial; they were challenged because of their likely prejudicial effect. It's inevitable that when juries consider the "uniqueness" of the victim, they'll find some victims more unique than others. They'll pass judgment on their unique worth, just as they pass judgment on defendants.

Perhaps criminal trials have always been, in part, popularity contests between victims and defendants. Jurors are human beings, influenced by human likes and dislikes, and a flesh and blood victim is a much more sympathetic party than some abstract concept of the state. But if we can't avoid the jury's tendency to base its judgments partly on affection for the victim, neither should we foster it or posit it as a goal, allowing feelings about the victim to displace facts about the defendant's culpability.

That, however, is a dispassionate statement, which seems wanly out of place in such a highly charged debate. "Believe the victim," people cry; in other words, presume their charges are true. Eroding the defendant's presumption of innocence is one implicit, unacknowledged goal of the victims rights movement, especially in cases involving sexual abuse, especially when the alleged victims are children ("Believe the children"). Victims rights advocates who work with sexual abuse cases deny that they oppose the presumption of innocence, and, of course, not all do; but many are apt to dismiss questions about the credibility of self-proclaimed victims and the insistence that they prove their cases as "backlash" to assertion of their rights.

In the spring of 1994, I appeared on a panel on sexual abuse and victims rights. I represented backlash partly because I suggested that we should not automatically believe the victim's accusations anymore than we automatically believe the defendant's denials. Reading materials distributed to the audience included other examples of backlash, such as attempts to ensure fair trials in abuse cases by excluding the testimony of children who had been exposed to suggestive interrogation techniques. The mere notion of false memory syndrome, questioning the reliability of repressed memories of abuse, allegedly recovered after many years, was labeled backlash too. "There are no false memories," some people insisted, denying the possibility of ever confusing memory and imagination.

"This is a political movement," some proclaimed, inadvertently explaining their utter intolerance of a trial process open to truths that might differ from the truth offered by the victim. This was a historic power struggle between victim and abusers, one panelist said, suggesting that you had to choose sides. You couldn't choose a fair trial process; instead, in the advocate's view, your notions of fairness would be shaped by your biases in favor of victims or abusers. There is no belief in neutral process in this world. You are either for victims or against them, categorically. To challenge the claim of a particular victim, even if it is false, is to endorse victimization in general.

In a political struggle, truth is less important than choosing sides; or, you might say, in a political struggle, there are no truths independent of politics. Truth is a matter of ideological, not factual correctness. From a zealot's perspective, the truth of whether a particular defendant raped a particular victim is subordinate to larger "truths" about men's systematic brutalization of women. Waiting for my panel on sexual abuse and "backlash" to convene, I overheard two women discussing a controversial rape case. "So what if he didn't rape her," one woman said. "You can be sure he raped someone else. How many men aren't guilty of rape?"

Remarks like this do not represent mainstream approaches to justice. They probably don't even represent the victims rights movement; they're the ravings of its loudest and least thoughtful members. But even though the belief that all men are rapists is shared only by a fanatical minority, the tendency to disregard the truth of a particular case, in service to some notion of rough justice, is still pervasive. Police officers routinely perjure themselves to make their cases, New York City's Mollen Commission on police corruption and brutality reported in 1994, to the surprise of few people who work in the court system. When police officers testify, you can sometimes see the judges suspend disbelief. Police regularly lie about the circumstances of arrests and searches to cover up Fourth Amendment violations. The commission found that perjury among police officers is so common that it has a name, "testilying."[18]

To many officers engaged in no other form of corruption, testilying may seem, at worst, a trivial offense and, at best, a moral imperative. If you search someone without reasonable cause, in violation of his rights, and find a gun or a considerable quantity of cocaine, wouldn't justice be served by claiming that you saw the gun or the drugs "in plain view" before you approached him, so that a guilty defendant doesn't go free on a "technicality"? Perhaps, in this particular case. (Police on TV tell what are supposed to be white lies about arrests all the time.) But if testilying facilitates the conviction of some offenders, it ensures that others will go free. Criminologist David Kennedy observes that testilying helps create the "conspiracy of silence" within police departments that protects officers who are guilty of worse crimes than perjury—drug dealing, illegal gun sales, and manslaughter. If everyone is a petty crook, no one can risk speaking out against major offenders.[19] And, when situational ethics replace the rule of law, lying becomes habitual, even dutiful, along with illegal searches and, in some cases, self-righteous brutality. The Los Angeles police officers who beat Rodney King displayed an unshakable belief in their own rectitude, as if their actions were justified because they were the good guys and he was bad.

If only we could depend on the police to cull the good from the bad unerringly. If only society were neatly divided into innocent victims and guilty defendants, with scarlet *I*'s and *G*'s emblazoned on their breasts. If only no one were ever falsely accused and there were never any mitigating circumstances to crimes. If only guilt were the equivalent of evil.

4 The Death Penalty— How It's Perceived

"Nothing is more cruel than righteous indignation," Clarence Darrow said, pleading for the lives of Leopold and Loeb. He meant, I think, that moral certainty is more dangerous than moral ambiguity, and this is often true. Cult leader David Koresh would surely have done less harm had he been more doubtful. Still, Darrow was indulging in hyperbole. Sadism exists in the absence of righteous indignation, and righteous indignation can inspire compassion as well as cruelty. Righteous indignation over vandalism fueled support for the caning of Michael Fay, while righteous indignation over torture fueled its opposition. Both advocates and critics of the death penalty call upon righteous indignation over violence committed by offenders or violence committed by the state. Each side accuses the other of cruelty and claims as its own the copyright on compassion. Critics of capital punishment focus on its cruelty to offenders; supporters argue that its abolition would be cruel to the families of murder victims. The choice between execution and life imprisonment is often falsely framed as a choice between compassion for the victims or compassion for the condemned, which is partly why executions are so popular. Siding with the executioner seems like siding with innocence instead of guilt.

This assumes, inexplicably, that compassion can only be demonstrated by an exacting commitment to retributive justice that demands a life for a life, and it ignores the anguish capital punishment inflicts on some murder victims' survivors, even those who support the death penalty. The prolonged process of trying and appealing capital cases is quite painful for victims' families, as advocates of limiting death penalty appeals constantly assert. But delay is inevitable in a system that takes seriously the business of killing people and tries to avoid mistakes, which sometimes come to light only years after conviction. In a notorious case, Randall Dale Adams, wrongly convicted of murder in 1977, spent twelve years in a Texas prison, including three years on death row, before the state dropped all charges against him. (His conviction was based on perjured testimony and prosecutorial misconduct, and he owed his eventual release to the fortuitous decision of filmmaker Errol Morris to make what became a celebrated movie about his case, *The Thin Blue Line*.)[1] Walter McMillian, arrested in 1987, spent six years on Alabama's death row before he was exonerated in 1993, through a federal appeal. His conviction was also based on perjured testimony and stank of racism. McMillian, an African American with no felony record, was convicted of murdering a young white woman; virtually the only evidence against him was the testimony of a white man who had confessed to another similar killing. McMillian offered the testimony of several alibi witnesses, friends and family members, who swore that he spent the morning of the murder at a charity event for a local church.[2]

The popular equation of opposition to capital punishment

with a preference for guilty defendants over innocent victims overlooks cases like these. Innocent people are occasionally sentenced to death. Are innocent people executed? It's quite difficult to prove the innocence of a dead man. When people die their cases usually die with them, and even in celebrated cases involving strong evidence of innocence, the state is not likely to admit that it has killed someone who was innocent or, at least, not clearly guilty. (Anyone who is executed despite reasonable doubt about his guilt has been executed wrongly.)

There is, then, considerable dispute about the number of wrongful executions. Abolitionists claim there have been many; supporters of capital punishment are apt to claim there have been none. Research by Michael Radelet and Hugo Bedau, first released in 1985, that carefully documented over 400 wrongful capital convictions and 23 wrongful executions[3] was attacked by the Reagan Justice Department as mere polemic, partly because it had been funded by the apparently nefarious Unitarian Universalist Society, which "has provided financial support to many liberal groups seeking to change national policy on social issues."[4] (Imagine that.) Yet, for all the sound and fury about wrongful executions, there is no dispute that innocent people, like Walter McMillian, have spent years on death row and in prison until gross misconduct and mistakes in their cases were uncovered.

But, if the unavoidable risk of executing the innocent is the most politically effective argument against the death penalty, it is not the primary motive for many abolitionists. People who oppose the death penalty generally believe that it is wrong to execute the guilty, even those who have committed the grisliest, most gratuitous crimes. This is why abolitionists, like defense attorneys, enjoy relatively little support. They are indeed advocates for the guilty, although that does not make them apologists for their crimes. So, it is tempting to rely on stories about wrongful convictions in arguing against the death penalty, but focusing on questions about innocent defendants evades harder questions about how to evaluate and punish guilt.

Who is executed in America and why, after what sort of trial process? Who cares? A majority of Americans may favor executions in general but they're essentially indifferent to particular executions that occur in particular cases. Most of us are oblivious to the numerous executions now carried out every year. Most of us know virtually nothing about the personal histories of people on death row and little about the characteristics of the death row population in general.

Practically all death row inmates are male. Many are mentally handicapped or mentally ill, according to Amnesty International. In Georgia, for example, according to a 1987 report (by the Clearinghouse on Georgia Jails and Prisons) an estimated 20 percent of the state's death row inmates may have been severely mentally handicapped or below normal intelligence.[5] The Supreme Court has ruled that the Constitution permits the execution of retarded people, although states may prohibit it if they choose.[6] Amnesty International estimated that at least six people diagnosed as mentally handicapped or borderline cases were executed during the late 1980s.[7] Probably the most famous mentally disabled person executed in recent years was Rickey Ray Rector, who suffered from extensive brain damage from a self-inflicted gunshot in the head and a subsequent partial lobotomy. (Rector shot himself after killing two people.) He was executed by the state of Arkansas and then Governor Bill Clinton during the 1992 presidential campaign. The Supreme Court declined to review this case, but the execution seemed to violate constitutional strictures against executing the incompetent. Rector was reported to have had virtually no understanding of his impending death; in the apparent belief that he would return to his cell after being executed, he saved the dessert from his last meal.[8]

Insane people are not supposed to be executed. A 1986 Supreme Court case, *Ford v. Wainwright* held that people must be sane or "competent" to be executed, meaning that they must understand that they are about to be killed for the crimes they have committed.[9] But determinations of competency are left to the states, and procedures for assessing a prisoner's mental state vary. Amnesty International estimates that in recent years several people with severe mental illnesses have been executed or "come close" to execution.[10] Indeed, the desire to execute people who have been sentenced to die, regardless of their states of mind, seems strong. In Louisiana, officials forcibly medicated an insane death row inmate in order to make him competent to be executed. Michael Perry, convicted in 1984 of killing both his parents and several other members of his family, had an extensive history of schizophrenia; he was paranoid, delusional, and heard voices. The state acknowledged his natural incompetence, but argued that he was competent when medicated. "Synthetic competency," according to the state, was as good as natural competence, for purposes of an execution. The state even argued that it had not just the right but a duty to medicate Perry against his will, arguing that it would be cruel and unusual punishment to deprive him of medication that would make him competent—if only for the sake of being executed—which was a tortured way of saying he was being killed for his own good.[11]

Louisiana lost this case on a state court appeal; the execution of severely mentally ill prisoners is apt to make people uncomfortable, as is the execution of the physically disabled, who have no formal protection against execution. In 1991, Texas executed a partially paralyzed man.[12] Executions like this are controversial—the image of a handicapped offender being wheeled to his death is unseemly and often labeled uncivilized. But why, after all, should we consider it especially immoral? Why should the execution of a healthy prisoner be considered more civilized than the execution of a paraplegic?

Juveniles once seemed less threatening and more redeemable than adult offenders but, today, dramatic increases in juvenile violence have increased demands to imprison juveniles for long periods of time and even execute them. The Supreme Court has declined to prohibit the execution of juvenile offenders. Instead, in 1989, it ruled that executing people as young as sixteen was constitutional.[13] A majority of death penalty states permit the execution of offenders who were under eighteen at the time of the crime. More than ninety juvenile offenders have received death sentences since the 1970s, and nine men have been executed for crimes committed as juveniles (1985 saw the execution of the first juvenile offender, Charles Rumbaugh, since 1964). As of 1991, according to Amnesty International, there were more juveniles facing execution in the United States than in any other country known. There were thirty-nine juvenile offenders on death row in 1994.[14]

In 1991, Amnesty International reviewed the cases and personal histories of twenty-three juveniles sentenced to death.[15] It found that "overwhelming" numbers of them came from "acutely deprived backgrounds." They were often the victims of severe physical and sexual abuse in childhood, and more than half were afflicted with mental illness or brain damage. They tended to have serious substance abuse problems and were often of below average intelligence. Their family histories lent new horror to the word "dysfunctional." They were abandoned by their parents and raised by abusive, alcoholic relatives, or they watched their fathers beat and rape their mothers or they were brutally beaten and raped themselves. Some were psychotic, schizophrenic, delusional, or retarded and were using drugs or alcohol at the time of their crimes. It's not at all uncommon for many factors like these to be ignored during their trials as they were ignored throughout their childhoods, before they erupted in violence. Nor is it uncommon for adults on death row to have similar histories of derangement, retardation, and abuse.

Turn on the TV and you see parades of people with less horrific histories of child abuse and familial dysfunction and less serious addictions demanding and receiving our support. Of course, most people on death row, juveniles included, have probably committed dreadful crimes; they require and arguably deserve long-term, maybe lifelong institutionalization. Still, you have to wonder, how does a culture so sensitive to the ravages of early childhood abuse and deprivation decide that they deserve to die?

◀ | Why do we execute people? Deterrence once seemed the most popular, socially acceptable justification for capital punishment. A 1973 Harris Poll showed that 76 percent of people surveyed who favored capital punishment said that it had greater deterrent effect than life imprisonment.[16] Support for deterrence may be exaggerated by the tendency to confuse deterrence—discouraging others from committing murder—with incapacitation—disabling or destroying convicted murders so that they can't murder again. Still, the concept of deterrence, the notion that the threat of punishment prevents people from committing crimes, has been central to the capital punishment debate.

To people who grow up in relative order, in families and communities with fundamental rules of behavior and reasonable systems of rewards and punishments, the deterrent value of law seems obvious. (I stopped speeding after receiving a very expensive traffic ticket.) For people who grow up in anarchy and violence, in worlds in which rewards are sparse and punishments arbitrary and harsh, the deterrent value of law can be minimal. Most of my legal aid clients did not appear to be people who thought through and weighed the legal costs of their crimes. They tended to be short-term thinkers, for whom the very concept of deterrence seemed irrelevant. The prospect of punishment also has little deterrent effect on violent offenders who lack the will or capacity to control their actions or on arrogant offenders who deem themselves above the law. (Richard Nixon probably never imagined that his own tapes would be used against him.)

Social science evidence that the death penalty deters is scant (some would say nonexistent). A 1975 study by Isaac Erlich that purported to prove that capital punishment deterred homicides has been so thoroughly discredited that even proponents of the death penalty have, in general, stopped citing it.[17] They now tend to rely on their own feelings about deterrence rather than facts. Massachusetts Governor William Weld has conceded that evidence of capital punishment's deterrent effect is inconclusive but has said that his "gut" tells him the death penalty deters. Alabama Assistant Attorney General Ken Nunnelley, who prosecutes capital cases, agrees, "My gut tells me that it has a deterrent effect. Let me put it that way."[18]

Gut instinct tells others that the death penalty brutalizes more people than it deters, encouraging more violence than it prevents. This is not a new feeling. The eighteenth-century reformer Cesare Beccaria observed that capital punishment served as an "example of barbarity." So far, however, social science has not been able to substantiate this contention. A few preliminary studies suggest that homicides may increase after an execution, but they do not constitute hard evidence of any brutalizing effect.[19] And, given the fact that so many executions are unnoticed, it's difficult to imagine that they have much effect on the public at all. Concern about capital punishment's brutalizing effect is at the center of discussion about televising executions, but it may be television's suspected brutalizing effect that's so worrisome.

We have no proof of how capital punishment affects people. Sometimes we can only rely on feelings and ideology. We can look at the experiences of states that impose the death penalty, which generally enjoy no corresponding decline in homicides or violence. Texas has the most populous death row in the nation and one of the highest homicide rates, but that proves nothing. You could easily argue that the high homicide rate causes the high rate of capital sentencing. Proponents of capital punishment also argue that the death penalty doesn't deter only because it isn't used often enough or because the appeals process makes the imposition of sentence seem a slim possibility rather than a certainty. Or, they assert that homicide rates would be even higher without the death penalty. None of these claims can be proved or disproved.

But the debate about deterrence is less important than it seems, given the inordinate amount of attention that has been paid to it. Abolitionists would not drop their opposition to the death penalty if it were proved to have a deterrent effect on homicide. Its deterrent value would be considered irrelevant to the perceived immorality of state-sanctioned executions (especially when there are alternative means of deterrence, like life imprisonment without parole). Proponents of capital punishment do not rely solely, or even primarily, on its presumed deterrent effect. How many have been persuaded by studies suggesting that the death penalty does not deter?

The debate about deterrence is also becoming less important as demands for retributive justice gain more and more support. The notion of retribution has always played a central role in capital punishment debates. In 1973, 40 percent of people surveyed by the Harris Poll cited biblical retribution as a reason for imposing the death penalty, and a striking 54 percent of people who supported the death penalty said they would support it if it had no deterrent effect. Studies conducted in the 1960s and 1970s suggest that the demand for retribution may have been stronger in some proponents of the death penalty than their belief in deterrence.[20]

Still, in the 1970s, deterrence seemed a more respectable reason for supporting the death penalty than retribution, a sentencing goal that can be hard to distinguish from revenge. Today, our culture is laced with the desire for revenge, and retribution is becoming eminently respectable. Some proponents of capital punishment contend it is necessary to stave off vigilantism.

The desire for revenge or retribution also seems stronger than any practical concern about the death penalty's excessive costs. It is considerably more expensive than life imprisonment. (There's relatively little debate about that, although supporters of the death penalty may blame the costs on the appeals process, which they'd like to eliminate.) According to the Death Penalty Information Center, Texas spends an estimated $2.3 million on every capital case, about three times the cost of a forty-year sentence to a maximum security prison. Florida spends some $3.2 million for each execution. In California, capital trials are said to be six times as expensive as noncapital murder trials.[21] The expense of capital litigation is unavoidable. Because "death is different," the trial process is different, generally longer and more complicated. Every capital case requires essentially two trials—one to determine guilt and one to determine sentence. Appeals to the state's higher courts are generally automatic. Pretrial expense can also be high, if the case is properly prepared. At every step along the way, a capital case costs more than a noncapital case. We could, of course, reduce these costs by reducing the due process afforded capital defendants. (In some states, costs are minimized by failing to provide defendants with competent counsel.) We could summarily try and execute people at relatively low cost and at the high risk of executing the innocent or the not entirely guilty—people whose guilt is mitigated by mental or emotional disabilities or the circumstances of the crime.

Confronted with the indisputable facts about the relative costs of capital punishment, fiscally conscious politicians who support the death penalty are suddenly apt to decide that costs should not influence policy. "You can't put a price on justice," Massachusetts Governor William Weld has said in defense of his admittedly costly death penalty bill.[22] Of course, Governor Weld regularly puts a price on justice when it comes to funding social services or welfare programs. He takes pride in putting a price on social justice. The state puts a price on criminal justice as well every time it sets salaries for court officers or corrections officials, considers programs for diverting juvenile offenders, or establishes shelters for battered women. Weld doesn't really mean he can't put a price on justice. He simply means that either for political reasons or out of a genuine personal conviction, he's willing to pay the price for the death penalty, however excessive it might be.

Meanwhile, opponents of capital punishment speculate that the public is more concerned with enacting capital punishment laws than enforcing them. Perhaps. But if that were true, politicians might garner few votes by railing against extended appeals in capital cases. What appears to be public indifference to the annual number of executions might instead reflect the relatively little attention they're paid by the media. What if every execution were televised and preceded by a talk show confrontation between advocates for the condemned and advocates for the victims who favor executions, or better yet, encounters between the condemned and the victim's family?

It's not hard to imagine television arousing public interest in executions without arousing interest in their fairness. Public demand for strict sentencing, in general, seems stronger than public concern about whether strict sentences are merited in particular cases. Popular support for imposing mandatory life sentences on three time felons didn't seem much diminished by the tendency of three time loser laws to include some petty offenders in their sweep. Popular endorsement of corporal punishment in Singapore didn't evince much concern about the quality of justice in the Singaporan courts.

Many Americans seem to like the idea of capital punishment the way they like the idea of caning, disregarding its practice. This is a hard thing to say but should perhaps be the first thing to say about strong majority support for capital punishment. Public support for capital punishment seems based on ignorance about how the death penalty is applied and what it does or does not achieve. In the 1980s, a *New York Times* poll on public attitudes toward the Reagan administration support of the contras in Nicaragua's civil war showed that a majority of Americans supported the president's position while only a minority could describe it. In other words, a majority opined that we were on the right side of the war although only a minority knew which side we were on. I suspect that the gap between information and opinion is equally dramatic on the subject of capital punishment, and criminal justice in general.

At least, public knowledge about the practice of capital punishment seems vague and essentially irrelevant to opinion. Some polling data does indicate public suspicion that racism and economic discrimination help determine whether defendants are sentenced to live or die. A 1991 Gallup Poll found that although 76 percent of Americans favored the death penalty, 72 percent of blacks and 59 percent of whites agreed that poor defendants are more likely to receive death sentences than middle- or upper-class defendants convicted of the same crime. Further, 73 percent of blacks and 41 percent of whites agreed that blacks were more likely to be sentenced to death than whites in similar cases.

It's difficult to know whether to be slightly encouraged or very depressed by this poll. It may show some awareness of inequities in the criminal justice system, but it also shows willingness to tolerate inequities, even when they're fatal. You can easily infer from these figures that more than half of the people who support the death penalty prefer a biased capital punishment system to no capital punishment at all.

Am I being unfair? Perhaps. Polls that point to a suspicion that poor people and racial minorities are treated more harshly in the criminal courts than affluent whites may reflect a general cynicism about the advantages of wealth and status, not specific knowledge about racial and economic discrimination. Nor does it necessarily reflect a belief that disadvantaged defendants are being railroaded. Perhaps some people tell themselves that determination of guilt and innocence are reliable even when sentences are partly affected by class and racial biases. The Gallup Poll doesn't indicate a belief that innocent defendants are being executed. It may, instead, evince concern that guilty defendants with the privileges of race, class, and high-priced lawyers are going free. Then again, it may be that some people are willing to sacrifice an occasional innocent in order to execute the guilty. We can only speculate. A 1988 random survey of 353 adults showed that 80 percent of respondents favored the death penalty, although only 64 percent believed that "innocent people are only rarely executed."[23]

What does the public know about the death penalty and

how much does it care about the way the death penalty is applied? Social scientists confirm that people are generally ill-informed about capital punishment, as they are about a range of public issues.[24] Still, support for the death penalty has steadily risen in the past twenty-five years, as people ill-informed about the criminal justice system have become increasingly fearful of crime.

In the mid-1960s public opinion was almost evenly divided on the subject of the death penalty. In 1966, polling data showed 47 percent of the public opposed to capital punishment and 42 percent in favor of it (11 percent had no opinion). Endorsement of capital punishment was popularly associated with right-of-center political views, and a few provocative studies conducted in the 1960s and 1970s confirmed that proponents of the death penalty tended to be politically and socially conservative, more authoritarian than opponents of the death penalty, and more likely to endorse statements sympathetic to racial discrimination and restrictions on civil liberties. But these findings may tell us less about the nature of support for capital punishment than the political and social divisions of the time, when antiwar protesters, civil rights activists, feminists, and hippies or former hippies were still squared off against a less than silent majority. In any case, support for capital punishment began broadening in the late 1960s (when concern about law and order was on the rise); by 1973, 59 percent of the public favored the death penalty. Less than ten years later support for the death penalty was at 66 percent and by 1988 it had reached 79 percent, with only 16 percent of the public opposed. Today, nearly 80 percent of the public continues to profess support for the death penalty and not many politicians, liberal or conservative, dare oppose it.[25]

Some evidence suggests, however, that support for capital punishment may be more equivocal than these figures suggest. A 1973 Harris Poll showed that while 59 percent of the public favored the death penalty, only 39 percent said that, as jurors, they would always vote guilty if the defendant were proven guilty of a capital crime with a mandatory sentence of death.[26] Support for capital punishment may be more qualified than it appears, like support for abortion rights. Many people who endorse abortion rights in general oppose making abortions available to women in particular cases, when they don't approve of the reasons abortions are sought. A 1989 *New York Times* poll showed that 63 percent of the public favored abortion rights but only 26 percent favored making abortions available because pregnancy interfered with a woman's education or career.[27]

What are we to make of the polls by which we try and measure the public mood? Novelists might do a better job than pollsters in illuminating the logic of public opinion. Polls sometimes confuse more than clarify. People who are ashamed to admit ignorance are apt to answer questions they don't understand, or, as *New York Times* reporter Daniel Goleman has explained, people offer opinions on subjects they know nothing about. In a 1981 study, 30 percent of respondents asked their opinion about a fictitious law obediently offered one, claiming they opposed or supported it. In a 1941 study, college students offered opinions about three nonexistent nationalities.[28] People are also highly suggestible—biased questions produce biased results—and people are inconsistent. Simple yes and no answers to questions about morally ambiguous subjects, like capital punishment or abortion rights, cloak a complex mix of conflicting feelings and ideas.

What, then, does it mean to say that 75 percent or 80 percent of the public favors the death penalty? Would 75 percent or 80 percent participate in an execution? Do widespread expressions of support for the death penalty reflect a rational assessment of its usefulness in controlling homicide or emotional reactions to crime and disorder, or both?

Putting aside polling data, for the moment, and talking to people who support the death penalty or listening to them talking to each other on radio and TV, you quickly sense the correlation between a deep belief in the death penalty and shallow understanding of its practice. There does seem to be an inverse relationship between knowledge and belief on the subject of capital punishment: the more people know, the more equivocal and uncomfortable they are about supporting the death penalty; the less people know, the more adamant they are in their support.

This apparent discrepancy between opinion and information about capital punishment was underscored by the late Justice Thurgood Marshall in 1976. Asserting that "American citizens know almost nothing about the death penalty," Justice Marshall dismissed the importance of public opinion polls indicating its popular support. This buttressed his argument that capital punishment violated the Eighth Amendment stricture against cruel and unusual punishment, which is generally defined by the prevailing public conscience and "sense of justice." Public support of capital punishment, expressed in the polls, arguably showed that it did not violate the public conscience, unless the polls were meaningless because the public didn't know precisely what it professed to be supporting. In Marshall's view, capital punishment violated the Eighth Amendment because if people were fully informed, they would find it "barbarously cruel . . . shocking, unjust, and unacceptable."[29]

Marshall listed what he believed the public ought to know about the death penalty and didn't: that it has no particular deterrent effect; that it is more expensive than life imprisonment; that it is not selectively applied to the most dangerous recidivist offenders; that it discriminates against poor people, minorities, and men (women are rarely executed); and that innocent people are sometimes sentenced to die.

Most of these facts are the subject of considerable dispute. Proponents of the death penalty might dismiss them as opinions. But accepting, for the sake of argument, the truth of Marshall's assertions, you might still question his conclusion about what an informed public would and would not tolerate. For some people, a desire for vengeance or anger spawned by an overwhelming fear of crime or anxiety about social chaos can easily outweigh concerns about justice. Whether or not the death penalty is a rational, morally justifiable response to violence and disorder, the mere idea of it can provide emotional satisfaction. Marshall himself noted that the more people based their support for the death penalty on a desire for vengeance, the less likely they were to be swayed by information about its inefficiencies.

Again, we can only speculate. Attempts to test Marshall's hypothesis have been inconclusive. A 1976 study by political scientist Austin Sarat and psychologist Neil Vidmar tentatively confirmed Marshall's belief that information about the death penalty would decrease support for it, particularly information questioning its deterrent effect. Sarat and Vidmar also confirmed Marshall's suspicion that a public bent on exacting vengeance would care less about the death penalty's practical utility or cost.[30] A recent study by criminologists William Bowers, Margaret Vandiver, and Patricia Dugan suggested that Marshall was overly optimistic in predicting the effect of knowledge on opinion. They found that people whose support for the death penalty is moderate or qualified may become less supportive as they become more informed. But knowledge has relatively little effect on people who support the death penalty enthusiastically. "People who say they feel 'strongly' about the death penalty tend to incorporate information about capital punishment selectively so as to reinforce their preconceived attitudes." In other words, information may act on weak opinions, shaping what people believe;

strong opinions act on information, shaping what people know.[31]

Information does seem to be of limited value in the campaign to abolish the death penalty. Strongest support for capital punishment seems to be essentially emotional (as is strongest opposition to it). According to Bowers and colleagues, "strong death penalty proponents have tended to maintain their expressed commitment even when they conceded that the death penalty did not or would not comport with standards of utility or fairness they themselves gave as grounds for their support."[32]

This doesn't necessarily bespeak hypocrisy. It may be that people don't really base their support for the death penalty on the notions of "utility or fairness" that they cite as the basis of their support to pollsters. Perhaps utilitarian arguments seem more respectable; perhaps they're simply easier to articulate. Many people may be unwilling or unable to express their emotional reasons for supporting the death penalty—anger, fear, frustration. Bowers, Vandiver, and Dugan suggest that support for the death penalty reflected in the polls is, in part, a symbolic response to "social turmoil and disorder."

They find striking evidence that people who are most supportive of the death penalty tend to be least affected by violent crime. "Such support is more widespread not among African Americans, former crime victims, or city dwellers who most need the law's protection against violent crime, but among reasonably well-to-do, white, male suburbanites."[33] The 1993 Gallup Poll on crime tends to support this assertion. Support for the death penalty is higher among suburbanites and rural dwellers than in urban areas, and it's substantially higher among whites than blacks.

If hard-core support for the death penalty is an emotional response to disorder, it can be easily exacerbated by politicians who make emotional appeals to voters, linking capital punishment to law and order. If some politicians profess support for the death penalty because they believe the public demands it, others generate support for the death penalty by turning it into a symbol for toughness on crime.

It's difficult to know how many people support the death penalty as an end in itself, for the sake of emotional satisfaction it affords, and how many people support the death penalty as a means of controlling crime, in general, and protecting the public against particularly dangerous criminals. But recent polls, aimed at teasing out the nuances of public opinion, do indicate that a significant segment of the public is not blindly committed to capital punishment and might prefer alternative sentences.

According to a 1993 poll (sponsored by the Death Penalty Information Center), support for capital punishment drops dramatically when people are presented with alternatives to it, notably life without parole, coupled with a requirement that the offender make restitution to the victim's family: 44 percent of respondents preferred life without parole, plus restitution, while 41 percent continued to prefer capital punishment.[34] The 1993 Gallup Poll, however, shows that while the death penalty commands diminished support when people are presented with alternative sentences, it still commands a majority: 59 percent of people surveyed by Gallup preferred the death penalty; 29 percent preferred life without parole. Again, there were striking differences in the attitudes of blacks and whites. Of whites, 62 percent preferred the death penalty and 26 percent preferred life without parole. Of blacks, 38 percent preferred the death penalty and 45 percent preferred life without parole.

Battles over these polls are central to the battle over capital punishment; prevailing perceptions of public opinion have obvious political and legal consequences. Supreme Court Justices, as well as state and federal legislators, respond to opinion polls. The Court has pointed to the apparent popularity of the death penalty in declining to strike it down under the Eighth Amendment prohibition of cruel and unusual punishment.[35]

Have the Justices as well as legislators been wrong in their assessment of public opinion? William Bowers believes that support for the death penalty has been greatly overestimated. His surveys also indicate that "people will abandon the death penalty when presented with a harsh and meaningful alternative," mainly life without parole with restitution. Many people support the death penalty with discomfort, according to Bowers's surveys. Four out of five people agreed that the death penalty was "too arbitrary." (Fewer people agreed that the death penalty had a deterrent effect.) People will say that they favor the death penalty when asked a simple yes or no question about it, Bowers suggests, because they believe that the system offers no alternatives.[36] The public is generally ill-informed about stringent mandatory minimum sentences in murder cases. Thirty-three states have life without parole statutes and an additional twelve states impose mandatory sentences of at least twenty-five years to life. But it is conventional wisdom, reinforced by political rhetoric, that convicted murderers commonly serve as little as seven or ten years.

What would polls on capital punishment show if people were presented with sentence alternatives in murder cases? Bowers reports that surveys conducted in Florida, Georgia, New York, California, and Nebraska (from 1985 to 1991) showed that "in all instances where this alternative of life without parole combined with a restitution requirement . . . was posed, expressed death penalty support plummeted." (In New York, support for the death penalty dropped from 71 to 19 percent; in Nebraska, it dropped from 80 to 26 percent. In Georgia, it dropped from 75 to 43 percent, and in Florida from 84 to 24 percent.)[37]

Perhaps because we rely on traditional polls that do not ask people about alternative sentences, legislators tend to over-estimate public support for the death penalty, Bowers suggests. For example, New York legislators surveyed in 1991 wrongly believed that their constituents would prefer the death penalty to a life without parole alternative. The New York legislators were also much less likely than their constituents to abandon their own professed support for capital punishment, given the choice of harsh sentence alternative. Bowers suggests that "legislators are under an illusion of staunch public support for capital punishment." In his view, polls showing strong majority support for the death penalty indicate acceptance of it, as a necessary evil, not a preference for it.[38] (Bowers, however, is an abolitionist, as proponents of capital punishment will be sure to point out.)

In my own thoroughly unscientific speculation about public attitudes toward the death penalty, I've found it useful to compare what, I suspect, people don't know about capital punishment with what they need to believe.

They don't know that many death row inmates have not had fair trials, in many cases because they have not been represented by competent counsel. They don't know that what are commonly derided as legal technicalities—rules prohibiting the use of coerced confessions or suggestive identification procedures—bear directly on questions of innocence and guilt. They don't know the extent of class and racial biases in capital cases, although knowing about bias does not necessarily translate into caring about it. And, in general, people may suspect that the death penalty is not always applied with pristine fairness, without knowing the extent of its unfairness. After conducting a study of capital cases in six southern states, the *National Law Journal* concluded that "justice in capital murder trials is more like a random flip of the coin than a delicate balancing of the scales."[39]

What do people need to believe? I suspect they need to believe that all defendants condemned to die are both guilty and evil. The belief that they are redeemable and still human complicates the decision to kill them. The belief that they might be innocent acknowledges that yet another murder has gone unsolved. Audiences may love movies about people who are wrongly tried and convicted for murder, but in real life, it's frightening to believe that the innocent are convicted while the guilty go free. People need to believe that life only imitates art in exceptional cases. They need to believe that the vast majority of defendants have been fairly tried and so have relatively little need for protracted appeals, although a widespread belief in the presumption of guilt may make this need to believe in fair trials less pressing. When all defendants are deemed guilty, all errors are deemed harmless. Finally, people need to believe that the death penalty could restore a sense of order, that it could control crime, at least a little, if only its enforcement weren't hampered by lawyers armed with technicalities, if only every death sentence were a promise, not a threat.

◄ 5 The Death Penalty— How It's Applied

To many of us, constitutional rights are a bit like tax breaks: we endorse the ones we use. To some people, a low rate on capital gains is just another loophole for the rich; others claim it indirectly benefits the poor, by triggering investment. Someone who expects never to be arrested might regard constitutional guarantees of fair trial as technicalities and, in the long run, prescriptions for disorder. To criminal defendants, they're inalienable rights.

The "technicality" most maligned in the capital punishment debate has been the writ of habeas corpus, which allows for federal appeals of state court convictions. Habeas corpus petitions, blamed for delays in executions, have been the primary focus of efforts to expand or restrict the death penalty. Proponents of capital punishment advocate strictly limiting or eliminating such appeals, to expedite executions. Abolitionists fight to preserve habeas corpus, viewing it as the last defense against capital punishment and an invaluable safeguard of a fair trial process. Habeas corpus reform was a primary point of contention in Congress for about a decade, beginning in the early 1980s, and was widely credited with preventing passage of comprehensive federal crime control legislation during the Bush administration. Opposition to gun control may have been a more important reason for congressional inaction, but the drive to restrict habeas corpus petitions exemplified the demagogic approach to crime control that has retarded federal and state policy for years. The habeas debate also reflects deep divisions about what Americans should value most in their criminal justice system—fairness or efficiency—particularly in the imposition of the death penalty.

A majority of Americans may oppose maintaining the writ of habeas corpus, that is, they may oppose extensive federal review of capital convictions—but relatively few Americans understand the habeas debate, which has become hopelessly technical and arcane. (Few members of Congress understand habeas corpus either, Republican Senator Arlen Specter remarks.[1]) Few Americans know that a habeas corpus petition is a vehicle for obtaining federal review of a state court conviction, nor do they know the rationale for this review: that federal remedies must be provided for federal rights. It's likely that few Americans understand the federal system and the division of power between the states and the federal government; few realize that the federal courts are the arbiters of the federal Constitution, just as state courts are the arbiters of state constitutions. How much of these matters a majority of Congress understands is impossible to say.

This is not intended as criticism of the American public. It is not even a plea for civic education. (While most students probably know less about civics than they do about sex, at least civic ignorance won't kill them.) There's no particular reason why educated voters should understand the debate over habeas corpus—unless they find themselves wrongly convicted of a crime in state court. Most people are busy and distraught enough trying to manage their lives, hold on to their jobs, and address law enforcement problems closer to home—gun violence and a variety of street crimes. People pay their elected officials to manage the criminal justice system, among other things, and many take on faith what politicians say about how the system does or does not work. (Some take on faith what may be the ravings of their favorite columnist or talk show host.) So, for a great many people, fear of crime is matched by ignorance of the criminal justice system, which is why support for restricting habeas appeals is easy to muster.

"Convicted killers who have been duly tried and sentenced to death by state courts are endlessly delaying their executions with federal appeals, based on legal technicalities, at the taxpayer's expense." That's how the debate about habeas corpus has been framed. Voters who don't understand criminal procedure or the role of the federal courts in vindicating federal rights can surely understand what sounds like a common sense appeal for swift and sure punishment.

What if the debate were framed, instead, like this? Every year a small number of people convicted of crimes, perhaps less than 2 percent of all state inmates, appeal the constitutionality of their convictions in federal court. Only a handful of these are death row cases. Most petitions fail (over 95 percent of petitions in noncapital cases), and habeas corpus petitions are not, in general, a burden for the federal courts: in 1988, for example, habeas petitions constituted less than 4 percent of the district courts' total caseload.[2]

No one can seriously suggest that restricting or eliminating habeas review will have a noticeable effect on violent crime. All petitioners are in custody and are not released to roam the streets while their usually unsuccessful petitions are considered. Occasionally, habeas proceedings do result in long delays in executions of convicted murderers. Occasionally, they prevent the execution of innocent people or, at least, of not clearly guilty people who have been wrongfully tried and convicted in state court. The habeas debate is not a debate about crime; it is a debate about justice.

The writ of habeas corpus, the "Great Writ," enshrines a right not to be wrongfully imprisoned. Congress created federal habeas remedies, for wrongful imprisonment by federal authorities, when it created the federal courts, in 1789. Federal habeas review was extended to state prisoners after the Civil War, when the Fourteenth Amendment was adopted.

The current debate over habeas corpus dates back to the early 1980s, when the Reagan administration began a campaign to eliminate, effectively, federal review of state convictions. The administration proposed denying review in cases in which petitioners' claims had been "fully and fairly adjudicated" by the state courts; given the broad view of what constitutes full and fair adjudication, this would have precluded federal review in practically all cases. A 1991 report by the American Bar Association (ABA) notes that the "full and fair" standard had an ugly history. It was essentially the standard invoked by the Supreme Court in 1915 to deny habeas corpus relief to Leo Frank, a Jewish man convicted of the rape and murder of a young woman in Georgia, in an outburst of antisemitism. Frank was lynched shortly after the Court denied his appeal.[3]

Seventy years later, however, the public was more concerned with crime in the streets than crime in the courts, and Republican administrations, along with several conservative Republican senators, continued pressing for the practical elimination of habeas review. The restrictive proposals were not enacted into law, but they were the subject of much congressional debate about crime legislation during the 1980s and the cause of considerable congressional stasis.[4]

What Congress declined to do by legislation, however, the Supreme Court did, in part, by judicial review. While the Warren Court approach to state court convictions had been suspicious, evincing concern for defendants' rights, the Rehnquist Court approach has been deferential, evincing concern for state sovereignty. To protect state court convictions from federal review, the Court erected formidable new procedural barriers to habeas corpus appeals, including a virtual ban on successive petitions (repeated petitions from the same prisoner) and limitations on the retroactivity of "new rules" of law enunciated after petitioner's conviction.[5] Both these rules seem reasonable on their face; both are easy to defend in a sound bite and practically impossible to discredit. But both were unnecessary and unfair. The courts have long been wary of second and third petitions and allowed for dismissal of petitions involving new claims that petitioners had deliberately failed to raise previously. What the Rehnquist Court essentially did in a 1991 case, *McCleskey v. Zant,* was hold petitioners strictly liable for failing to present all claims in their first petitions, regardless of whether their failure was deliberate; this made it easier to execute people despite serious constitutional errors in their convictions, because their lawyers made mistakes. The Court's decision regarding the retroactivity of "new rules" was equally harsh, because "new rules" have been defined so broadly as to preclude the federal courts from correcting mistaken state court interpretations of constitutional law. (This correction would constitute a new rule.) As the ABA points out, this decision, *Teague v. Lane,* essentially sacrificed legal consistency to judicial efficiency: the Constitution will confer different rights on people in different states if state courts can mistakenly adjudicate them with impunity.[6]

These are the kind of arcane legal issues that dominate the habeas corpus debate. The political issues are much simpler: if you're for restricting habeas, you're against crime; if you're against restricting habeas, you're for crime, even though, as a practical matter, habeas review has very little to do with violent crime. Like the political debate, the legal debate is mostly ideological. The campaign for procedural restrictions on habeas does not reflect any empirical evidence of abuses in the current system. In fact, an empirical study conducted by Richard Faust, Tina Rubenstein, and Larry Yackle (published in the *Review of Law and Social Change*) suggests that alleged abuses of the writ have been considerably exaggerated.[7] Even advocates of restricting habeas are apt to concede that evidence of abuse is anecdotal. "We've been dealing with horror stories of individual cases," former Bush administration official Paul McNulty says, and "that drives the debate more than empirical data."[8]

Horror stories from both sides dominate the habeas debate, as they dominate the debate about capital punishment. Parents of murdered children testify before Congress on one side; innocent men who were sentenced to die testify on the other. At a congressional hearing in May 1993, Robert Stearns described the brutal murder of his son and the agonizing nineteen-and-a-half-year period between the murder and the conclusion of the killer's appeal; ten and a half years were taken up by federal appeals.[9] Rubin Carter testified to the nineteen agonizing years he spent in prison on a false murder conviction, before being released in a habeas corpus proceeding by a federal judge who found that his conviction was based on gross prosecutorial misconduct and racial bias. Carter, who spent years appealing his conviction in the New Jersey courts, noted that his long series of appeals was necessitated by the prosecution's illegal "piecemeal" disclosure of evidence, and "every step took years and at every stage I was the one accused of abusing the system and wasting the court's valuable time on 'frivolous' appeals."[10]

What's striking about these horror stories, on both sides, is their apparently minimal effect. People in favor of habeas restrictions rationalize the stories about innocent people condemned to die by labeling them "anomalous." Or they point with pride to the eventual release of a man who spent years on death row; "the system worked," they say. (The system, of course, has relied heavily on the writ of habeas corpus.) People who want to preserve habeas consider prolonged delays in execution a necessary cost of fairness, and besides, they tend to oppose capital punishment, in any case—just as proponents of habeas restrictions tend to favor it.

Putting the question of capital punishment aside, what you believe about the need for restrictions on federal appeals generally reflects what you believe about the quality of justice in the state courts. Restrictions on habeas expand state judicial authority at the expense of federal authority (and the rights of individual defendants), so the more you trust the states to comply with the Constitution and provide fair trials, the less you believe in the need for generous habeas review.

Defense attorneys opposed to restricting habeas review insist that the states routinely discriminate against African Americans and poor people, particularly in death penalty cases. They point primarily to the dearth of competent counsel. Nationwide, in noncapital cases as well, public defender services are in crisis, because of budget cuts, increasing caseloads, and the limited public commitment to defense: criminal defendants are not exactly a popular or powerful interest group. The crisis in defense is "as bad as I've seen it in twenty years," remarks Mary Broderick, director of the National Legal Aid and Defender Association. "There's a saying that judges and prosecutors use: 'Poor people aren't entitled to a Cadillac defense; they're entitled to a Chevrolet.' But at this point they're not even getting a horse and buggy."[11]

The taxpayers, however, may still be paying for Chevrolets. States are required by the Constitution to provide attorneys for indigent defendants. When jurisdictions don't maintain public defender services, or when public defenders are inadequately funded or used, courts rely on untrained, unsupervised attorneys, who function like independent contractors, or consultants. (Legal aid lawyers, like assistant district attorneys, are salaried public employees.) According to a 1994 report by the *New York Times*, some 40 percent of poor defendants in New York City had been represented by court-appointed attorneys, who range from good to grossly incompetent. They cost the city about $55 million per year, over two-thirds of the cost to maintain the New York Legal Aid Society. Private attorneys, however, are often less likely to conduct investigations or even consult with their clients, and they have had ample opportunities to overbill. One study of 124 cases in New York City found that in 27 percent of them, private attorneys submitted bills for court appearances they never made.[12]

The problem of incompetence is particularly acute in capital cases, where it is most dangerous, partly because these cases are often handled not by public defenders but by private attorneys appointed by local judges in what tends to be a highly politicized process, not a meritocratic one. Incompetent or inexperienced and untrained defense counsels are routinely assigned to represent indigent defendants on trial for their lives. A 1990 study by the *National Law Journal* found that in six southern states, which have inadequate public defender services and relatively large numbers of capital cases, death row inmates were represented by lawyers who had been "disbarred, suspended, or otherwise disciplined at a rate of three to forty-six times the discipline rates for those states."[13] Sometimes court-appointed attorneys barely present a defense; capital trials may last only one or two days; the penalty phase of the trial, during which the jury decides between life and death, may last only a matter of hours. (Compare this to a celebrated capital case—the Menendez trials—which lasted for months.)

The systematic failures of defense attorneys in capital cases is a systematic violation of the Sixth Amendment right to effective assistance of counsel, which the Supreme Court has the job of defining. The Court could, then, have responded to the crisis in defense by setting high standards of competency for counsel in capital cases in order to ensure fair trials. Instead, it set low standards of competence and effective counsel, in order to limit the number of successful appeals. In a 1984 case, *Strickland v. Washington,* the Court held that defendants must not only show that the defense counsel's performance was "deficient," but that the counsel's deficiencies "prejudiced the defense," meaning that the outcome would have been different if the counsel hadn't erred.[14] This ruling has become an almost insurmountable bar to appeals based on Sixth Amendment counsel rights.

The Court did not define "deficiency" of counsel or establish specific standards by which counsel's performance could be measured: did counsel consult with defendant, investigate the facts, or present any defense witnesses? The Court simply declared that appellate judges should be "highly deferential" to decisions made by trial counsel and left the determination of competency to individual judges in individual cases. Since the Strickland decision, appellate judges have been deferential indeed in evaluating defense counsels' performance. According to the *National Law Journal,* "appeals courts have upheld convictions and sentences even though trial counsel presented no expert or character witnesses when many were available, or failed to investigate circumstances of the crime, the defendant's background and mental health. At the bleakest end of the spectrum, defendants have been given no relief when their trial attorneys referred to them using racial slurs in front of the jury, abused alcohol or drugs during the trial, or had clear ethical conflicts."[15]

Establishing that defense counsel was incompetent—difficult as it seems—is, however, only the first step for defendants raising Sixth Amendment claims. A petitioner convicted of murder who manages to convince an appeals court that, say, a drunken real estate lawyer was deficient counsel must still prove that counsel's errors determined the outcome of the case. This is an extremely difficult if not impossible task, especially long after the trial is concluded, when most appeals are likely to be heard.

Providing competent counsel to indigent defendants is an important constitutional mandate in any criminal case, but it is, of course, most compelling in capital cases—not just because the defendant's life depends on it but because capital litigation is particularly demanding, requiring particular skills. Trial lawyers need to be schooled in the complicated, changing rules governing appeals in capital cases, so that errors at trial can be preserved for appeal. (They need to understand the law on habeas corpus much better than do members of Congress.) And they need to be familiar with the unique format of a capital trial, which separates determinations of guilt from determinations of sentence. Conscientious, well-intentioned attorneys with no experience in capital cases may not be competent to try them unassisted. (At a lecture on capital litigation, which is much too complicated for me to follow, an eminent law professor sitting next to me says, "I have to remind myself that I know this.")

Serious mistakes are inevitable in a system that only a relative handful of expert litigators truly understand. Yet the Supreme Court has also severely restricted the right to appeal a defense counsel's mistakes. In 1977, in *Wainwright v. Sykes*, the Court held that a defendant loses the right to habeas review of a constitutional claim if defense counsel makes procedural mistakes that did not preserve the claim.[16]

Given these Supreme Court rulings, the states have little incentive to provide indigent defendants facing execution with adequate representation. Instead, as defense attorney Stephen Bright aptly charges, the Court's holdings "reward [the states] for providing inadequate counsel. The state obtains two benefits from the poor representation the defendant receives: the likelihood of obtaining the death sentence is increased and any constitutional deficiencies that occur in the process may be insulated from review."[17]

Concern about the quality of defense counsel in capital cases is not limited to advocates for death row inmates and members of the defense bar, like Bright, who specialize in capital litigation. A 1991 report by the American Bar Association also focused on the problem of inadequate defense and the burden it places on the entire court system. Despite restrictions on habeas appeals, federal courts do overturn about 40 percent of the convictions they review in capital habeas proceedings, because of serious constitutional errors by defense, according to the ABA. It identified the provision of inadequate counsel as the primary reason for long and costly appeals: "The expensive and time-consuming proceedings necessary to uncover that astonishing number of constitutional violations and to retry and re-review all those cases are without doubt the single largest cause of delay in capital litigation." Comparing the time and money spent on capital trials with the time and money spent on federal appeals, the ABA found a "legal process stood on its head." It recommended greatly improving the representation provided to defendants by the states, so that the trial could once again become the "main event" in a capital case and not the prelude to a lengthy appeal.[18]

Reports like this made the problem of incompetent counsel in capital cases increasingly difficult to ignore. In the early 1990s, even Congress began to acknowledge it. An aborted congressional compromise on habeas corpus reform, introduced in 1993 by Democratic Senator Joseph Biden, proposed establishing new counsel standards for capital trials and appeals. The price for these standards was new statutory limits on habeas corpus review—limits which are likely to be enacted by the Republican Congress elected in 1994, with or without counsel standards. Questions about the general fairness of state court proceedings have, however, prompted occasional expressions of concern from advocates of restricting habeas. Senator Arlen Specter, a former prosecutor, favors procedural restrictions on habeas but also wants to maintain substantive federal review of death penalty convictions, because "there are still a lot of problems in the southern states."[19] (After being wrongfully incarcerated for nineteen years in a New Jersey prison, Rubin Carter might point to problems in the northern states as well.) Still, with few exceptions, advocates of limiting the writ of habeas corpus put their faith in state court systems, as does the Supreme Court.

In its recent decisions restricting habeas, the Court made clear a strong presumption that states can be trusted with defendants' constitutional rights, that finality is more at risk in capital cases, if not of more importance. If the liberal Supreme Court of the 1960s and early 1970s elevated concern for procedures ("legal technicalities") over evidence of a defendant's guilt, the conservative or centrist Court of the 1980s and early 1990s elevated concern for procedures over evidence of defendants' innocence.

"A claim of 'actual innocence' is not itself a constitutional claim," Chief Justice Rehnquist declared in *Herrera v. Collins,* suggesting that it is not unconstitutional to execute an innocent person, as long as constitutionally mandated procedures have been followed. In part, Rehnquist meant that questions of innocence were not the province of appellate courts. Appeals courts review questions of law (deciding whether prosecutions were procedurally correct); the trial courts decide questions of fact. That is a basic principle of litigation. Rehnquist affirmed that this principle would be strictly applied, even to capital cases in which questions of fact were questions of life and death. In habeas appeals, the federal courts "sit to insure that individuals are not imprisoned in violation of the Constitution not to correct errors of fact," Rehnquist wrote. A dissent in this case from Justice Harry Blackmun called the majority's decision "perilously close to murder."[20]

Defenders of this decision argue that convicted murderers often assert their innocence; if appellate courts reversed the conviction of every defendant who claimed to be innocent, relatively few convictions would stand. It was also clear that the majority in this case was skeptical of Herrera's claim of innocence; the Justices seemed to believe in his guilt (meaning that they did consider the facts, after all). In her concurring opinion, Justice Sandra Day O'Connor suggested that in a "truly extraordinary case," involving a "truly persuasive demonstration of actual innocence," the federal courts might intervene, but it was unclear what a "truly persuasive" demonstration of innocence might comprise.

The claim at issue in Lionel Herrera's case rested on newly discovered evidence (unavailable at trial) implicating his brother Raul Herrera in the murder for which Lionel was condemned. This evidence was uncovered nine years after Herrera's trial; it could not be considered by the state courts because under Texas law, newly discovered evidence must be presented within thirty days after the conviction. A federal district court judge had found the new evidence persuasive enough to order a stay of execution so that the state courts would consider Herrera's claim. The Federal Court of Appeals lifted the stay, and in the interest of finality, the Supreme Court agreed that the sentence should be carried out. Herrera was executed some five months later.*

Deference to state procedural technicalities also dominated the Court's opinion in another notorious case involving the right of a condemned man to obtain a hearing on the constitutionality of his conviction. "This is a case about federalism," Justice O'Connor wrote in a famous lead to her opinion in *Coleman v. Thompson*, denying habeas corpus review to petitioner Coleman (who'd been convicted of rape and murder) because he'd missed a state filing deadline by three days. Coleman, who had a relatively strong claim of innocence that received considerable attention in the media, was subsequently executed. But you'd never know that an execution was pending from the Court's opinion in this case. O'Connor's dry, bloodless prose is Dickensian in its attention to procedural niceties and the principles of federal-state relations. She might as well have been resolving a commercial fraud case. Reading her lawyerly exegesis on federal-state comity, you have to remind yourself that this is not a case about federalism but a case about life and death and principles of justice. As the dissent observed, "one searches in vain . . . for any mention of Coleman's right to a criminal proceeding free from constitutional challenge to his convictions and sentence of death." In the view of the dissent, the Court had elevated "abstract federalism over fundamental precepts of liberty and fairness."[21]

---

*In 1995, the Court allowed the execution of Jesse Dewayne Jacobs, convicted of fatally shooting a twenty-five-year-old woman, even though the state subsequently convicted Jacob's sister of the shooting, claiming that Jacobs had only been an accomplice who didn't even know his sister had a gun. Since, in theory, Jacobs could have been sentenced to death as an accomplice, the state essentially dismissed his innocence of the actual shooting as a mere technicality.

⤳ | Inattention to the routine inequities of the criminal justice system has become a hallmark of the Supreme Court's approach to capital punishment. This may reflect a little ignorance or self-deception, as well as ideology. The Court has much at stake—its sense of its own integrity—in believing that laws are applied rationally and fairly, in good faith, and with occasional exceptions it is composed of jurists from the upper echelons of the profession—scholars and judges who lack ordinary experience litigating cases in the lower criminal courts and representing individual, ordinary clients at trial. You might expect that the Court's opinions in capital cases would sometimes have an air of unreality—particularly since opinions are often drafted by clerks, recent law school graduates whose theories have yet to be tested by experience.

The Supreme Court has been downright delusional on the subject of capital punishment, Justice Harry Blackmun suggested shortly before retiring in 1994. Since the late 1970s, Blackmun noted, the Court has crafted "procedural rules and verbal formulas" designed to make the death penalty efficient and fair. Blackmun had joined in these efforts, defending the constitutionality of the death penalty until he was about to step down from the Court. Then, in his last capital case, he concluded that after some twenty years of rule making "the death penalty remains fraught with arbitrariness, discrimination, caprice, and mistake." Asserting that "the death penalty experiment has failed," Blackmun declared, "From this day forward, I no longer shall tinker with the machinery of death."[22]

The tinkering began in 1972, with *Furman v. Georgia*, the Supreme Court case that struck down death penalty laws then in existence.[23] *Furman* was a confusing 5 to 4 decision that offered no clear consensus on the constitutionality of the death penalty. Two Justices, Thurgood Marshall and William

Brennan, argued that capital punishment was inherently cruel and unusual, in violation of the Eighth Amendment. Three Justices, William Douglas, Potter Stewart, and Byron White, held that capital punishment was unconstitutional as it was then administered because it was susceptible to arbitrary, discriminatory enforcement. The *Furman* case itself involved three capital convictions, one for murder, two for rape. All three defendants were black males, two of whom had been diagnosed with serious mental or emotional problems. You might say, with only a little hyperbole, that all three were sentenced to die at the whim of the courts, as the majority of the Justices suggested. Death penalty statutes at the time gave juries unfettered discretion to impose the death sentence for any reason, or no particular reason at all.

Concern about arbitrary death sentences was what united the five Justices who voted to strike down the death penalty in *Furman v. Georgia.* "These death sentences are cruel and unusual in the same way that being struck by lightning is cruel and unusual," Justice Stewart wrote, offering what became the most famous line from this case. "Indeed it smacks of little more than a lottery system," Justice Brennan concurred, noting that the death penalty was rarely applied (in no more than fifty cases a year), and only to a tiny percentage of homicide cases. The rarity of application strongly implied capriciousness, Brennan wrote: "When the rate of infliction is at this low level, it is highly implausible that only the worst criminals or the criminals who commit the worst crimes are selected for this punishment." There was simply no "rational basis" for distinguishing "the few who die from the many who go to prison."

Of course, there was an apparent basis for sentencing decisions in capital cases, but it was not what the Court would consider "rational," meaning arguably legal or just. The death penalty was consistently applied to the most powerless people in society—poor people, racial minorities, and social outcasts, several Justices noted. Thanks to their biased application, death penalty laws covertly accomplished in fact what could not be accomplished overtly, under law, as Justice Douglas observed: "A law that stated that anyone making more than $50,000 would be exempt from the death penalty would plainly fall, as would a law that in terms said that blacks, those who never went beyond the 5th grade in school, those who make less than $3,000 a year, or those who were unpopular or unstable would be the only people executed. A law which in the general view reached that result in practice has no more sanctity than a law which in terms provides the same."

The challenge of formulating standards for jurors in capital cases to ensure unbiased judgments had long bedeviled judges and legislators. Only one year before *Furman* struck down existing death penalty laws because of their arbitrary, highly discretionary application, the Court upheld laws giving jurors absolute discretion to impose sentence of life or death. In *McGautha v. California,* the Court noted that the challenge to unlimited jury discretion had "undeniable surface appeal," but suggested that standards governing jury discretion were not only extremely difficult to devise but impossible to enforce. Indeed, jurors had been granted discretion in capital cases by law because they were exercising it in fact, the Court observed, summarizing the history of capital punishment laws.[24]

Two hundred years ago, the Court noted, common law made the death penalty mandatory for all convicted murderers. In an attempt to mitigate this rule, reformers in the late eighteenth century wrote new laws applying the death penalty only to first degree murder cases, involving murders that were willful and premeditated. Jurors still disregarded this limited mandate, issuing prison sentences even in some cases of premeditated murder. Legislators responded to this problem of jury nullification (decisions by jurors that effectively nullify the law they are supposed to apply) by rewriting the laws and giving juries sentencing discretion they were exercising anyway.

The Court thus presented jury discretion as a boon to defendants, an instrument of mercy not bias, vengeance, or fear. The underlying assumption of *McGautha* is that jurors are compassionate, that their instincts are benign, that they use discretion wisely, morally, with the best intentions, in accordance with the spirit of the law. The Court put its faith in the fabled good sense of jurors. "The States are entitled to assume that jurors confronted with the truly awesome responsibility of deciding life or death for a fellow human being will act with due regard for the consequences of their decisions."

Capital cases are, no doubt, particularly sobering for many jurors, who try to act responsibly. But to suggest, as the Court does, that jurors can, in general, be trusted to render unbiased decisions ignores human nature and history, particularly the history of the American South, where the death penalty has been most frequently used. (Between 1935 and 1969, the southern states accounted for more executions than all the other regions of the country combined.)[25] The racial animus behind this reliance on capital punishment was unmistakable: blacks accounted for two-thirds of all state-sanctioned executions from the 1890s through the 1960s. This did not reflect offense rate by blacks: they were executed for less serious crimes than whites and for crimes that were not generally punishable by death (primarily rape). They were younger at execution and less likely to have had the benefit of appeals. They were also less likely to receive commutations.[26] Death sentences imposed on blacks were, therefore, more likely to be carried out. Discrimination was perhaps most grievous in the prosecution of rape cases. Historically, black defendants have accounted for about 9 out of every 10 executions for rape. Between 1930 and 1972, for example, 455 people were executed for rape; 405 of them were black.[27]

These appalling figures were, of course, the legacy of slavery. In the antebellum South, laws expressly provided for differential sentencing of blacks and whites: some crimes were capital only when committed by blacks or only if the victims were white. The letter of the law changed with Reconstruction and passage of the Fourteenth Amendment, but prosecution and sentencing practices remained extremely biased.

In the first half of this century, all-white southern juries convicted black men of capital crimes, without much regard for the evidence, conducting what some considered official lynchings. (As lynchings declined after 1900, legal executions increased.) Take the celebrated Depression-era case of the Scottsboro Boys, involving nine young black men sentenced to death for the rape of two white women, on the basis of fabricated evidence. (History has made clear that the rape never occurred.) For many Americans, this case became a symbol of racial injustice, historian Dan T. Carter observes in *Scottsboro*, while for white Alabamans it stood for the dangers of social equality, as well as the failure of northerners to understand the "Negro problem." Southern whites were also likely to see this case as a symbol for progress on racial justice, Carter adds: a lynching had been averted; the community exercised self-restraint, agreeing to try the defendants before they were hung.[28]

The Scottsboro case dragged on for nearly thirty years, with successive trials and appeals; the Supreme Court reversed convictions and sent the cases back to the state several times; the juries kept on convicting. (The nine defendants whose innocence was eventually conceded spent a total of 104 years in prison.) In the fourth and final trial of one defendant, the jury, recognizing his innocence, sentenced him to 75 years in prison, instead of death. Eleven of the jurors in this case reportedly informed the foreman, who sought a not guilty verdict, that they feared returning to their communities if they voted to acquit.[29]

The willingness of juries like this to convict blacks of capital crimes they did not commit was matched by a willingness to acquit whites of capital crimes against blacks during the civil rights era. Byron de la Beckwith, convicted in February 1994 of assassinating civil rights activist Medgar Evers some thirty years ago, escaped conviction in two previous trials when all-white juries deadlocked.

Advocates for the death penalty and the jury system will protest that these cases are merely history, irrelevant to capital cases today, that racism is a sin of the past. And it's true that we've made considerable legal progress since the days of the Scottsboro Boys and the early years of the civil rights movement, although racism is not simply a legal problem, and we do regress occasionally. (Consider the acquittal in the first, state trial of the white police officers who assaulted Rodney King.) My point is not to compare racial problems today with racial problems thirty or sixty years ago. My point is that juries, in any era, are capable of arbitrary, irrational, or frightened behavior. They reflect the biases and bad faith of their communities and culture, as well as the good will. Of course, the most famous cases don't represent the jury system in general, but they are part of the system that the Court in *McGautha v. California* extolled.

Perhaps the Justices in *McGautha* felt they had no alternative but to presume jurors' fairness and rationality. The fiction that jurors know best underlies the jury system, in general, not just the exercise of sentence discretion in capital cases. No doubt many jurors vindicate our faith in them, while others do not. Why should jurors, as a class, be less biased and gullible and less likely to make ill-considered judgments than the rest of us? You might even argue that traditional customs and rules governing jury selection help ensure that people chosen to serve as jurors were more biased, gullible, and ill-equipped to make judgments than the people rejected for service.

The more you know about the law in general or about a particular case, the less likely you are to end up on a jury. States have routinely exempted lawyers and other professionals who work in the courts precisely because they know too much about the system. Knowledgeable people who do make it into the jury pool run the risk of being rejected by trial attorneys during the selection process. Litigators don't seek objective, unbiased jurors; they seek jurors who seem to harbor biases that favor their respective cases (as jury selection in the O.J. Simpson case showed). Finally, concern about the effect of pretrial publicity can favor uninformed jurors over the informed, as Mark Twain deftly observed.

The jury system was the "most ingenious and infallible agency for *defeating* justice that human wisdom could contrive," Twain wrote. The notion that jurors should have no prior knowledge of the case they were called to decide "compels us to swear in fools and rascals . . . [and] rigidly excludes honest men and men of brains."

> I remember one of those sorrowful farces, in Virginia, which we call a jury trial. A noted desperado killed Mr. B, a good citizen, in the most wanton and cold-blooded way. Of course the papers were full of it, and all men capable of reading read about it. And of course all men not deaf and dumb and idiotic talked about it. A jury list was made out. . . .
>
> When the preemptory challenges were all exhausted, a jury of twelve men was impaneled—a jury who swore they had neither heard, read, talked about, nor expressed an opinion concerning a murder which the very cattle in the corrals . . . were cognizant of! . . . It was a jury composed of two desperados, two beerhouse politicians, three barkeepers, two ranchmen who could not read,

and three dull, stupid human donkeys! It actually came out afterward that one of these latter thought that incest and arson were the same thing.[30]

Many people who have served on juries or argued before them or presided over them may recognize some discomfiting partial truths in Twain's jaundiced view of the jury system. Still, we can assume that common sense will be as widely distributed among jurors as bias, ignorance, and inanity; no one has yet proposed an appealing alternative to trial by jury; and, as long as we're stuck with it, we adapt. Finding value in the system is particularly important to people who are part of it. Twain had the luxury of noninvolvement. People who have any integrity or self-respect find it practically impossible to work within a system they thoroughly disdain. Unlike satirists, jurists are compelled to tinker with the machinery of justice in the belief that they can make it work. Those who support capital punishment or defer to the public demand for it must tinker as well with the machinery of death, as the Supreme Court discovered. Juries do sometimes need guidance, the Supreme Court conceded in *Gregg v. Georgia,* the 1976 case that resurrected the death penalty in America by upholding state laws that purported to guide juries' sentencing discretion.[31]

In *Gregg* and companion cases handed down the same day, the Court reviewed the constitutionality of death penalty statues the states had enacted after the *Furman* decision, four years earlier. In *Furman,* the Court's invalidation of laws giving absolute sentence discretion to juries left states intent on preserving capital punishment with two alternatives: limit the jury's discretion by writing standards telling it when the death penalty should or should not be applied; or eliminate the jury's discretion by making death sentences mandatory for certain crimes. The Court stuck down mandatory death sentences, because they did not allow for "particularized" evaluations of the defendant's character and motivation: all defendants found guilty of capital crimes would be executed, regardless of any mitigating circumstances. But the Court upheld "guided discretion" statutes, which took several forms.

The Georgia law at issue in *Gregg* established six categories of capital crimes: murder, armed robbery, rape, kidnapping, treason, and hijacking could each be punishable by death. Juries had practically unfettered discretion to impose death sentences in hijacking and treason cases, but in cases involving other capital crimes, death sentences could be imposed only if the jury found evidence beyond a reasonable doubt of certain aggravating circumstances listed by statute. These ten factors included the facts that (1) the defendant had a record of serious crimes; (2) the defendant committed murder for money; (3) the defendant's crime was "outrageously or wantonly vile, horrible or inhuman in that it involved torture, depravity of mind, or an aggravated battery to the victim." Juries finding evidence of any one of the ten aggravating factors listed had the option but not the mandate to impose a death sentence.

A Florida law upheld in *Proffit v. Florida* listed eight aggravating circumstances and seven mitigating circumstances for the jurors to weigh in making a sentence recommendation to the judge.[32] (Georgia juries were directed to consider mitigating circumstances, although none were expressly cited by statute.) A Texas law upheld in *Jurek v. Texas* adopted a somewhat different approach to guided discretion: Texas listed five types of aggravated murder for which juries could impose death sentences, depending on how they answered three statutory questions: was the murder deliberate; was there insufficient provocation for it; and is the defendant likely to commit acts of violence in the future—a question to which the only reliable response is "It depends."[33]

In addition to sentencing standards, guided discretion statutes entailed a bifurcation of the trial process. A capital trial was divided into guilt phase, in which the jury evaluated evidence of defendant's guilt and rendered a verdict, and a penalty phase, in which the jury evaluated evidence of defendant's evil, examining the nature of his or her crime and character. The new standards governing the determination of sentence (all the aggravating and mitigating factors and questions about future dangerousness) came into play during this second, penalty phase. Guided discretion remains the model for death penalty statutes today.

Readers who have, by now, glazed over in the attempt to follow and make sense of these legalisms might appreciate the challenge posed to jurors in capital cases, for whom making sense of the facts and the law before them is a matter of life and death.

The Court, however, seemed oblivious to the prospect that jurors who would never read and, in many cases, never understand its opinions might have trouble applying them. Nor did it consider the possibility that jurors who once ignored statutory mandates to impose death sentences might also ignore statutory standards intended to guide their sentencing decisions. Or they might interpret the standards in varying and unpredictable ways. What, after all, is a particularly heinous or horrible crime? What is depravity of mind? Deciding which murders should be punishable by death under these statutes is a bit like deciding which pornographic video should be censored under an obscenity law. Assessments of the wantonness or cruelty of a particular crime are as subjective as assessments of obscenity. "I know it when I see it," Justice Stewart once declared about obscenity, and he might have said the same thing about capital murder in the opinion he authored in *Gregg*.

Gregg reinstated the death penalty only four years after it had been disavowed in *Furman*. During these years, between 1972 and 1976, the makeup of the Court changed: Justice Douglas, who voted against the death penalty, was replaced by Justice John Paul Stevens, who voted for it. And Justice Stewart changed sides; having voted to strike down state death penalty laws in *Furman* because they were arbitrary, he voted to uphold guided discretion statutes in *Gregg*.

Justice Stewart argued that the new jury standards and establishment of a separate penalty phase of trial would rationalize the administration of the death penalty. But he may have been persuaded less by the substance of the new laws than by their prevalence, which reflected a surge of popular support for the death penalty. Writing for the plurality in *Gregg*, Stewart underscored the "deference we owe to the decisions of state legislatures under our federal system."

State legislative response to *Furman* had been swift. Within one year twenty states had drafted new death penalty laws to replace the laws struck down by the Court. By the time *Gregg* was decided in 1976, thirty-five states had enacted new laws. Like *Roe v. Wade*, which invalidated state prohibitions of abortion, *Furman v. Georgia* had been met with considerable outrage about judicial activism and federal court interference with state democratic processes. But, unlike abortion rights, the abolition of capital punishment was generating decreasing public support. In invalidating the death penalty, the Court was accused of frustrating the will of the majority, which, in a way, means that the Court was accused of doing its job.

Protecting the minority against the excesses of majority rule is a primary purpose of the Bill of Rights and a primary responsibility of the Court. Individual rights—First Amendment rights of speech and religion or Fifth Amendment rights of due process—are guaranteed by the Constitution precisely so that the majority can't vote to take them away (without a constitutional amendment). Neither can the majority decide to ignore

Eighth Amendment prohibitions of cruel and unusual punishment, even with regard to a small minority of people convicted of terrible crimes. Proponents of capital punishment argue that executions cannot be considered cruel and unusual precisely because the public supports them, although as Justice Marshall pointed out, public support shouldn't count for much when it's based on public ignorance.

In *Furman,* Justice Brennan had argued that the history of the death penalty, the gradual but steady restriction of the number of capital crimes, indicated that capital punishment had become "progressively more troublesome to the national conscience."[34] Even the spate of new post-*Furman* death penalty laws did not signal the resolution of debates about the morality of capital punishment. In the mid-1970s when *Gregg* was decided, and the death penalty reinstated, 30 to 40 percent of Americans still opposed it. The majority that supported the death penalty did not have its support tested by frequent executions, and most Americans on both sides of the debate (86 percent of the public) had enough qualms about executions to oppose televising them.[35]

As arbiter of the Constitution, the Court was bound to mediate the moral controversy over capital punishment, Justice Brennan suggested. In interpreting the Eighth Amendment, the Court had no choice but to decide that "when individuals condemned to death stand before the Bar, 'moral concepts' require us to hold that the law has progressed to the point where we should declare that the punishment of death, like punishments on the rack, the screw, and the wheel, is not longer tolerable in our civilized society."[36]

Legal theorists argue about whether or how much Supreme Court Justices are bound by the knowledge and understanding of the Framers in construing the Constitution. If capital punishment was legal when the Eighth Amendment was written, must it remain legal today? If abortion rights weren't specifically mentioned in the Fourteenth Amendment can the Court locate them there a century later? This is a debate about whether the Bill of Rights is a statement of general principle or a list of specific rules to be interpreted according to the beliefs and biases that prevailed when they were drafted. It is a debate about the appropriate context for the Court's definitions of fundamental rights. Does the Court rely on its own, modern notions of equality, liberty, and the individual's relationship to government in construing the Constitution or must it take an imaginary trip back in time to the eighteenth or nineteenth centuries so that rights can be understood in the context of what was known and believed when the Bill of Rights and the Fourteenth Amendment were written?

It's difficult to imagine what use the Constitution might have served if its meanings were so bound by time. The Bill of Rights is not quite as clear-cut as the Ten Commandments, after all; people who agree about the meaning of "adultery" might have widely divergent views about "due process." The Bill of Rights traffics in abstractions as New York University Law Professor Dworkin has stressed. The Court can't simply refer to an eighteenth- or nineteenth-century dictionary to define such terms as "due process," "equal protection," or "cruel and unusual punishment" in deciding a late twentieth-century case.[37]

But, these are intellectual, juridical arguments. How most people feel about a judge defining moral behavior for the rest of us, as Justice Brennan did in declaring capital punishment immoral, probably depends on whether they subscribe to the judge's moral code. Abolitionists will applaud Brennan's moral courage, while proponents of capital punishment will deplore his moral presumptiveness. But, instead of asking whether judges are entitled or obliged to make moral judgments, we might ask how they can manage not to make them, particularly when the consequences of judging are life or death.

How do jurors make judgments in these cases? Do capital cases decided during the decades since *Gregg v. Georgia* vindicate the Court's faith in guided discretion? Has arbitrariness been purged from the system and replaced with fairness and rationality?

◣ | The evidence is clear that guided discretion has done little to eliminate racism, in one of its more subtle forms, from the prosecution of capital cases. Today, racial discrimination is most striking in the treatment of black and white victims.

In 1988, the General Accounting Office reviewed studies of sentencing practice in capital cases and found "a pattern of evidence" of race discrimination. The great majority of sentencing studies examined by the GAO found that people who murdered whites were "more likely to be sentenced to death than those who murdered blacks."[38] Victim-based discrimination can be dramatic. Studies of prosecutions in the 1970s indicated remarkable leniency in black victim cases: in Florida, for example, black offenders who killed whites were forty times more likely to receive the death penalty than blacks who killed blacks. Blacks were five times more likely than whites to be sentenced to death in cases involving white victims.[39]

Since murder is, in general, an intraracial crime (blacks kill blacks; whites kill whites), the bias against black victims probably works in favor of black offenders. In New Jersey, for example, urban homicide cases involving poor black offenders and poor black urban victims are less likely to result in death penalty prosecutions and death sentences than homicides involving middle-class suburban or rural white victims.[40] Harvard Law School Professor Randall Kennedy has pointed out that law-abiding black citizens, not black offenders, are the people generally deprived of equal protection by victim-biased sentencing.[41]

The dismissive attitudes toward black victim cases that Kennedy underscores was captured in a brief by the Florida Attorney General in a 1978 case involving a white victim and a white offender, John Spenkelink (subsequently executed). Confronted with statistical disparities in cases involving black and white victims, the state of Florida argued that murders of blacks tended not to qualify as capital murders because they were more likely to have involved "family quarrels, lover's quarrels, [and] barroom quarrels." Putting aside the highly questionable assertion that black homicides differed qualitatively in this way from white homicides, studies of homicide cases demonstrated that differences in categories of crime did not account for differences in the treatment of black and white victim cases.[42]

The Supreme Court was faced with unpalatable evidence of victim-based racial discrimination in the administration of the death penalty in the 1986 case of *McCleskey v. Kemp.* Warren McCleskey, a black man sentenced (and subsequently executed) for killing a white police officer in Georgia, argued that the death penalty was unconstitutional because it was applied disproportionately in cases involving white victims. As Justice Brennan observed, in his dissent, studies of sentencing patterns showed that "the jury more likely would have spared McCleskey's life had his victim been black."[43]

McCleskey's appeal was based on a frequently cited study by David Baldus, showing that, in Georgia, killers of whites were, by conservative estimates, four times more likely to receive the death penalty than killers of blacks. The Court did not question the Baldus study. Instead it assumed its validity and effectively excused the discrimination it showed. The

Court held that statistical evidence of discrimination in capital sentencing, in general, however persuasive, was not evidence of discrimination in McCleskey's particular case. To prevail on his claim of unequal justice, McCleskey would have had to prove that decisions made in his case were purposefully discriminatory.

Proving particularized intent to discriminate is, however, extremely difficult, and often impossible (people don't usually admit their discriminatory motives). That is partly why federal employment law long allowed statistical evidence of discrimination, in general, to establish an inference of discrimination in a particular case. The Court in *McCleskey* acknowledged this, but, because McCleskey's claim challenged decisions "at the heart of the criminal justice system," it ruled that the kind of statistical evidence that might have saved McCleskey from discrimination in employment could not save him from discrimination in capital sentencing.

Congress has proved equally unsympathetic to claims of racial discrimination in capital cases, repeatedly refusing to pass the Racial Justice Act, introduced in response to the McCleskey case. The Racial Justice Act would essentially extend evidentiary practices in employment cases to capital appeals, allowing challenges to death sentences in particular cases based on statistical evidence of discriminatory practices in general. President Bill Clinton obliquely dismissed this as a special interest bill during debates about federal crime control legislation passed in 1994. Republican proponents of the death penalty derided it as a quota bill that would somehow require the death penalty to be imposed on "an equal number of persons from all races."[44] All the bill would do, in fact, is require courts to review statistical evidence of discrimination and require the prosecution to rebut any inference of discrimination, if the evidence is found persuasive. In other words, statistical evidence would not invalidate a death sentence; it would only require the state to demonstrate that the sentence was not imposed on account of race. It is, however, nearly impossible to explain the Racial Justice Act in a sound bite. The truth of the proposal doesn't matter; if Senator D'Amato says it's a quota bill, then for many of his constituents it's a quota bill.

Opposition to the Racial Justice Act has obvious political benefits to senators who get to rail against quotas and further delays in executions. The Supreme Court's discomfort with the use of statistical evidence of discriminatory sentencing seemed more logistic than political. As Justice Powell observed in his majority opinion in *McCleskey,* allegations of biased sentencing were not limited to capital cases or to allegations of racial bias. The criminal justice system involved subjective, discretionary decision making by judges, juries, and prosecutors; laws could not eliminate all apparent bias—whether based on race, sex, ethnicity, or appearance. "Thus, if we accepted McCleskey's claim that racial bias has impermissibly tainted the capital sentencing decision, we could soon be faced with similar claims as to other types of penalty."

The majority in *McCleskey* seemed to harbor "a fear of too much justice," Justice Brennan observed in his dissent. And, as Brennan also noted, the Court could have limited a ruling in McCleskey's favor to capital cases, avoiding a wholesale challenge to criminal sentencing, if it had been willing to acknowledge the truth of a familiar refrain in capital litigation—that death is different. As the Court had observed ten years earlier, "Death in its finality, differs more from life imprisonment than a 100 year prison term differs from a term of only a year or two."[45]

There was also something else at stake for the Court in this case: McCleskey's claim questioned the success of guided discretion statutes in exorcising prejudice from capital cases. In denying McCleskey's appeal, Justice Powell carefully chronicled the various rules safeguarding against bias, required by *Gregg v. Georgia* and subsequent cases—as if the mere existence of safeguards were proof that they worked.

Justice Powell, now retired from the Court, has since changed his mind about the *McCleskey* case, because he's changed his mind about the death penalty. Like Justice Blackmun, he has come to believe that the rules haven't worked—that the death penalty is not and probably cannot be fairly applied. Recent studies of jury deliberations support his change of heart, confirming that guided discretion statutes have resoundingly failed.

In-depth, post-trial interviews with jurors conducted by the Capital Jury Project indicate that they often do not understand sentence guidelines.[46] One study of jurors in North Carolina indicated that while jurors had "reasonably good understanding" of aggravating factors (factors that could demand the death penalty) they had "poor understanding" of instructions regarding mitigating factors, which would militate against execution. Many jurors did not consider all appropriate mitigating factors, they applied the wrong burden of proof to evidence of mitigating factors, and they did not understand that they were supposed to vote for imprisonment instead of execution if mitigating factors outweighed aggravating factors. The North Carolina jurors also misunderstood the consequences of a failure to reach a unanimous decision on sentence. Only 16 percent understood that if they failed to agree on a sentence, the judge was required to impose a prison sentence on the defendant. One-half of the jurors mistakenly believed that their failure to agree would result in a new trial—a misconception that increases pressure on jurors in the minority to compromise their beliefs and join the majority, in order to reach a verdict in the interests of efficiency.[47]

Juror interviews also indicate that juries find it difficult to abide by the division of trial into a guilt and a penalty phase. Social psychologist Marla Sandys believes that jurors tend to make decisions about guilt and sentencing simultaneously; they base their sentencing decision on evidence heard during the guilt phase. Sandys notes that 70 percent of jurors interviewed in a Kentucky study said that they had been absolutely convinced of their own sentence preferences before the penalty phase. (A majority of these jurors maintained their preferences throughout deliberations on sentence.) About half of the jurors acknowledged that discussions of sentence took place during the guilt phase.[48] This suggests that, contrary to law, jurors are determining sentence when they hear evidence of guilt, before they hear evidence about a defendant's state of mind or character that might call for a life sentence. Mitigating evidence is only presented during the penalty phase, after the jury has decided on a defendant's guilt.

Jurors not only make their sentencing decision at the wrong stage of the trial, before they have heard all the evidence, they tend to be swayed by factors that are not legally relevant, such as a defendant's silence when given a chance to testify or a defendant's courtroom demeanor. Under law, jurors are not supposed to consider a defendant's silence as evidence of guilt (defendants have a Fifth Amendment right to remain silent and force the prosecution to prove its case), but, as Marla Sandys reports, jurors are suspicious of defendants who don't testify. "If I were innocent, I'd be up there fighting," jurors say. One juror was prejudiced by the defendant's impassivity on hearing a guilty verdict: "When he didn't change his expression after the guilty verdict, I felt more for the death penalty."[49]

You could, I suppose, blame errors like this on the individual juror who makes them, but they are such natural mistakes. What's striking about all these mistakes and misconceptions by jurors is that they are not, in general, particularly foolish or surprising. They reflect what might be considered the common sense for which jurors are so widely praised. It's natural to assume that innocent defendants will want to speak out on their own behalf (although many do not). It's natural, although maybe not thoughtful, to judge defendants by the emotions they display and to be suspicious of self-control. It's natural for people to think about the appropriate punishment for a defendant while they hear evidence of guilt, especially in a capital case, involving a grisly crime. The division of capital trials into guilt and penalty phases is unrealistic. And it is natural for people unschooled in the law to be confused by complicated jury instructions about aggravating and mitigating circumstances and burdens of proof.

The jury system probably demands more of people than they can be expected to deliver, especially under stress. Jury service is, after all, an ordeal. It's often uncomfortable and unpleasant (courtrooms can be dingy, depressing places); it's often boring but sometimes frightening, especially in cases involving considerable violence in which people are badly harmed. Jurors are asked to examine evidence of brutalized, bloody bodies, which many of us would rather not see, and they feel the burden of passing judgment on people, in a context in which judgments have consequences. (In casual conversation, most of us have little trouble passing judgment on notorious defendants—O.J. Simpson or Claus von Bulow—when we know the judgments are moot.) After difficult trials, jurors report suffering insomnia, sexual dysfunctions, eating problems, and other stress-related disorders, and post-trial counseling or debriefing for jurors is beginning to gain publicity and support.[50]

It's not only the cases themselves that disturb jurors; deliberations in the jury room can be quite stressful, even hostile. (Being locked in a room and forced to reason with eleven of my fellow citizens, chosen at random, is, for me, one vision of hell.) Deliberations are particularly difficult for "hold-out" jurors, people who find themselves in the minority, frustrating the majority's will. "I had to know that I had given him every benefit of the doubt, that I had looked at everything," one juror reported, explaining her difficulty in joining the majority in their verdict. She was attacked by her fellow jurors as "spineless, gutless, unable to make up [her] mind."[51]

Sometimes jurors in the minority report adopting the majority view simply to conclude deliberations so that everyone can go home. "When the judge was going to sequester everybody . . . all of a sudden those holding out changed their minds because they didn't want to be sequestered," one juror recalled. "I told my husband about it . . . 'Can you imagine if [you were on trial] . . . and because they were going to hold the jury overnight they decided to change their minds and you're guilty?' That's scary. That's what scared the pants off me."[52]

Stories like this challenge one of our most cherished beliefs about juries—that they respect and rely upon individual acts of conscience. We like to imagine a lone juror with a commitment to truth—Henry Fonda in *Twelve Angry Men*—withstanding the pressure to conform and leading the jury to justice. In real life, out of fear, self-doubt, or sheer exhaustion, many people are more likely to vote with the majority than according to their conscience.

Of course, sometimes, the majority may be right. Lone jurors may hold out for no good reason—out of a mere desire to be contrary or sheer irrationalism and an inability to evaluate the evidence. Sometimes, justice may be served when the majority rules, but sometimes the majority itself may rule irrationally. In a sensational child abuse case in North Carolina, explored by a 1993 *Frontline* documentary, the jury found the operator of a child care center guilty of multiple acts of abuse, based on the highly questionable, often fantastic allegations of children who had been subjected to suggestive interrogations that encouraged them to offer stories of abuse. Two jurors said that they joined the majority in finding the defendant guilty, after long deliberations, because the stress of holding out was taking a toll on their health (one man said he feared having a heart attack if he continued resisting pressure to convict). A third juror holding out for acquittal said he began to doubt his beliefs about the case precisely because he was outnumbered. The defendant in this case, whom several jurors believed was not guilty, was sentenced to life in prison and awaits appeal.[53]

No appeals are possible for William Henry Hance, executed by the state of Georgia on March 31, 1994, even though one juror in his case, Gayle Daniels, swore that she had not voted for the death penalty and that the jury foreman had lied in presenting the sentence decision as unanimous. The reported tension on the jury was racial. Daniels was the only black on the jury (the defendant was a black man, diagnosed by one psychiatrist as borderline retarded), and, according to another juror who corroborated Daniels's statement, jury deliberations were marked by racial slurs. Daniels also said that she felt pressured by the other jurors to join them in voting for death so that they could go home for Mother's Day.[54]

In capital cases, it appears particularly difficult for jurors to hold out for life sentences. Data from the Capital Jury Project indicate that jurors begin the penalty phase of the trial with a "substantial bias in favor of death." (They have, after all, already found the defendant guilty of a terrible crime.) Commenting on juror interviews in South Carolina, Theodore Eisenberg and Martin T. Wells observe that "a defendant on trial for life in the punishment stage has one foot in the grave. The defendant needs affirmative action by jurors to pluck him from the crypt, action that is likely to annoy other jurors, at least initially. The juror favoring life faces a struggle against initial opposition that will last throughout the deliberations and continue to annoy fellow jurors in post-trial interviews." Confusion and indecision in capital cases "tend to be resolved in favor of death," Eisenberg and Wells add, and since confusion seems inevitable, given the intellectual and emotional demands on jurors, it's fair to say that the capital trial begins with a built-in bias toward death.[55] Guided discretion in practice, begins to look like biased discretion.

One crucial source of confusion and bias is the common belief that a defendant who is not sentenced to death will be out in the community after a relatively brief prison term. As a general rule, jurors in criminal cases are not informed of sentence options for the defendant or eligibility for parole when they determine guilt or innocence. This reflects the traditional division of labor between juries and judges: the jury evaluates questions of fact and renders a verdict; the judge determines sentence (although judges determine fewer sentences today because of the popularity of mandatory minimum sentencing laws; legislators are determining sentences for a variety of defendants convicted of the same crime.) In capital cases, however, the jury decides or recommends the sentence, sometimes with insufficient information or understanding of the law.

More than half of the death penalty states that provide the option of life without parole do tell jurors about the defendant's parole ineligibility. And a recent Supreme Court case held that if the prosecution argues that the defendant should be executed because of future dangerousness, the jury must be informed of the life without parole alternative.[56] But it's not clear that juries believe that life without parole really means life without parole.

Only 11 percent of people surveyed in 1993 believed that someone sentenced to life without parole would actually serve a life sentence.[57] About one-third of jurors surveyed in

California, Florida, and South Carolina believed that convicted murderers sentenced to life imprisonment would only serve fifteen years or less, when in South Carolina, the mandatory term was thirty years, in Florida it was twenty-five years, and in California it was life without parole.[58]

Juror misconceptions about prison terms in capital cases reflect even more pervasive misconceptions of the public at large, shaped by publicity about dangerous felons serving very little jail time and some misleading claims by death penalty proponents. They often argue that people convicted of homicide are routinely released after serving as little as five or seven years in prison. If these claims are true (the cases are usually unspecified), it probably means that the people being prosecuted for homicide are not being convicted of categories of homicide that would qualify for the death penalty, even if one was in place. They're probably released in five or seven years because they were convicted of lesser crimes (at trial or pursuant to a plea bargain)—not because of the absence of a death penalty. After all, a defendant in a homicide case may plead guilty or be found guilty of manslaughter instead of first degree murder in a state with or without the death penalty. Defendants who are convicted for aggravated homicide that would qualify as a capital crime are not generally going to be released in five or seven years, whether or not the state has a death penalty. Mandatory prison terms in these cases are considerably longer than that.

It is understandable that jurors who underestimate prison terms in capital cases are more likely to vote for death. Executions must seem like the only means of keeping dangerous offenders off the streets. At the same time, at least some jurors believe that death sentences are not likely to be carried out (partly because of the appeals process). It may be that jurors sometimes vote for death as a way of ensuring that a defendant gets life or at least a very long prison term.

Preliminary interviews with Indiana jurors indicate that some may actually take comfort in the belief that the death penalties they impose may not be exacted. Joseph Hoffmann has reported that jurors demonstrate a strong desire to evade responsibility for deciding if another human being should live or die. They worry about the "right" to pass sentence, and pray for guidance (and, perhaps, for permission). Or, Hoffmann has found, they may tell themselves that they're not exercising any discretion at all. Some jurors regard the jury instructions not as guidelines for their own independent decision making but as a formula to be applied mechanically, "eliminating most of their own personal responsibility for making a 'choice' between life and death for the defendant." In Indiana where the judge has the power to override the jury's sentencing decision—power that is rarely exercised to set aside a death penalty—jurors may also seize upon the characterization of their decision as a mere recommendation. The belief that any sentence they pass will not be final can be particularly useful in persuading jurors holding out for life to join the majority in voting for death. And, like the insistence that jury instructions present jurors with a formula to apply, unthinkingly, the notion that a sentence decision by the jury is a "recommendation" allows jurors to abdicate the responsibility of making choices: "I really had no thought about [the death penalty] because it wasn't my choice to make," one juror explained, after voting for a death sentence. "It just really doesn't mean a whole lot what I say because it's ultimately up to the judge . . . it's not my call."[59]

"It's not my call." The death penalty is possible partly because responsibility for imposing it is so widely shared by groups of people that it can easily be denied by individuals. Prosecutors who make crucial decisions about how to classify a crime and whether to charge an offender with capital murder can say that the jury will decide the case. The jury can say it is only heeding the arguments of the prosecuting attorney and following instructions from the judge about how to evaluate evidence and determine sentence, and, in any case, jurors can always tell themselves that the trial judge or appellate judges will decide whether their sentence should stand. Trial judges, in turn, hesitate to second guess juries; appellate judges will not generally review findings of fact. The jury has spoken, the judges will say. Governors confronted with clemency petitions defer, as well, to prosecutors, juries, and judges and are fearful of frustrating what they believe is the public will. Corrections officials, the people who conduct executions, are merely carrying out the wishes of prosecutors, juries, judges, and governors who came before them. As one corrections officer remarks, "I am an instrument of the state," although the public never sees him go about his business.[60]

Capital punishment is possible partly because, in the end, it's private, impersonal, bureaucratic. By the time condemned prisoners are executed, they have been thoroughly dehumanized. It is likely that from the time of their arrest through trial they've been regarded as less than human (or they would not have been condemned to die.) "They're animals," people say of violent offenders in general. But, shuffling off to their deaths, in prison garb and shaven heads, after years on death row, they seem less like animals than mere automatons. "We first kill the person . . . by a process of dehumanization," Robert Johnson observes in *Death Work*. "Then we kill and dispose of the body."[61]

An incremental, bureaucratic killing is better than what they deserve, many people will say. Condemned prisoners enjoy "civilized" deaths compared to the deaths of their victims, people point out—as if we should take credit for being less cruel than the cruelest among us. And we have not turned executions into bureaucratic processes out of compassion for the condemned (for them, waiting on death row is torture).

We have depersonalized executions and even denied their reality, providing life-saving surgery to the condemned, in order to make the act of killing easier on ourselves.

The death watch that Robert Johnson describes exemplifies this need to make an execution manageable for the people who conduct it. An execution is broken down into a series of discrete tasks, shared by a team of corrections officers. It begins with a death watch, twenty-four to forty-eight hours before the execution. The prisoner is kept under supervision and surveillance by at least two guards who keep the condemned placid, compliant, and "on schedule." The goal is to ensure that he cooperates in his own death, so that it goes "like clockwork," with no disruptive displays of emotion. It is as if he is volunteering to be killed, with corrections officers merely walking him through the motions—motions ordained by legislators, prosecutors, juries, judges, and governors. Someone dies at the end of a long process, but there is no executioner.

➷ 6 | The Prosecutor's Perspective

If you favor capital punishment, you characterize the trial and execution process differently. Instead of focusing on what "we"—law-abiding citizens—do to "them"—convicted murderers—you focus on what they have done to us. You describe their savage, senseless crimes, you evoke the terror of their victims and the lifelong pain of the victims' survivors. You stress that if the death penalty is a lottery, it is a lottery that only violent offenders can play. More than bad luck—a brutal childhood, a mental or emotional disorder, an incompetent attorney—put them on death row, you say; they were put there as well by their acts.

So what if other murderers manage to escape execution. If you favor capital punishment, you may concede that it's not always imposed on the worst offenders for the best reasons (retribution perhaps, instead of vengeance). But you are likely to assert that the people we execute are bad enough and the reasons for the executions are good enough: if there are a great many worse or equally bad offenders receiving prison terms, you argue, then we should extend the death penalty to the many, not restrict it to the few.

Capital punishment is necessary, you may assert. If it doesn't deter others from committing murder, at least it incapacitates the person who is executed, while providing retribution to the victim's family, as well as a semblance of order. (Such necessity is the "mark of human wretchedness," Saint Augustine wrote. "How much more mature reflection it shows, how much more worthy of a human being it is when . . . he cries out to God, 'Deliver me from my necessities!' ")[1]

You trust that what is necessary will also be just, that no one will be executed by mistake and every condemned prisoner "deserves" to die. The system isn't perfect, you admit (how could it be?), but it works well enough. In general, prosecutors are honest, unbiased, and uninfluenced by political pressures; juries are wells of common sense; defense attorneys are always competent, even slick, or they can be made competent. If you favor capital punishment, you argue that whatever is broken within the system can be fixed; you support establishing higher standards for defense counsel, perhaps, and even increasing the resources available to defense. Or, you dismiss claims about incompetent counsel and other inequities as ploys to abolish the death penalty by people who oppose it, regardless of systematic safeguards. And it's true that the most vociferous critics of the system for administering capital punishment are not reformers seeking a fair death penalty; they are abolitionists seeking no death penalty at all. But if some people begin with the belief that capital punishment is inherently immoral and seek to abolish it by attacking the way it is applied, others, like Supreme Court Justices Blackmun and Powell, begin with the belief that capital punishment is, in theory, permissible and end by opposing it precisely because of the way it is applied.

How are people who have no firsthand experience with the

death penalty or the criminal justice system in general and no particular knowledge of law or history supposed to evaluate the conflicting claims made by advocates intent on abolishing the death penalty and advocates intent on maintaining it? They describe completely different systems of justice—one pervaded by arbitrariness, mistakes, and discrimination and one that successfully guards against arbitrariness, mistakes, and discrimination. It is not as if each side were describing a different part of the elephant from their different perspectives. It is as if one side were describing an elephant and the other side were describing a frog.

❧ | Doug Pullen has been a prosecutor for more than twenty years and district attorney for Chattahoochee Judicial Circuit in Georgia since 1989. He is a forthright supporter of the death penalty who has prosecuted numerous capital cases (anywhere from ten to twenty to a couple of dozen, his assistant estimates). Pullen is anathema to some of the defense attorneys in Georgia who defend capital cases and are intent on abolishing the death penalty. He has been described to me as a white-collar redneck—biased, dishonest, and mean, with a deceptively civilized veneer. By repeating this, I'm not telling Pullen anything he doesn't already know: "People opposed to the death penalty have no respect for me as a person or a lawyer," he stresses at the outset of our meeting. His relations with abolitionist attorneys are generally shaped by "nastiness and name-calling . . . they'll do anything but spit on me."[2]

Pullen knows that I am opposed to the death penalty too, but I have been recommended to him by one defense attorney with whom he has respectful relations, so he's agreed to see me. He's generous with his time, spending nearly two hours with me in his office in Columbus, Georgia, on a hot

June afternoon. But he is also defensive and harbors as many preconceptions about me (which are partly true) as I have about him. He seems to assume that I am a northern liberal with a strong bias against the South; that I'm completely uncritical of abolitionist attorneys and take all their assertions about him, and the system in general, at face value; that I have a strong bias, in general, in favor of the defense and feel undue sympathy for the murderers on death row, whom "not even a mother could love." When I tell him I was once a legal aid lawyer, he says, "Surprise, surprise, surprise."

Still, he gives me his side of the story, emphasizing that the abolitionists tell lies about him and prosecutors in general. He cites as an example allegations that his predecessor was guilty of influence peddling in a capital case involving a prominent local citizen, described by abolitionists as a wealthy contractor. His daughter was murdered, and, the story goes, the district attorney called this man to ask him if he wanted prosecutors to seek the death penalty in the case against his daughter's killer. The death penalty was requested and obtained, and the victim's father contributed to the D.A.'s campaign.

Pullen tells the story like this. The victim's father was not a wealthy contractor: "He worked and he made some money; when he died he owned a house and a truck and about $37,000. His estate was worth maybe $250,000. His influence came from being a decent human being. It wasn't because he had a lot of money, and he got his money from throwing some shingles on his back and climbing a ladder, throwing them up on the roof and nailing them down. If he ever went to the country club, it was to put a roof on it."

Pullen doesn't exactly deny that the district attorney consulted this man about seeking a death penalty in the case against his daughter's killer (and he might say there's nothing inappropriate about a prosecutor consulting a victim's family).

He does claim, however, that the D.A. decided not to go for the death penalty and offered the defendant a life sentence, which he turned down. The offer was then withdrawn.

Abolitionists knew this was not a case of influence peddling according to Pullen, but they circulated their allegations to the House Judiciary Committee, during hearings on the death penalty. "They let the Congress believe that we're sitting down here like little stooges and this rich and powerful man comes in and says, 'I want the man who killed my daughter electrocuted,' and we say, 'Yes, sir, yes, sir.' "

I don't know the truth of this case. (I suspect that each version I've heard is partly true.) But I haven't conducted my own investigation into the facts, because I'm less interested in which version of the story is more true than I am impressed by how true each version sounds. The vast majority of voters who hear these stories have no way to confirm their veracity and perhaps little inclination to do so. Which side do they believe? They believe the side that seems to share their values and ideals, trusting them to tell the truth. Sorting out the facts about the death penalty is a formidable challenge. With equal passion and conviction, advocates on either side present different versions of reality, different stories about the same cases.

Even when there is general agreement about the facts of a case, the truth is difficult to discern. Justice is not self-evident. Defense attorneys and abolitionists, in general, tell stories about the defendants aimed at eliciting sympathy for them. Prosecutors tell stories about their victims' grisly deaths.

Pullen describes several gory, brutal murders, partly, I think, to unsettle me:

> Think about someone you love, walking into a convenience store, being impatient to make a purchase and go home because it's late in the evening and hearing muffled cries out of

the back of the store. Your loved one walks in to take a look and sees this person in the back room with the clerk, torturing her, making sexual and obscene gestures among other things. He tells her to hold out her hand; he's going to give her the knife and he cuts her across the hand and ultimately stabs her in the chest with the knife, twists it and starts picking her up off the floor. Then he comes out and your loved one is standing there, this person stabs him through the heart. Your loved one walks out the door, falls down in a greasy parking lot and the testimony from the only witness is that "he was laying there, just a-floppin' and a-twitchin'." That's the only time that momma and grandmother lost it during the whole trial. . . . Then this guy, so repentant about leaving your loved one layin' there in the parking lot drives 7 miles, breaks in on an elderly couple, beats the old man over the head with a shotgun, rapes the old woman and stabs both of them, stabs the old man so much he cut the muscles that operate his voice; leaves both of them for dead and drives another 30 miles, goes into another convenience store, asks for a pack of cigarettes, and stabs the clerk square in the back. She survives. Do you really want that individual sitting there on Thanksgiving Day eating turkey?

Another shorter story—a throw-away:

A mile from where we're sitting, a man walked into a convenience store with a shard of glass from a bottle, grabbed a woman and stabbed her through the throat with this piece of glass, took the cash register and ran out. She walks from the place, across the road to a car and falls dead. She falls to death with her blood in the gutter.

"You might think that's socially acceptable behavior," Pullen concludes. "I think the man who did that ought to be on trial for his life."

I don't bother assuring Pullen that I don't consider this behavior "socially acceptable." I simply tell him that I don't think we should kill people unless it's absolutely necessary. Why not sentence this man and others like him to life without parole? Pullen says that he supports life without parole, but as a supplement, not a substitute for the death penalty. "It ought to be an option . . . I'm afraid it's all too necessary," he says of the death penalty. He concedes later that its role in crime control is primarily symbolic but would argue, I think, that the death penalty would have some practical value if it were more efficiently enforced. Far from being barbaric, our criminal justice system is all too civilized, Pullen asserts. The "criminals are winning. . . . We have civilized ourselves to the point where if everybody takes advantage of the system, it will collapse."

Pullen refers approvingly to public impatience with the rights of the suspects, describing a movie in which the cop batters "the bad guy" while reading him his rights. "The people in the movie theater are standing up and cheering because they know that our side is losing, and the very notion that criminals need to be advised of their constitutional rights— the only place it'll ever wash is in this country."

We might learn something from other countries in which cops are not restricted by the constitutional rights of people they arrest, Pullen suggests.

> The absolutely snottiest people in the world about our Fourth and Fifth Amendments are the Swedes, who don't have any problems because they don't put up with them. They will snatch you up and take your eyeteeth out. The very notion that a suspect doesn't have to talk is lunacy to them. . . . The Italians say you'd be amazed at what kind of confession you can get by taking a soft drink, shaking it up, and sticking it under a guy's nose.

I'd be amazed if confessions obtained under these circumstances were reliable. People confess to all sorts of crimes they didn't commit under torture or even under a suggestive inter-rogation conducted over a long period of time during which they're held in isolation. Rules prohibiting the mistreatment of suspects are aimed, in large part, at ensuring the reliability of any confessions they might make. Pullen implies, however, that the rules reflect mere squeamishness and too much civi-lization: "We have civilized ourselves to the point where the average citizen feels that the only thing he can do in the criminal justice system is to pay for air-conditioned prisons and color TV sets."

In fact, there may be more people getting raped in prison and infected with AIDS than kicking back in air-conditioned comfort watching TV. But this mythical image of prisons as places where criminals are coddled still seems to resonate with people across the country, just as the death penalty resonates with people angry about crime. In any case, Pullen sees capital punishment as a matter of states' rights. "I'm not fussin' Wis-consin because they don't have a death penalty." Why should out-of-staters, like me, fuss with Georgia? Pullen is sensitive to stereotypes of southern justice and quick to remind me that the North has perpetuated its share of abuses: "We didn't have the Salem witch trials in Atlanta." Racism is a fact of life across the country, he points out, and outside the South, it's become more rather than less respectable. In his thick southern drawl, Pullen concludes, "Used to be if you talked like me you didn't want to leave this part of the country. You didn't get treated so well. That's changed, but I don't know if it's changed for a good reason." What does he mean? "Used to be that talkin' like this was associated with being a racist and that was a bad thing; now it's not considered so bad."

◣ | If the rest of the country has become more overtly racist, as Pullen implies, the South is becoming less so, according to Susan Bolyn, assistant attorney general for the state of Georgia. Southern justice has changed considerably, Bolyn says; at least the players are changing:

> A lot of the old line prosecutors have retired; you have younger people and a lot of former public defenders and women prosecutors and black judges—the whole complexion of the system is changing, so you are going to see changes because you have people who look at things differently. I used to say that when I went to argue a death penalty case, they'd expect some big fat redneck with a white belt and white shoes to represent the death penalty in Georgia; they didn't expect someone like me, that was not the image of the southern prosecutor. But the good old boys are on the way out, the ones that used to get by elbowing the sheriff; they're on the way out, partly because they couldn't stand up to public scrutiny anymore.[3]

Bolyn represents the state of Georgia in appeals of death penalty cases in state and federal court. She has "mixed feelings" about the death penalty, for moral and practical reasons. As a "preacher's daughter," she wonders about the "religious questions" raised by the taking of life, and, as a lawyer, she wonders about the death penalty's deterrent effect, given the fact that most murders involve people who know each other. But, as a lawyer for the state, she says, it is her job to enforce the law, not pass judgment on it. Nor does she pass judgment on the fairness of the prosecutions she defends on appeal. The Georgia Attorney General's Office is known for never confessing error in capital cases, meaning they don't concede on appeal that a prosecution was wrongly conducted; they defend capital trials regardless of mistakes or misconduct by the state. Bolyn defends this tradition, explaining that deciding whether a trial was fair is the job of the appellate court. Her job is to present the facts about how the case was prosecuted and let the judge decide the law.

Lawyers are taught to have tunnel vision, to focus on particulars—the interests of their clients—instead of the general public good. Not that they don't care about justice, in general (some do, of course), but they will argue that it's best served when lawyers advocate for their clients without passing judgment on the merits of their cases or characters. Both defense attorneys and prosecutors are, therefore, often in the position of defending the indefensible.

Several years ago, Susan Bolyn represented the state of Georgia in a notorious case involving charges of jury tampering by a local prosecutor, which reached the Supreme Court. On appeal, the defense presented evidence that the prosecutor had conspired to keep blacks out of the jury pools. (The federal Court of Appeals granted a writ of habeas corpus in this case, which was upheld by the Supreme Court.) Bolyn says she doesn't know whether or not the allegations of jury tampering were true. She argued before the Supreme Court that the defense had essentially forfeited the right to present the allegations because of a procedural default, and she was "flabbergasted" when Justice Stevens pointed out to her that if the charges of jury tampering were true, they would be serious. "Everybody held on to my every word, and it flabbergasted me that there would be any question that I wouldn't think that these charges were serious. I looked at him and said, 'Yes, that would be wrong.' " Bolyn expresses outrage that "in a death penalty case" because she is defending the state, people assume she has a "different view of right and wrong. How could you agree that jury tampering is right?" But as Bolyn stresses, it wasn't her job to decide the merits of the claim of jury tampering. It was her job to argue that the claim was forfeited and, in the alternative, to argue that evidence of jury tampering was insufficient.

Bolyn is not sure whether she would have declined to defend this case if she believed the prosecutor was guilty of fixing the juries. "I don't know if a state lawyer can do that [refuse to take on a case] and still keep her job. You can always say, 'I have a problem with this,' but why should I get to choose what my cases are?" How she "feels" about a case or law she is charged with defending, like Georgia's law against consensual sodomy, for example, "is irrelevant."

Bolyn knows that by agreeing to handle every appeal that crosses her desk, regardless of her own opinion about the justice of it, she is offering something like a Nuremberg defense. "Since the first day I came here I've heard, 'All you are is a Nazi taking orders.' " In her view, however, she is supposed to play a very narrowly proscribed role in this system; she presents the state's side of a case on appeal, the defense presents its side, and the judge determines which side should prevail. In Bolyn's view, she is upholding the integrity of the advocacy system, in which she has a lawyerly faith.

> What you really want is to get good people in every role: a good defense attorney, a prosecutor with integrity, a good judge, a good appellate court, and when you get good, thinking, feeling moral people and everyone does his or her job, the result will be as just as we can get.

This is the textbook description of the advocacy ideal. Defense attorneys are apt to respond by arguing that, in practice, the trial of capital cases is far from ideal, that advocates are not evenly matched because of incompetent or inexperienced defense attorneys with relatively few resources. Bolyn says she "hears all these stories" about inadequate defenses, but she doesn't see them.

Her boss, Attorney General Mike Bowers, has a similar response to the charge that capital defendants are not provided with adequate counsel: it's fabricated, he says. Bowers denies any familiarity with the *National Law Journal* report documenting the problem of ineffective counsel, and other inequi-

ties, in the southern states, although he was cited in the
report as conceding Georgia's need for good capital trial lawyers.[4] (The Chief Justice of Georgia's Supreme Court, Harold
Clarke, told the *National Law Journal* that Georgia needed
"substantial improvement in the trial representation of indigent defendants.")[5] Today, Bowers simply says that if the *National Law Journal* reported serious inequities in death penalty
trials, "It was wrong."

Bowers dismisses charges about incompetent counsel as
part of the game abolitionist defense attorneys play to discredit the death penalty:

> Ten years ago, the issue was racial discrimination, 'til that got
> busted. . . . [Today] if it weren't trial counsel, it would be some
> other issue; it's just the issue of the day. If I were on the other
> side, I'd be doing the same thing, trying to find the issue to tie
> these cases up and achieve delay. Delay is winning for those
> who are against the death penalty.

Bowers says that the system should "grind out a result in
two or three years. . . . The whole process is so drawn out
that people forget what the crime was by the time it comes
round to execution."[6]

Perhaps. But if appeals were so restricted that sentences
were imposed in two or three years, several innocent men
recently released from death row, like Walter McMillian,
would be dead. For Bowers, this does not appear to be a serious concern, because, he says, innocent people are almost
never, if ever, convicted of murder. "Guilt or innocence in 99
out of 100 cases isn't even debatable; it's not a question, not
even close." Abolitionists, of course, disagree, naming people
who have been released from prison after being exonerated
of murder and citing cases of people who were never
exonerated but presented strong claims of innocence. Whom
should we believe? Most of us will not investigate these cases

ourselves or even read reports on them. Most of us accept the assertions of one side or the other on faith, depending on where our sympathies lie.

Do people understand the capital system? "My sense is they don't understand it too well," Georgia's Chief Justice Harold Clarke remarks. "I'm not sure that I understand it, working with it as much as I do. I've got to believe most folks don't understand it. They may have some conviction on it, but they may be misinformed."[7]

Most folks don't understand that constitutional rights are not mere technicalities, Justice Clarke adds. They don't understand the most elemental principle of the criminal justice system—that "you can't protect the innocent without also protecting the guilty," because it is the presumption of innocence that prevents us from prejudging a case. But, Justice Clarke agrees, given public concern about crime, some may be willing to sacrifice a few innocent defendants in order to convict more of the guilty. In any case, capital punishment is an emotional issue, Clarke stresses, and "when people become emotional [about it], you're almost wasting your time talking to them."

But how do we impose rationality on death penalty cases that evoke such strong emotional responses? The Supreme Court tried to rationalize the trial process, with guided discretion statutes governing jury deliberations, but it has not addressed the matter of prosecutorial discretion. The prosecutor's decisions about how to charge cases and whether to negotiate pleas are generally outside the purview of courts. Prosecutors have to play by procedural rules governing the way cases are tried, but in making decisions about whether to try them at all, prosecutors generally regulate themselves. Some will be influenced by politics, some by gut instincts, and some will try to standardize their charging decisions, just as courts and legislatures have tried to standardize the decisions of juries.

In his twelve years as District Attorney of Fulton County, Georgia, Bob Wilson recalls that he evaluated 200 to 300 murders eligible for the death penalty. About 100 to 120 of these cases were categorized as capital cases and the majority of these were resolved by plea negotiations. About 25 or 30 cases went to trial under the Georgia death penalty statute (about 10 percent of all death penalty eligible cases) and some 15 of these trials resulted in death sentences.[8]

How were 200 to 300 death penalty eligible murders winnowed down to 25 or 35 capital trials? Bob Wilson (now in private practice) acknowledges that prosecutorial discretion in selecting capital cases is "one of the weak points of the system," although he stresses that discretion can be used to alleviate as well as inflict injustice. (Opponents of mandatory minimum sentence statutes, which don't allow judges to exercise discretion and mitigate mandated prison terms, would agree.) Wilson says he tried to guide the discretion of his office with a set of written procedures, but he remarks that "there was not a whole lot to be said" about the handling of capital cases, which took up a small section of an office manual.

Wilson describes the process for evaluating murder cases briefly. Cases came into his office through the investigative unit; death eligible cases were identified at this initial stage. They constituted a small minority. "Most cases don't even come close to fitting within Georgia's death penalty statute. . . . Homicides come in a wide variety, from truly accidental killings to premeditated conspiracies." Domestic murders range from sudden outbursts of a husband against wife or a wife against husband "to cases in which one spouse buys a new insurance policy thinking 'I don't want this mate to be with me anymore.' "

Charges were drawn up by assistant district attorneys in the next stage of the process. Cases marked "death penalty eligible" eventually moved up to a special prosecution team, which considered the defendant's record (was he a career criminal with several armed robbery convictions?) and the nature of the crime (was this a random shooting of four people at a McDonalds or a quarrel between two people that ended in death?). Eventually all death penalty eligible cases reached Wilson with a recommendation. The final decision about whether or not to seek a death penalty was his, although he consulted with senior staff.

What standards guided Wilson in making his final charging decision? The largest "catch-all" category of capital murder under Georgia law, Wilson notes, is the category of "heinous" or "vile" homicides. The majority of Georgia's death row inmates have been sentenced under this relatively vague provision, according to Wilson. What exactly does "torture" or "outrageously vile" mean? Wilson says his staff studied case law defining these terms; his bottom line interpretation of this provision of Georgia's law is "that you've got to be a pretty bad son of a bitch to fall into it."

Apart from aggravating circumstances, like a consensus that the defendant is a "son of a bitch," prosecutors are also expected to consider factors that mitigate against seeking the death penalty. Wilson says that the primary mitigating factors for him were defendant's age, criminal record, mental capacity, and the involvement of a codefendant who was not subject to the death penalty. "If, for example, you had a case involving two boys, one 17 and one 16, it seemed unjust to me that you could seek the death penalty against the 17-year-old but not the 16-year-old. I'm not saying the law is unjust, but it does give you discretion. I think defendants ought to be treated as closely alike as possible for similar conduct." So, in the case he describes, Wilson might offer the 17-year-old a plea. Another D.A. who did not believe in equal treatment of codefendants could, however, seek the death penalty for one and offer a prison term to another. As Wilson notes, the treatment of codefendants is a matter of prosecutorial discretion, so they are often treated differently.

Different prosecutors handle the same cases differently; Wilson agrees that the application of the death penalty can vary from county to county. But, he stresses, "the question is not who gets the death penalty but who doesn't get it. You'd be hard pressed to find someone on death row whose case didn't meet the aggravating circumstance requirements of Georgia's law." You might, however, find people whose cases are marked by a broad range of mitigating factors, Wilson admits. Factors that might convince one D.A. not to seek a death penalty (such as a defendant's mental capacity) might be ignored by another.

Juries are supposed to act as checks on arbitrary exercises of prosecutorial discretion. (Rarely will a judge rule that evidence is insufficient on its face.) It is mostly the jury's job to second guess the prosecutor, making an independent evaluation of guilt and all the aggravating and mitigating factors. "Ultimately, the jury decides," Wilson says. "We present the case and the jury decides what the ultimate punishment will be." But, as surveys of capital jurors show, jurors don't necessarily see themselves as the ultimate arbiters of punishment. They may not understand instructions about how to evaluate aggravating and mitigating factors, and, even if they do, they are apt to know very little about the prosecutor's decision to seek the death penalty, and they may not know about the fate of any codefendants. They may be equally ignorant of all the mitigating factors of the case, if the defense is inadequate. As a check on prosecutorial discretion, juries aren't necessarily effective.

Wilson, however, puts his faith in the jury system and the appellate process: if there is an abuse of discretion by one player in the system, a prosecutor, for example, there are other players to review his or her conduct along the way.

Each case has to survive a "series of traps. It's got to clear the judge, the jury, and a multitude of appeals. If something's been done wrong, the chances are it's going to show up and be rectified. You've got to have some faith that the system has done the best it can. . . . You've got to have some faith in the integrity of people who took an oath that they'll do their duty. . . . I do not believe that anyone goes through the system encountering unfairness at every step."

In Wilson's view, today the system is "as close as we can make it to being fair." (In the past, he notes, it was "woefully inadequate.") Still, he suggests that the death penalty will eventually be abolished ("and I'm not sure we won't be the better for it"). Wilson says that some crimes merit the death penalty and that virtually everyone on death row has earned a place there, but, he observes, we may find ourselves unable to "create a system which we can be certain will always be fair." Wilson seems to contradict himself at times, both affirming and questioning the system's fairness; that is perhaps a reflection of what he says are his mixed feelings about the death penalty.

Something will be lost if or when we abolish the death penalty, Wilson suggests—the capacity to make a "more profound statement" about communal outrage over a crime than we can make with a term of life in prison. But we will not lose a solution to violent crime, he adds. "People who present the death penalty as an answer to crime are wrong." In defending the death penalty, Wilson does not focus on its arguable practical value, as a deterrent or a method of incapacitation. He evokes its sentimental or religious value, as an occasional affirmation of moral order.

◄ | Religion naturally infuses the practice as well as the theory of criminal justice. Jurors asked to sit in judgment on their peers are apt to pray for guidance from a higher power than the judge. Offenders are supposed to atone. (The establishment of penitentiaries in the nineteenth century reflected a belief that convicts would be rehabilitated through solitude, prayer, and reconciliation with God.) Religious beliefs—about forgiveness and retribution and the promise of eternal life—have been central to debates about capital punishment. The movement to abolish the death penalty, like the movement to abolish slavery or abortion, is partly grounded in religion. Many proponents of the death penalty also rely on Scripture and the belief that the condemned may find salvation by confession and atonement. We execute people but provide them with chaplains to pray for their souls.

The belief that execution only terminates the life of the body, not the soul, makes it seem less horrible. If the soul is immortal, then capital punishment is not the ultimate punishment; it is only death, not damnation. It may even be the path to redemption.

When we execute people, "we're eliminating the physical presence on this earth," Bob Wilson says. "We are not trying to condemn people to Hell; that is not our place." Wilson's view of body and soul and human stewardship of earthly matters provides him with a rationale for the death penalty:

> God has given us a world to run, to try and order. . . . There's some territory that's not ours. It's not for me to say what your relationship is to God and how your spirit is in tune with God. . . . But I am enough of a realist to say, "Okay God, I can't touch the spirit, but you've given us a world and it's run amok." . . . and I think the best thing to do is eliminate this person from our presence. I pray that in God's presence, things will be better.

Some people simply pose too great a threat to the "order of

the world," Wilson explains, raising the specter of Adolf Hitler. "I believe that you execute a Hitler, but as a Christian, I believe I have a duty to pray for his soul." (As a Jew, I wouldn't execute Hitler, but neither would I pray for his soul; although I'm not convinced he had one or that he faced the prospect of eternity.)

Confidence that death is a portal to eternal life provided the most powerful historical justification for capital punishment. Public executions were, in part, religious rituals: a condemned prisoner repenting on the gallows was supposed to remind spectators of the possibility of salvation, while the execution proved the wages of sin, Louis Masur writes in his history of the death penalty. In the early years of the republic, before public executions were abolished, "criminals were encouraged and manipulated to recant publicly their sins and plead for the mercy of God . . . the execution spectacle dangled before spectators [sic] eyes the journey 'from the gallows to glory.' " It was, in part, the failure of this spectacle, the refusal of attendant crowds to be converted or even sobered by it, that ended public executions.[9]

Abolitionists sometimes argue that when executions were shorn of their religious meaning and rituals, they were shorn of their reason. Private executions exclude rather than involve the community; they're conducted mechanistically, without passion or any ennobling ideal.

Executions have no legitimate secular purpose, Albert Camus wrote, in a justly famous argument against the death penalty. He did not believe that capital punishment had any deterrent effect, considering the utter lack of evidence that it deterred crime and the irrationality of violent criminals: "Fear of death, however great it may be, has never sufficed to quell human passions. . . . For capital punishment to be really intimidating, human nature would have to be different." Religious belief, the certainty that the soul survives and that all human judgments will be second guessed by God provided the only rationale for state-sanctioned killings, Camus argued; and religious beliefs did not predominate in the postwar Western state. Executions were conducted by secular bureaucracies, with no notions of immortality:

> When an atheist or skeptical or agnostic judge inflicts the death penalty on an unbelieving criminal, he is pronouncing a definitive judgment that cannot be reconsidered. He takes his place on the throne of God, without having the same powers and even without believing in God. He kills, in short, because his ancestors believed in eternal life.[10]

The great majority of Americans today, however, believe in eternal life; at least they profess belief in God, and many buy a lot of books about angels. The United States is officially a nonsectarian country (to the chagrin of some who believe it should be a Christian one); but it's hardly irreligious. Still, Camus's critique applies. If many people involved in sentencing offenders to die are not skeptics or atheists but believers, the system itself is still bereft of any transcendent purpose. Only vestiges of the religiosity that justified capital punishment remain, and they seem out of place: we assign chaplains to counsel and comfort the condemned, and we prohibit executing incompetent offenders who don't understand the nature of their punishment or the reason for it and so have no opportunity to repent before they die. Our shallow commitment to the principle of repentance is evidenced by the inconsistency with which it's applied (considering the number of mentally disabled people on death row), and the religious logic of the rule against executing the incompetent is lost on a secular bureaucracy, in which it seems arbitrary. If there is no promise of eternal life and no need for the condemned to repent, there is no moral difference between executing the sane and the insane. Why should we kill one and not the other if we have no concern for their souls?

From a secular perspective, discomfort with executing the insane seems particularly irrational: the greatest cruelty we inflict on the condemned is not death but anticipation of it, in isolation on death row. Death sentences seem so much less cruel when imposed on people who don't understand them. Rickey Ray Rector's execution was criticized because he was brain damaged and apparently oblivious to his impending death; but from a secular perspective, his incompetence only made his execution more merciful than most.

Still, this is not an execution that inspires pride in people—the pride they take in bravely standing up to criminals on the streets or in their homes. The execution of a helpless man, already rendered harmless, may satisfy some notion of justice (Rector committed the crime for which he was killed), but it hardly seems like the act of moral courage some proponents of capital punishment make it out to be.

The rhetoric in support of capital punishment is much more ennobling than the practice of it. Walter Berns, an eloquent defender of the death penalty, has described it as an expression of "moral strength," likening it to the Israeli raid in Entebbe (a high-risk hostage rescue mission that had nothing in common with the assembly line executions of tranquilized prisoners). The death penalty dignified the condemned as well as his executioners, Berns has written, recalling the execution of American revolutionary hero, Nathan Hale, "whose statue stands in the Yale Yard with hands tied behind the back and head held high, presumably as an inspiration to the undergraduates who are supposed to look upon their country—'For God, for Country, and for Yale'—as something worth dying for."[11]

Nathan Hale? In a discussion of the death penalty in late twentieth-century America—a penalty applied to a random assortment of vicious, abused, and disabled people, many of whom committed terrible crimes for no discernible reason, much less for God or country—why are we talking about Nathan Hale? What did Rickey Ray Rector have in common with him? How many undergraduates would be inspired by the image of a brain-damaged lunatic, shuffling to his death, looking forward to eating his dessert when his execution was over?

The best evidence of the "moral strength" and dignity of capital punishment is conjured by a world more fictional than real—the world of Sidney Carton, sacrificing himself in *A Tale of Two Cities*, for love of Lucy Manette, peacefully facing the guillotine; the world of Billy Budd. Capital punishment has long been associated with honor, glory, and salvation—that's true—but when we talk about the prisoners on death row in America today, we're hardly talking about Christ on the cross or even Barabbas.

To illustrate the moral necessity of capital punishment, its essential role in enforcing a collective sense of right and wrong and maintaining order, Berns must also turn to fiction. Shakespeare serves him well. Berns's most powerful rhetoric follows from an account of Macbeth, who killed not blindly or senselessly or as a result of some mental defect, but out of "vaulting ambition" to be king. What our world needs, Berns says, is the poetic justice handed out to Macbeth, who paid with his life for his crime. Berns stresses our obligation to reassert the moral order whenever it is flouted. He talks about the importance of affirming that whenever someone is murdered, whenever an injustice occurs, the universe responds. "The cosmos rebelled" against Macbeth, he says. "Can we imagine the play in which Macbeth does not die?"[12]

Punishment is like "dramatic poetry," Berns writes, and it's hard not to wish that were true.[13] His poignant argument reflects the yearning for a world in which every murder is a sacrilege and every execution an act of atonement. But there are no Macbeths on death row, no Nathan Hales, and not even any Hannibal Lectors. Instead there are dull-witted people, damaged and crazy people, along with inexplicably cruel people whose sordid, secret deaths do nothing to set the universe in order. It's not the universe rebelling that lands people on death row; it's merely the bureaucracy plodding through its paces.

Former prosecutor Bob Wilson suggests that people of good faith, applying consistent, reasoned standards of law can make capital punishment more like a passage of dramatic poetry and less like a day at the Motor Vehicle Bureau. But he professes ambivalence about the death penalty and expresses confidence that the public will eventually accept its abolition: "I'm absolutely convinced that we never give the public enough credit," he says, sounding for the moment as if he's running for office. (Politicians, a few editorial page writers, and the occasional talk show host like to praise the judgment, good sense, and essential decency of the American public; the rest of us, cognizant, perhaps of all the Americans we neither like nor respect, often know better.) There is some demagoguery "around" the issue of the death penalty, Wilson admits, but "ultimately demagogues fall by the wayside." Consider the abortion debate, he adds: moderates, not demagogues, have prevailed.

Perhaps. (Wilson made these remarks before the murders of abortion clinic doctors and staff.) In general, however, abortion rights advocates have always had a natural advantage over those opponents of abortion who demonize it. Too many women and men have firsthand experience with unplanned or unwanted pregnancies, too many women have had or desired abortions, with the sympathy and support of too many men for the public to condemn abortion as a cardinal sin. Far fewer people have had firsthand experience with capital trials, as relatives of victims or defendants, much less as defendants themselves. Assertions about the value of capital punishment or the fairness of the system aren't subjected to much reality testing by the public at large.

We don't, after all, make purely dispassionate moral or intellectual judgments about such life and death issues as abortion and capital punishment; we base our judgments on experience and temperament, as well. I can still remember my outrage when my mother explained to me that abortion was illegal. I was twelve years old with no expectation of becoming pregnant in the imaginable future. Still I took abortion prohibitions personally, with the visceral sense that they might someday be applied to me. What if other criminal laws might apply to me as well? What if instead of seeing themselves as potential victims of crime, the majority of voters saw themselves as potential victims of the criminal justice system?

7 Knowledge Is Irrelevant— Federal Crime Control

If a conservative is a liberal who's been mugged, a liberal is a conservative once arrested. Former Reagan administration official Lyn Nofziger, prosecuted in the Wedtech scandal, gives thanks to the American Civil Liberties Union. Hollywood liberals buy guns. Sometimes, ideology is sorely tested by experience.

The politics of crime control sometimes seems a simple matter of arithmetic. There are more crime victims than criminal defendants, particularly among the voting public, so there are likely to be more conservatives than liberals on the subject of crime—many more. Given the daily barrage of crime reports on TV news and in daily papers and the low clearance rates for violent crimes, it's likely that even people who've never been victims or defendants worry more about being victimized by violence than being prosecuted for it. Polling data indicating that a majority of the American public supports the death penalty are probably part testimony to the fact that a majority of Americans fear being murdered more than they fear being prosecuted, much less convicted for murder.

Of course, in any marginally civilized society, victims of violent crime will outnumber perpetrators, giving conservative approaches to crime a natural advantage over liberalism—an advantage that has been decisive during recent years of intense social anxiety. Liberalism held sway briefly during the 1960s, at least until the Nixon law and order campaign of 1968, not because crime was down (it rose sharply), but, in part, because hope was up. Hope fueled the war on poverty, the civil rights movement, and feminism; even the angriest protests of the Vietnam War reflected hope in the possibility of peace.

Today, hope seems as out of date as beehive hairdos reaching improbably for the sky. The hopeful notion that prisons might rehabilitate people has long been dismissed as naive, displaced by a belief in retributive justice and the demand that prisons serve as places of near permanent exile for the incorrigible among us. Some liberals still protest America's uniquely high incarceration rate, tirelessly pointing out that we imprison more people per capita than any other country in the world, except for Russia, but a majority of Americans favor building more prisons, despite their costs, and believe that sentencing practices are excessively lenient.

It's hardly surprising that the 1990s' answer to violent crime at the state and federal levels has been the "three time loser" statute, imposing mandatory life sentences without parole on repeat felony offenders, without much regard for the nature of their crimes or their characters. In Washington, which became the first state to enact a three time loser law by referendum in November 1993, qualifying "violent" felonies include promoting prostitution and petty robberies, in which no one is hurt. One of the first people sentenced to life in prison under the Washington law was Larry Fisher, a nonviolent small-time thief. His first strike was pushing his grandfather and taking $390 from him; his second strike was holding up a pizza parlor for $100, by pretending his finger in his pocket was a gun; for his third strike he once again stuck his finger in his pocket and robbed a sandwich shop.[1] Larry Fisher is not someone I'd invite home for dinner, but neither would I imprison him for life.

"I feel that we're sort of pulling one over on the public," Chase Riveland, director of Corrections for Washington state, remarked on the *MacNeil-Lehrer Newshour*, asserting that three time loser laws were not "really dealing with violence on our streets."[2] In fact, preliminary anecdotal evidence suggested that the law might increase violence in the streets: police reported that when offenders were cornered, they were more likely to shoot their way out, rather than surrender and face life imprisonment. Another unintended but easily foreseeable consequence of the law will probably be an increase in trials (people aren't likely to plead guilty even to petty crimes that can be used as "strikes" against them.) In California, the increase in trials occasioned by the three time loser laws has contributed to prison overcrowding and to the early release of other, convicted offenders.[3] To the extent that they contribute to court congestion and delays in trying cases, these laws could decrease overall conviction rates; delay almost always favors the defense.

Three time loser laws may also be redundant, especially if they are drafted carefully so that they only apply to violent offenders. Violent crimes already carry lengthy sentences and many states have career criminal laws that impose strict mandatory terms on repeat offenders. (These laws have not been shown to ameliorate crime.)[4] The problem that is supposed to be addressed by three time loser laws—the early release of violent felons—might be best solved not by inflexible life sentences but by more rational allocations of prison space, decreases in the sentences of nonviolent offenders, and increases in strictly supervised prison alternatives for them. Prison overcrowding puts more felons back on the streets than soft-hearted judges, creatures more mythic than real.

Still it's been practically impossible for politicians to oppose three time loser laws. The 1993 Washington law was supported by more than three-quarters of the voters and was credited with sparking a national trend. The drive to imprison more people for longer periods of time seems unstoppable. It is as if all we can do is warehouse people until they die or are too old and decrepit to threaten anyone on the outside again.

Public dismay about crime posed more than a rhetorical challenge to an administration that came to power urging people to vote their hopes, not their fears. The adoption of violence-prevention programs, Attorney General Janet Reno's rhetorical theme for her first months in office, requires the hope that the federal government, in partnership with localities, can successfully treat social pathologies that contribute to crime. Indeed, the assumption that there is an identifiable, treatable connection between pathologies—such as the neglect and abuse of children—and crime reflects the hopeful notion that violent people are made, not born, and can sometimes be unmade, if intervention comes early enough. Early childhood intervention programs, violence-prevention curriculum, and alternative sentencing are more resonant of Lyndon Johnson's War on Poverty than Nixon's War on Crime. Along with an increasingly rare belief in the curative powers of good government, they reflect faith in the malleability of human beings and the capacity of distressed people and communities for self-improvement.

For all his sunniness about America, Ronald Reagan presented a much darker view of criminality that still holds its appeal. There are no social solutions to crime, Reagan asserted in a 1981 address to the International Association of Chiefs of Police, because crime is not a social problem. "It's a problem of the human heart." For most criminals, crime was a calculated choice, Reagan said, inspired not by need but by greed and a false sense of entitlement. Most offenders "do really believe that they're better than the rest of us," Reagan told the police chiefs, and "a lot of them are making as much money or a great deal more than you or I do." Reagan cited what he viewed as a dual liberal fallacy about crime—the conviction that ameliorating poverty might reduce crime and the assumption that "there was nothing permanent or absolute about man's nature."[5]

This bleak vision of crime as an untreatable fact of life, the implicit equation of crime with original sin, dismisses liberalism as utopian. Government can merely respond to the symptoms, by arrest and incarceration; only God can treat the disease, Reagan implied. He had a penchant for using religious rhetoric in talking about crime: "We have seen license allowed to the wicked and abuse heaped upon the decent and innocent," he preached in 1968.[6]

Reagan offered the more traditional view of crime—as badness, not madness, as a result of nature, not nurture. This was the view that dominated in colonial America, historian David Rothman has observed. Calvinism associated crime with sin, which essentially made it easier to bear. Crime was, as Reagan suggested 300 years later, a fact of life or human nature, not a function of social failures. With a strong belief in original sin, the colonists had low expectations of human nature, Rothman writes, and "little faith in the possibility of reform," which gave them little reason to assume responsibility for it. The individual, not the community, was responsible for deviant behavior, which could be checked—by painful, public punishment, perhaps—but not cured. Corporal punishment and executions were the primary forms of "correction," aimed not at rehabilitating people but scaring them, making clear to offenders and the public at large the awful consequences of disobedience.[7]

The utility and morality of corporal punishment and, to some extent, execution began to be questioned in the eighteenth century by reformers who preached moderation and the new idea that punishment might rehabilitate people. The landmark modern critique of capital punishment was Italian theorist Cesare Beccaria's *On Crimes and Punishments* published in 1764. American reformer Benjamin Rush published an argument against the death penalty in 1792 and was instrumental in limiting Pennsylvania's use of capital punishment to first degree murder. Rush also helped found the movement to establish penitentiaries; as an alternative to the death penalty and other harsh, public punishments, he proposed establishing houses of repentance, in which offenders could contemplate and cast off sin.

In the nineteenth century, prisons became the dominant response to crime and, as originally conceived, prisons were supposed to reform. An American ethic of self-improvement was displacing Calvinist beliefs in determinism, and in the early 1800s penitentiaries were established in the hope of improving offenders with isolation, work, and discipline. The explanation of crime was changing, David Rothman writes: Crime was not preordained, the product of original sin; it was the product of human institutions and human mistakes and was amenable to human correction. Urbanization, industrialization, and changing patterns of family life created considerable concern about disorder in Jacksonian America. While this generated some rather bleak views about society and its effect on individuals, it also offered considerable optimism, as Rothman notes. Social problems that caused crime, as opposed to existential ones, were amenable to social solutions.[8]

This was the optimism that became and remains entrenched in popular culture. It is the optimism of the personal development tradition. We are all diseased and dysfunctional, according to personal development experts, because of what was done to us in childhood; but our dysfunctions are not genetic or ordained by God, so we can all recover. The diagnosis of dysfunction, or disease, holds out the promise of a cure.

But the optimistic view of selfhood that shaped personal development movements had much less effect on notions of criminal justice. Optimism about the chances of recovery for criminal offenders did not long survive the creation of penitentiaries, which quickly became places for punishment, not penitence. In the 1830s, officials at New York's Sing Sing were meting out harsh punishments like whipping for slight offenses as a means of maintaining discipline. By the 1860s, the penitentiaries were primarily places for storing people, generally from the margins of society, lower income groups, and immigrants.[9]

The decline of efforts to rehabilitate offenders was accompanied, not surprisingly, by the rise of "scientific" theories about the inevitability of their offenses. Criminal behavior was said to be based in biology, not culture. Italian physician Cesare Lombroso, whose 1887 book *Criminal Man* popularized the notion of "born criminals," identified and classified offenders by the shape of their skulls and other physical characteristics he considered ape-like, such as long arms. In Lombroso's view, criminals were literally atavistic creatures, lower on the evolutionary scale than law-abiding, white men like himself. Blacks were considered less evolved (as were women); Lombroso cited dark skin as one indication of criminality.[10] Thus, science, like religion (notably Calvinist belief in predestination) offered an explanation for criminal behavior that did not indict society: the criminals' genetic inheritance was a kind of original sin.

It's hard to know whether penologists embraced Lombroso's work because their efforts at rehabilitation had failed or whether their efforts failed because they embraced such a crackpot notion of human behavior—but embrace it they did. Lombroso's work and the field he founded, criminal anthropology, greatly influenced penology for decades, Stephen Jay

Gould observes, in *The Mismeasure of Man.* Criminal anthropology was "*the* subject of discussion in legal and penal circles for years. It evoked numerous 'reforms,' and was, until World War I, the subject of an international conference held every four years for judges, jurists, and government officials, as well as for scientists."[11]

Modern systems of indeterminate sentencing owed much to Lombroso, as Gould explains. Indeterminate sentencing, which has been out of favor since the 1970s, was differential sentencing that focused strictly on the criminal, not the crime. "Born criminals," in Lombroso's view, ought to be treated differently than noncriminal types who just happened to commit illegal acts, like murdering their spouses in the grip of passion. Today, determinate, mandatory minimum sentencing aimed at strictly punishing the crime regardless of character and motivations of the criminal generates different sorts of inequities (like three time loser laws).

But, if Lombroso's theories of sentencing no longer hold sway, his pessimistic view of criminality as an immutable character flaw, whether genetically or divinely ordained, retains appeal, as Reagan's statements show. Lombroso's theories were particularly influential in obviating calls for social reforms that address what we've now come to deride as the root causes of crime.

Recently, biological determinism has been revived by genetic explanations for a broad range of behaviors, from alcoholism to homosexuality to intellectualism and violent crime. In 1985, James Q. Wilson and the late Richard Herrnstein published a controversial book, *Crime and Human Nature,* devoted, in part, to a discussion of genetic causes of crime. Herrnstein's more recent book, co-authored with Charles Murray, raised the inflammatory claim that intelligence is genetic and linked to race. Scientists tend to be skeptical, if not dismissive of fairly simple notions of genetics that make their way into the mainstream, often through the social sciences. As biologist Evan Balaban told the *Boston Globe*, "All this talk of biological determinism is being driven by people who have the least training in genetics."[12]

The political appeal of genetic explanations for crime and other behaviors considered deviant is obvious. Gay rights activists can argue that homosexuality is an immutable characteristic, absolving homosexuals from the foolish charge that they have chosen an immoral life style. Criminal defendants, as well, can argue that a tendency toward violence is inborn. In 1994, a Georgia man sentenced to death for the gratuitous murder of a store manager during a robbery claimed, on appeal, that he was predisposed to kill by his genetic inheritance. "His actions may not have been a product of free will," one of his lawyers explained, noting a strong strain of violence in his family.[13] In one view, this defense represented the ultimate form of victimism. What chance do you have if you're born to be bad? But while the view of crime as genetic can bolster arguments for leniency, by making criminals seem less responsible for their acts, it also encourages harshness. A simplistic belief in genetics relieves many people from any pangs of conscience about what was done to violent offenders that made them violent, and it absolves society of responsibility for rehabilitating offenders, a task that seems increasingly hopeless. Genetic explanations for crime becomes excuses for giving up on people.

Today, resignation about the need for harsh punishments seems less based in science or religion than in sheer exhaustion—the sense that crime is out of control, particularly among juveniles—and complete disenchantment with government programs. In the popular view, social programs not only failed to alleviate crime; they increased it, by creating a culture of dependency and endorsing a moral relativism that declined to condemn single motherhood and other deviations from traditional family life.

That may sound like yesterday's editorial from the *Wall Street Journal,* but it was also one theme of Richard Nixon's 1968 campaign for president: "For the past five years we have been deluged by government programs for the unemployed, programs for the cities, programs for the poor," Nixon declaimed in his acceptance speech at the 1968 Republican Convention, "and we have reaped from these programs an ugly harvest of frustrations, violence, and failure across the land."[14]

Crime was a major issue in the 1968 presidential campaign. Crime rates rose in the course of the 1960s, along with dissent and social disorder, demands for racial justice, and illicit drug use among the children of the middle class. In the culture of Nixon's silent majority, all these phenomena, from violent crime to casual marijuana use, were linked, all reflected undue permissiveness, disrespect for authority, and a decline of moral values. Nixon successfully harnessed anxiety at the close of that disruptive decade, with his promise of law and order, and he changed the dominant rhetoric about crime focusing on order more than justice, and punishment more than poverty.

Lyndon Johnson had talked about crime in the context of poverty, which he urged the nation to combat:

> At its heart, the law enforcement problem has always been—and will remain—a human problem. Wretched living conditions produced high crime rates a century ago in immigrant neighborhoods. Today, slum conditions are producing equally serious problems among the new immigrants to our cities.[15]

The 1968 Democratic presidential candidate, Vice President Hubert Humphrey, noted that the increase in crime during the 1960s was primarily an increase in youth crime, as it is today, so he proposed "more extensive day care programs" for wage-earning mothers and after-school programs for kids. The enemy in the war against crime was poverty, Humphrey suggested.

Crime rates are highest among the poor and disadvantaged who commit more crime, but who also suffer more crime. In the long run we can only cut crime by getting at its causes: slums, unemployment, rundown schools and houses. This is where crime begins and that is where it must end.[16]

The Democratic platform of 1968, while promising increased support for local police as well as court reforms, persisted in stressing the need to attack the "root causes of crime." It offered a rather benign view of social disorder (one that might have been co-authored by psychologist Abraham Maslow): "The giant American nation, on the move, with giant strides, has never moved—and can never move—in silence. We are an acting, doing, feeling people. We are a people whose deepest emotions are the source of the creative noise we make."

To Republicans, however, who won in 1968, the creative noise of political protest was mere lawlessness, which was "crumbling the foundations of American society." Instead of talking about the evils of poverty, Nixon talked about the evils of welfare. Instead of blaming society for crime, the Republican platform blamed the individual committing it, calling for greater individual accountability: "We must re-establish the principle that criminals are responsible for their crimes, that while the youth's environment may help to explain the man's crime, it does not excuse that crime." In the view championed by Nixon in 1968, the root causes of crime were moral laxness, liberal Supreme Court decisions strengthening the "criminal forces" at the expense of the "peace forces" (Nixon's term for police); and, of course, the liberal focus on prevention. Crime was not a problem for psychologists; it was a problem for police. In his first term, Nixon allocated some $1.5 billion to state and local law enforcement, through the newly created Law Enforcement Assistance Administration (LEAA) block grants.

Rising public concern about crime and support for law enforcement in the late 1960s was captured and, perhaps, exacerbated by the popular press. "Whatever the actual blood count, the psychological reality is that crime is rising—and a sour pall of fear pervades the cities," *Newsweek* reported in 1969. "Everywhere man's eye is on his neighbor; from Harlem to Los Angeles, citizens are banding together to demand better street lighting and more police vigilantism, forming crime councils to patrol their own streets."[17] In 1972, *Life* magazine surveyed its readers about their fear of crime. "Are You Afraid of Crime?" the headline asked; beneath, in bold type, *Life* published the results of its survey: "78% sometimes feel unsafe in their own homes; 80% are afraid in the streets at night; 43% of families were crime victims last year; 30% keep a gun for self-protection; 41% say their police protection is inadequate; 70% would pay higher taxes for better protection."[18] Six months later, *Life* published a collection of expert responses to the crime survey. The liberal approach to crime was not entirely defunct, despite its decreasing political clout; the experts generally stressed the need to address social problems creating crime, while improving law enforcement.[19]

This was not rocket science. Yet, at the same time that America was sending a man to the moon, it was unable to confront the obvious need for effective crime prevention as well as apprehension and punishment of offenders. It's not as if the problem of crime had not been thoroughly analyzed. In 1969, the year of the moonshot, the Eisenhower Commission on the Causes and Prevention of Violence issued its voluminous final report. Chair Milton Eisenhower released a well-publicized statement noting that rising crime was primarily an urban problem and urging a commitment to combat urban ills; at the same time he urged that we upgrade the criminal justice system, particularly in high crime areas. Eisenhower also included chilling predictions of what the future might hold if we failed to take "effective public action," predictions that have come at least partly true: central business districts in the heart of the cities would be dangerously deserted at night and "surrounded by mixed areas of accelerating deterioration"; high-rise apartments and "residential compounds," protected by private guards and security systems would be "fortified cells for upper-middle class and high-income populations living at prime locations in the city." Suburban neighborhoods would be protected by "economic homogeneity" and distance from the cities; gun ownership would increase, along with private home security systems; inner cities would be "places of terror" and armed guards would patrol the public schools.[20]

Not even these dire prognostications, not even rising public anxiety about crime prompted any large-scale "effective public actions." The Nixon administration focused much of its crime control efforts on funneling federal funds to local law enforcement, the success of which was highly debatable. (Critics assert that too much money was spent on hardware.) Crime continued to rise in the 1970s, and by 1980, LEAA, which administered grants to localities, had fallen far from grace, although the public preference for funding law enforcement efforts at the expense of social programs now seemed entrenched. In the early 1970s, the Nixon administration also targeted the procedural rights of criminal suspects, introducing highly controversial anticrime legislation to authorize preventative detention and warrantless searches.

Crime control fell victim to the culture wars. Conservatives were becoming increasingly successful in casting crime as a moral failure, blaming it on the breakdown of the nuclear family, the decline of religion and traditional values, as well as the "coddling" of criminals mandated by the Warren Court. As law professor William Stanmeyer charged in a 1972 speech, crime was a result of the weakened internal controls of a "populace morally adrift" combined with a "failure of external sanction." In other words, crime was rampant partly because in our permissive society its costs to the criminal were low. Rhetoric about crime was heated and hyperbolic: "Our nation has almost reached the point where the safest person in America is the man accused of a serious crime," Stanmeyer declared, with equal measures of passion and ignorance—the untested certainty of a man who (I assume) had never been indicted for a serious crime.[21]

Some three years later in *Thinking About Crime*, James Q. Wilson offered a more thoughtful variation on this theme—that permissiveness at home and in the criminal justice system caused crime or, at least, made it difficult to control.[22] Wilson chided liberals for focusing on social injustice as the root cause of crime. ("If we are to eliminate crime and violence in this country, we must eliminate the hopelessness, futility, and alienation from which they spring," New York City Mayor John Lindsay said in 1968, offering what was then the typical liberal analysis, which Wilson attacked.)[23] It's not that social reasons for crime don't exist, Wilson wrote, but they are practically impossible to address: "The more we understand the causes of crime, the more we are drawn into the complex and subtle world of attitudes, predispositions, and beliefs, a world in which planned intervention is exceptionally difficult."[24]

For Wilson, the liberal fallacy was the notion that "no problem is adequately addressed unless its causes are eliminated."[25] This was a sophisticated version of a message Republican politicians had been offering for years. As Attorney General John Mitchell charged in 1969, whenever the Democratic administration had taken action against crime, "it tended to ignore the practical and immediate solutions in favor of the approach of social scientists who can explain the motivations of the criminal, but who can do little to protect the innocent against the mugger or armed robber."[26]

This rejection of liberal concern for social inequities as causes of crime was presented not just as a moral imperative but a pragmatic one. Wilson argued that policy is most effective when it focuses on objective matters such as the costs and benefits of crime, not the realm of "the subjective and the familial."[27] He posited criminals as essentially rational beings who would be deterred from crime when the cost of punishment became impractical.

It's impossible to know how many violent offenders are weighing the consequences of their actions. (It's likely that many who do engage in cost benefit analyses never get past assuming they won't get arrested.) Certainly thirteen-year-old boys with guns, a wide range of neurotics, psychotics, and apparently sane, smart killers like Gary Gilmore tend to act impulsively, without regard for harsh sentencing laws. Nor would the prospect of a prison sentence necessarily deter a young man for whom imprisonment has become a rite of passage, or a haven from the streets—"three hots and a cot." It might not even distress his parents. One Boston defense attorney remembers the first time the mother of a client encouraged her not to free her son from prison. "At least I'll know where he is," she said.

At times it has seemed that the poignancy of this appeal and the threatened destruction of several young generations might persuade liberals and conservatives alike to reconsider some of their basic assumptions, at least rhetorically. "Those mothers in the ghetto love their children," Republican Senator Orrin Hatch asserted in 1994 with all the force of revelation, acknowledging that poverty is related to crime (as well as a welfare system that "does not stimulate the desire to make something of yourself"). "Some people become locked in poverty and become embittered in the process . . . that's why drugs are so rampant in our society. Kids in the ghetto can make more money pushing drugs than working for the minimum wage."[28] Meanwhile, Jesse Jackson was preaching self-help—an ethic of individual and communal responsibility, telling African Americans to "look inward to go forward." President Clinton was emboldened to exhort an African American congregation to address the violence within their own community.

The public might have been persuaded to reconsider its approach to crime control as well, by embracing crime prevention programs in addition to tough new law enforcement measures. In fact, a 1989 Gallup Poll showed surprising support for social programs aimed at deterring crime: Asked to choose between spending additional funds attacking "the social and economic problems that lead to crime" and spending more to improve law enforcement, 61 percent of respondents chose "attack social problems," while 32 percent chose "improve law enforcement." It's probably wise not to read too much into this finding; the question includes an unstated assumption—that social and economic problems do indeed lead to crime—an assumption that, on second thought, respondents might question. It's difficult to reconcile support for focusing on "social problems" with current demands for harsher sentences and more spending for cops and prisons. Still, a poll that shows twice as much support for social spending as law enforcement makes you wonder. A 1994 Times Mirror poll found that while the public put most faith in longer prison terms for violent offenders (70 percent of respondents rated longer sentences very effective in the fight against crime), people expressed nearly as much support for more police, more prisons, and more inner city jobs programs.

Perhaps an even more telling indication of at least inchoate public support for social programs was the Republican attack on prevention programs in the 1994 crime bill as "pork." They didn't focus their attack on the notion of prevention, which makes you suspect that they suspected that prevention might have had a constituency. They appealed to public mistrust of big government and political venality.

But, as soon as they won control of Congress, Republicans vowed to slash the new prevention programs; in the end, the new talk about crime did not presage new approaches to controlling it. Although in the 1994 crime bill a considerable amount of money ($6.9 billion) was allocated to prevention, it represented less than one-fourth of the total $30 billion dollar bill—and before prevention funds were even allocated, they were in jeopardy of being eliminated by the new Republican Congress. Crime prevention is easily denigrated, not just because the public is more concerned with punishment but because prevention programs may be mistaken for rehabilitation programs. In other words, initiatives intended to ensure that young people won't become criminals are confused with initiatives to help or "coddle" those who have already begun committing crimes. Some people apparently believed that the much maligned "midnight basketball" program proposed in 1994 was one form of alternative sentencing, according to a report in the *New York Times*.[29] Remarks by conservatives, like Pat Buchanan, referring to the kids that would benefit from this program as "thugs" (why weren't they home in bed at midnight?) did little to clarify matters.

Even when it's clearly explained to the public, crime prevention is, at best, a secondary consideration, an acceptable or even desirable supplement to harsher, surer punishment. People will support programs that offer to curtail violence tomorrow only when their fear of crime today has been allayed, which is why the centerpiece of the 1994 bill championed by President Clinton was an array of traditional crime-fighting techniques. The law allocated close to $10 billion for new prisons, and $8.8 billion for 100,000 new cops, and established some sixty new federal death penalties, for crimes including train sabotage and sexual abuse resulting in death.

"This could be one of those turning points in our history in terms of positions of the parties and their public perceptions," then Senate Majority Leader George Mitchell said triumphantly, after passage of the crime bill. "I think the time is over when in fact or in perception the Republicans are seen as the party that's tougher on crime. It's the Democrats." Mitchell's statement turned out not to be prophetic. A *Wall Street Journal*/NBC poll conducted the day after the Republican sweep of Congress in the 1994 midterm elections found that the public preferred Republican approaches to crime by a two to one margin.[30]

The doomed Democratic effort to challenge Republicans on crime by enacting comprehensive federal anticrime legislation started relatively quietly, with Senator Biden's introduction of a "tough" bill in the early fall of 1993. Then came the 1993 election. Traditional anticrime rhetoric was credited with facilitating the elections of New York City Mayor Rudolph Giuliani and Virginia Governor George Allen, both of whom advocated abolishing parole for violent offenders. Polling data showed crime becoming an increasingly pressing national concern, although a substantial majority of people still felt safe in their neighborhoods.

Coincidentally, the day after the '93 election, the U.S. Senate was seized with a sense of urgency about crime. On November 4, the Senate voted to double the size and cost of the proposed crime bill, providing for 100,000 instead of 50,000 new police officers, as well as new prisons. In the next few frenzied weeks between the election and Thanksgiving recess, the Senate passed a variety of "tough" anticrime measures: The crime of the week—arson—was federalized (California had just suffered a series of catastrophic brush fires, some believed to have been deliberately set). Federal jurisdiction was also extended to crimes of the year (already covered by state laws)—carjacking, drive-by shootings, and gang violence. Drug "kingpins" were made subject to the death penalty, regardless of their involvement in any homicides. Federal penalties for hate crimes were toughened as well.

Many of these measures, including the new death penalties, were widely derided as less tough than symbolic, sometimes by the senators who supported them. "We are going to show everybody how tough we are," Senator Biden, sponsor of the Senate bill, remarked. "Maybe [these provisions] will have some effect. But I want to advertise as the author of the underlying bill, as the author of the death penalty amendments, they are not going to have much effect."[31] Senator Hatch agreed: "It's no use kidding ourselves; some of these tough on crime amendments may not have tremendous effect." Why do lawmakers pass bills, with much ado, that they know will be ineffective? Senator Hatch remarked that we "are sending a message across this country that the Congress had finally awakened,"[32] in time, of course, for the midterm elections.

Individual rights were sacrificed, predictably, to toughness. The federal Attorney General's Office was authorized to conduct secret prosecutions, using secret evidence, against aliens suspected of being a threat to the national security. New evidentiary rules of questionable legality were written for sexual abuse cases, which are rarely prosecuted in federal court, allowing juries to hear about evidence of similar acts allegedly committed by defendants in the past. (With some exceptions, evidence of a defendant's prior crimes, much less acts that did not lead to convictions, is generally excluded from trial because of the natural tendency of jurors to infer guilt in a present case from past behavior.) Federal funds were allocated to establish a national registry and national background check for child care workers. This background check provision, proposed by Oprah Winfrey, was informally dubbed the Oprah

Act. ("The Oprah Act?" someone asked. "Does that make it a crime to lose weight and gain it back?")

"If someone came to the Senate floor and said we should barbwire the ankles of anyone who jaywalks, I suspect it would pass," Senator Biden quipped, shortly after voting with ninety of his colleagues to impose mandatory life sentences on people with the bad luck or bad judgment to commit their third "violent" felony on federal property.[33] This provision would not have affected the majority of offenders nation-wide, and the small number to whom it could have applied was bound to include people more hapless than vicious. The Senate proposal could have applied to someone whose first two "strikes" were relatively minor property crimes involving threat of force—shoplifting and getting into a fight with a security guard, or holding up a sandwich shop with your fin-ger in your pocket—if those crimes were defined as violent felonies by the state in which they were committed. The only vote against this provision, which promised to be both harsh and ineffective, was cast by Bob Packwood, conscience of the Senate.

Such bipartisan shows of unanimity did not survive the process of negotiating anticrime legislation, nor did the origi-nal Senate bill escape some modifications. The three strikes provision was tempered (with a slightly more narrow defini-tion of violent felonies and a release option for prisoners over seventy years old who have served at least thirty years); pro-visions federalizing certain gun crimes and gang-related crimes were deleted. But the law that emerged was substan-tially similar to the bill that the Senate had passed so enthusi-astically in November 1993.

Watching the Senate march in lockstep on any controver-sial issue, however briefly, adds an extra *frisson* to the term "politically correct." Whether or not you favor cracking down on crime (who doesn't?), it's fair to say that the Senate was not acting reasonably in passing so many anticrime measures with near unanimity and relatively little debate. Reasonable, informed people disagree about the merits of the three time loser laws, extensions of federal jurisdiction, and other traditional strategies. Crime control is not a science; nor is it religion, a simple matter of revealed truth, expect perhaps to Pat Robertson who blames rising crime rates on the absence of prayer in schools.

God knows whether restoring school prayer might lower the crime rate. We mortals have to figure out the consequences of less mystical law enforcement policies, in the absence of any sensible debate. When Congress considers crime, symbolism almost always prevails over substance, and safety. Will more police, prisons, additional mandatory sentences, or extensions of federal jurisdiction make us any safer? Will they restore some peace to the nation's most troubled inner city communities where violence is so unavoidable? Probably not.

◀ | The primary anticrime measure of 1994 in which Democrats put their faith was the promise of federal dollars for 100,000 new cops. It had intuitive, common sense appeal (80 percent of people surveyed by Gallup in 1993 believed that increasing the number of police would significantly decrease violent crime). Even if police have no direct effect on crime, many people feel safer in their presence, absent suspicions of police brutality, and when people feel safer they're more apt to venture out of their homes to form safer neighborhoods. The new cops were partly intended to help revitalize neighborhood life. They're supposed to be trained in community policing, a progressive model of police work widely embraced, at least rhetorically: it calls for a partnership of police and local residents, and expands policing's focus from arrests to intervention and preventative "problem solving."

In its most reductive form, this approach is viewed as a shift from deploying police in patrol cars that randomly cruise the streets and answer calls for assistance to deploying police on the street and encouraging them to establish ongoing relationships with the residents. Community policing is often described simplistically as a return to beat cops who are integral parts of the neighborhood.

In its sophisticated form, however, community policing entails what New York City Police Commissioner William Bratton calls a "sea change" in the concept of policing, from reactive, "incident oriented" law enforcement to a hybrid of enforcement and community relations work, aimed partly at crime prevention.[34] It envisions the demilitarization of police departments, a shift in authority down through management ranks, so that cops on the street will have more discretion and can go beyond making arrests to analyzing underlying problems and responding to them, with community cooperation. At its most cosmic, community policing requires teaching critical thinking skills to people who have traditionally been taught to play by the book. Advocates of community policing stress that it is not a new program or strategy but a transformative new philosophy (what a New Age cop might call a paradigm shift).

Some observers are skeptical that funneling federal dollars into local police departments will facilitate community policing or enhance public safety. In general, community policing doesn't focus on an increase in the numbers of police. It focuses on increasing community participation in crime control. Police departments will increase their effectiveness not by increasing their numbers but by extending their reach into communities, Michael Smith, director of the Vera Institute of Justice explains. The ratio of police to citizens is, in fact, a "poor predictor of violent crime," according to Smith. People fear random street crime greatly, but while stranger-to-stranger crime is rising, violent crime still tends to occur between people who know each other. Private relationships need to be policed, as the history of domestic violence shows, but they need to be policed differently from hold-ups of convenience stores. Additional police will have only marginal impact in areas with grossly understaffed police departments, Smith believes. In New York City, he points out, "the number of cops won't make much difference. When cutbacks reduced the number of police, the number of arrests rose; crime went up and down during that period." Smith is dismissive of federal provisions for additional police: "The analytical work that tells you we need more cops doesn't exist. It was a campaign promise."[35]

This is how criminal justice policy is made. According to a report by Ruth Shalit in the *New Republic,* the Democratic proposal for 100,000 new cops was derived arbitrarily, during the heat of the campaign. It was an exercise in public relations, not policy. "Clinton had a big crime speech coming up," John Kroger, the campaign's deputy issues director, explained to Shalit. "We had no idea how many extra cops would be a good thing." So Kroger and Domestic Policy Deputy Bruce Reed called twenty-nine-year-old campaign aide Ron Klain for advice. "He said, 'Would 100,000 be enough?' "[36]

Ronald Hampton, executive director of the National Black Police Association, suggests that 100,000 is far too many. In general, we have enough police officers, he contends; we simply don't educate or use them properly. "We need to focus on what police do, not how many of them are doing it. If I take 100,000 police officers and put them through the present induction program, most of them won't end up on the street and they won't bring their heads with them if they go there. If we don't first change the philosophy of policing in this country, whatever police officers we add will fall into the black hole that exists in every police department."[37]

Many people talk about community policing, advocates agree, but few police departments practice it. Michael Smith calls it "rhetorical policing." Herman Goldstein, professor of law at the University of Wisconsin, stressed at a 1993 Justice Department conference on community policing that the term "is widely used without any concern for its substance. Political leaders and, unfortunately, many police leaders hook onto the label for the positive images it projects but do not engage with—or invest in—the concept." Goldstein warned that if community policing becomes a catch-all term (like empowerment or codependency) it will be regarded as a panacea for a catch-all litany of urban problems. Successful implementation of community policing means fundamentally redefining both police functions and community expectations of police, he said. Service-oriented policing is not intended to satisfy all the needs of communities that are "starved for social services."[38]

If communities are apt inadvertently to expect too much from community policing, many police departments are still prepared to deliver too little. The scope of reform and intensity of internal resistance to them are routinely underestimated or ignored. Police officer Ronald Hampton suggests that it could take up to ten years to implement community policing in a metropolitan police department, a task complicated by the fact that the average tenure for police chiefs today is only about three years. Mayors come and go as well, changing policing priorities. Shortly after taking office in 1994, New York City's new mayor, Rudolph Giuliani, called for reform of community policing programs adopted by his predecessor, David Dinkins. Giuliani, a former prosecutor with a penchant for talking tough, criticized community policing for its focus on social services. He suggested that social service is, at best, an "add-on" to police work and, at worst, a distraction from crime control. Giuliani's remarks typified the response of law enforcement traditionalists to new models of policing and missed the point made by advocates of community policing: crime control includes crime prevention, which requires an understanding of the community's needs and good, ongoing relationships with residents. Community policing is intended to be a law enforcement tool—detectives rely on leads from local residents in identifying and apprehending suspects.

Community policing still tends to be susceptible to political attacks at a time when a frightened and angry middle class is demanding a more punitive justice system, not a more conciliatory, cooperative one. "If you call 911, you get a social worker, instead of a cop," then House Republican Whip Newt Gingrich said repeatedly, in an attempt to discredit the 1994 crime bill.[39] But, even in the most judicious of times, community policing would be difficult to implement. The "ship of policing" will turn slowly, Commissioner Bratton agrees, because "we have to change everything we do," including recruitment, training and supervision, and militaristic management policies. Bratton says he is unaware of any program teaching community policing "the way we would like it to be taught." There is resistance from the "old guard" who fear losing authority and control as police departments are decentralized, and there's resistance from recruits "who come in expecting to chase people and do shoot-ups. 85% of police work is not that. The average police officer in America is never going to draw his gun in his entire career."

The image of policing is still shaped by the media, Ronald Hampton notes. "Some recruits expect to come here and be Dirty Harry or Don Johnson. We need to shift from a spirit of adventure to a spirit of service." Hampton adds that some recruits do enter the police academy with an ethic of service but leave with a taste for authority, which they find easier to satisfy by policing racial minorities. "The way you police in an affluent white community is not the way you police in a poor black community," he says, telling the story of a young black police officer engaged in on-the-job training in the predominantly black neighborhood where he was raised. "I asked him a few questions about his assignment. He said he was assigned to Georgetown, which is about 90% white, but he'd been training in a 99% black community. He said, 'I'm disappointed. I don't want to go to Georgetown.' He said he wanted to work where the police tell the people what to do, not where the people tell the police. That kid wouldn't have said that before he went into the police academy. Now he's calling the people he grew up with trash; he's calling them scum."

All these caveats about the prospects for community policing in the near future do not necessarily mean that the federal promise of new police is misguided. Democratic Congressman Barney Frank asserts that the failure to use the existing police force with utmost effectiveness and efficiency is no reason not to increase their numbers. Inefficiencies are built into any bureaucracy, he notes, adding that arguments about inefficiencies are fallbacks for liberals who have ideological objections to hiring more police. "Do they say this about housing? Do they say we shouldn't build any more housing units until we learn to use what we have efficiently? They don't say, 'No more aid to poor countries unless we learn to do that efficiently' either."[40] Commissioner Bratton believes that some police departments do need additional officers, although their needs will vary. The Boston Police Department lost people during the past decade through attrition; New York City gained police officers with assistance from the state.

The trouble is that because the government allocates funds for additional police, some cities may apply for them, regardless of need, Michael Smith points out. "Politically you take what you can get and try to deal with the downside of the gift." What might be the downside of new police officers? Federal funding is only partial; a less publicized provision of the bill required localities to cover 25 percent of the costs of new hirings, and federal funding runs out entirely in six years. There are also hidden, secondary costs in hiring new police. Additional police officers making additional arrests impose additional burdens on local prosecutors, defender services, courts, probation, and corrections. Community policing is not necessarily supposed to result in more arrests, since its focus is partly on prevention. But the standard measure of police effectiveness is arrest rate, and it will not be abandoned any time soon. All the talk about community policing is not likely to decrease political pressure on police to increase arrests. Senator Biden acknowledged that with an influx of new police officers, "Costs will go way up." (How far up an official at the Justice Department could not say.)

This is not to suggest that if the federal government can't cover all the costs of a new program for the states, it shouldn't cover any of the costs. Many local officials welcomed the 1994 crime bill because it did direct some federal money to them. Partial, temporary funding of new police officers and a federal incentive to adopt community-oriented policing may be helpful in some cities, although any actual reduction in crime effected by the community policing initiative will be gradual and very hard to measure. Democrats will probably not be able to cite a significant decrease in crime or increase in the public sense of security, attributable to the new federally funded cops in time for the 1996 election. Nor are Republicans likely to support any new community policing programs made possible by a Democratic initiative or concede whatever successes they may enjoy. Community policing could become a casualty of the intensifying rhetorical war on crime; as the battle to seem tough enough continues, community policing will have less and less political allure than old-fashioned authoritarianism.

Not that we should expect much diminution of federal

spending on local law enforcement. There is some bipartisan consensus that the federal government's primary role in the fight against unorganized crime is assisting cities and states, although there are abiding disagreements over how that assistance should be divided between prevention, rehabilitation efforts (like drug treatment), and punishment. (Most money in the foreseeable future is bound to be spent on punishment and policing.) But if there is one fact of life which politicians across the spectrum acknowledge it's that crime is a local affair.

Of course, until the 1994 elections, when dislike for President Clinton and anxiety about the state of the nation were credited with putting Republicans in control of Congress, it was universally acknowledged that all politics is local too. Facts of life can change. Considering the political potency of public outrage over crime, politicians at the federal level strive to be activists on crime control. Like local congressional elections, law enforcement has become, in part, a national affair.

◀ | In Congress, politicians right and left often begin a discussion of crime control by pointing out that 95 percent of all crime is local. Then they explain the rationale for imposing federal penalties on whatever crime is of particular concern at the moment—violence against women, including stalking and spouse abuse, along with carjacking, was targeted by Congress in 1994: stolen cars and parts move in interstate commerce, advocates of federalization say; violence against women is still ignored in many states, and if it is a form of discrimination, women have an arguable federal right to be free of it.

In fact, the federalization of a great many crimes can be rationalized, since an interstate nexus is rarely hard to find. (The 1964 Civil Rights Act prohibiting racial discrimination in public accommodations was based on the Commerce Clause.) Arguments about federalization tend to be more political than principled. Liberals tend to contest the federalization of criminal behavior, except when civil rights or hate crimes are involved. Conservatives tend to oppose federalizing racial or sexual discrimination, either in deference to states' rights or a free market. People usually want the federal government to extend jurisdiction in areas in which they favor stepped-up enforcement. Or, as Barney Frank remarks, "People favor federalizing what they don't like and oppose federalizing what they like."

No one likes juvenile violence, which has risen dramatically and disproportionately. According to a report from Northeastern University, from 1985 to 1991 the number of males aged thirteen to seventeen arrested for murder rose over 100 percent. Juveniles have been involved in high-profile cases—a thirteen-year-old was implicated in the fatal shooting of a German tourist in Florida in 1993—and they contribute to what has become a familiar barrage of stupid murders: in New York City a ten-year-old boy and his fourteen-year-old accomplice shoot and kill a woman during a robbery at a cash machine. A thirteen-year-old shoots and kills an eighteen-year-old in a dispute over a drug deal, in order to get money to buy sneakers. Five teenage boys on a robbery spree in Brooklyn kill three shop owners who hand over their money without resistance. In Davenport, Iowa, three teenage boys kill a seventeen-year-old female friend in order to get the keys to her car.[41]

Crimes like this are awful enough when committed by adults, but the cruelty of adults doesn't completely upend the natural order. We're not supposed to be afraid of our children. The spectacle of children with guns and no apparent empathy or conscience is particularly chilling. The rise in juvenile crime has overshadowed a recent modest decline in violent crime overall and accounts for much of the public outcry over violence.

So, the Senate voted to federalize a great deal of juvenile crime. Amendments passed hastily, without hearings, required that juveniles over the age of thirteen be federally prosecuted as adults for certain crimes involving firearms, federalized possession of handguns and ammunition by juveniles (already illegal in most states), and federalized gang activity by juveniles, loosely defined. (The attempt to federalize crime by thirteen-year-olds survived, in a modified form. The 1994 crime bill permits, but does not require, the prosecution of some thirteen-year-olds as adults.)

In voting for significant expansion of federal jurisdiction over juveniles, the Senate was undeterred by the absence of federal correctional facilities for incarcerating them. Juvenile justice has traditionally been the province of the states. Federalizing juvenile offenses could require the establishment of a redundant federal system and could also impose additional burdens on the states, if they're required to house juveniles subject to federal prosecution. New York City's Commissioner of Juvenile Justice opposed the Senate bill federalizing possession of guns and ammunition in the expectation that it would strain local facilities and increase delays in processing juvenile cases.[42]

Thus, if there are loose theoretical and few principled limits on the expansion of federal jurisdiction, there are practical limits to what federal prosecutors, defenders, and courts can manage. Federal district courts are already swamped by drug cases that ought to be tried in state court. It's becoming increasingly difficult to obtain a civil trial. Federal judges tend to oppose expansions of federal jurisdictions and the Justice Department has been wary of it as well. Political reasons for extending federal jurisdiction don't necessarily translate into practical reasons for exercising it. Congress may enact a broad range of federal laws that federal prosecutors may enforce only erratically, if at all—but there's no clamor yet for truth in legislating.

❧ | Protesting the influence of politics on policy, you feel a little like Claude Rains protesting gambling at Rick's. Still, it's hard not to be *shocked, shocked!* by the utter politicization of criminal justice debates. Informed discussions among elites about a range of criminal justice issues affecting public safety seem more than usually irrelevant to public debate. Replete with slogans and empty of information, they are exercises in demagoguery. Congress passes omnibus crime bills that you need a law degree and familiarity with the federal penal code to understand, covering everything from consumer fraud to genocide and arcane matters of federal procedure, with relatively little substantive debate and no reliable explanation. The public's capacity to evaluate criminal justice policy is minimal. Political leadership is nil. Politicians profess to believe what they must know is not true.

Take the matter of federal sentencing laws. Congress has long committed itself to legislation promising swift, sure sentencing, with little regard for consequences or facts. Every two years from 1984 to 1990, Congress demonstrated its toughness on crime by enacting mandatory minimum sentences for various drug and firearm offenses, including drug offenses committed near schools, violent crimes (broadly defined), or drug crimes involving the use of a firearm (the firearm triggers a mandatory sentence in addition to the sentence for the underlying offense), the possession of more than five grams of crack cocaine, and any degree of involvement in a drug conspiracy.[43]

These laws have had no demonstrable effect on drug- or gun-related violence, but they have greatly increased the number of people taking up space in federal prisons for non-violent, low-level drug offenses. According to the U.S. Sentencing Commission, in 1992 more than 3,000 drug offenders with no record of violent crime in the previous fifteen years were sentenced to minimum terms of at least five years.[44] Between 1984 and 1990, the proportion of people sent to federal prison for drug offenses rose 12 percent, while the proportion of people sentenced for violent crimes and property offenses declined.[45] Today, about 60 percent of all federal prisoners are serving time for drug offenses, some involving simple possession of marijuana or cocaine.[46]

These statistics are hardly news to legislators and policy-makers, and stories about people spending five to ten years in federal prison for playing minimal roles in drug conspiracies had begun to appear in the mainstream press by the time the 1994 crime bill was being debated. (In November 1993, the *New York Times* featured the case of a twenty-four-year-old man serving ten years in federal prison because he agreed to help an undercover agent find someone selling LSD at a Grateful Dead concert.)[47] Relatives of people sentenced to long federal prison terms for minor drug offenses formed a lobbying group, Families Against Mandatory Minimums, headed by Julie Stewart, whose brother was sentenced to five years for a first offense—growing marijuana at home.

Critics of mandatory minimums ranged from Janet Reno to Orrin Hatch. Hatch has expressed support for the mandatories in principle but acknowledged that they have been overused for nonviolent crimes.[48] Reno promised to issue a study on mandatory sentencing shortly after taking office, but it had yet to appear by the time the Senate recessed in November 1993, having passed a crime bill including still more mandatory minimums, and in the following months throughout negotiations of the bill, her criticisms of traditional tough on crime measures were greatly muted.

There is also strong opposition to mandatory sentencing from federal judges, both Republican and Democratic appointees. Ninety percent of all federal judges surveyed by Gallup for the *American Bar Association Journal* said that mandatory minimum sentences for drug offenses were "a bad idea," and 6 percent said they'd considered resigning from the bench in protest.[49] A majority of judges surveyed by the Sentencing Commission and a majority of probation officers, in addition to most defense attorneys, viewed mandatory minimums unfavorably, as did slightly less than one-third of federal prosecutors. Prosecutors were most critical of the fact that the mandatory statutes resulted in more trials. (Once defendants are charged under these statutes, they have relatively little incentive not to go to trial; the time to plea bargain is before charges are brought. Plea bargains are not exactly popular with the public at large, but the system would collapse without them.) Slightly more than one-third of the prosecutors expressed unmitigated support for mandatory minimums; the remaining one-third were neutral or had mixed feelings about them.[50]

In general, mandatory minimums are criticized for being excessively harsh as well as inflexible, for arbitrarily imposing five- or ten-year sentences on "mules," the most hapless, least culpable people in drug trafficking. The laws don't "differentiate between the kingpin and the schnook," federal District Court Judge Terry J. Hatter has said.[51] Some of the schnooks are women with children: mandatory sentences have increased the number of mothers in prison for nonviolent crime.

The inequities, the sheer idiocies of mandatory minimum sentencing laws shaped an extraordinary consensus favoring reform among people who work in the system. Criticisms became difficult to ignore, as did the burden these laws placed on a system struggling to keep pace with violent crime, and the

1994 crime bill included marginal modifications of mandatory minimum drug statutes. In some cases, first-time nonviolent offenders may now be sentenced under federal sentencing guidelines instead of the mandatory statutes; as a practical matter this means on a first-time marijuana offense you may serve two to three years in federal prison, instead of five. The relief afforded by this "safety valve" to the mandatory minimums was originally intended to be retroactive: it would have allowed people already in prison to apply for reductions of their sentences, if they qualified as low-level nonviolent offenders. The retroactivity provision was dropped when it was attacked by Republican opponents of the crime bill, for allowing the wholesale release of dangerous drug dealers from prison.

Even when Democrats dominated Congress, substantial reform, much less repeal, of the mandatory minimum sentencing laws was about as likely as socialized medicine. Congressman Barney Frank has said that members of Congress will condemn the excesses of mandatory minimums as applied to low-level drug offenses, "but they're not ready to vote for reform. There's a perception that you pay a big price for being soft on drugs. People are afraid of the 30-second spot." Proposals for sentence reform are utterly unrealistic, Senator Biden remarked: "I can count . . . 80% of the Congress and about 85% of the public still believes the misinformed rhetoric about sentencing."

The list of what people don't know and aren't often told about mandatory minimums in general is included in a 1991 report on mandatory minimum penalties, by the U.S. Sentencing Commission, which gently recommended their repeal. The story begins with a little history.

In 1984, Congress established the U.S. Sentencing Commission, charged with promulgating guidelines for sentences in federal cases. This represented a revolution in sentencing that was initially sparked by liberal protests of undue sentence disparity resulting from the broad discretion exercised by judges and parole boards. Federal Judge Marvin Frankel called for a sentence commission in an influential 1972 book, *Criminal Sentences: Law Without Order,* and a bill to establish a commission was introduced by Senator Edward Kennedy in 1975. During the 1970s, the states were also turning to mandatory minimum sentencing; concern about crime was rising, and people were losing faith in the ideal of rehabilitation, which partly underlay the system of indeterminate sentences. New York's Rockefeller Drug Laws, which went into effect in 1973, were among the most notorious experiments in sentencing. Mandating stringent minimum sentences and prohibitions on plea bargains, they resulted in longer sentences, but arrests declined as did indictment and conviction rates, while court congestion increased.[52] (No pleas meant considerably more trials.)

At the federal level, it took nearly ten years for Kennedy's bill to pass the Senate, and in 1984, when the Sentencing Commission was established, the political climate had changed considerably. As Kate Stith and Steve Koh point out in a 1993 article in the *Wake Forest Law Review* tracing the history of federal guidelines, sentence reform was "conceived by liberal reformers as an anti-imprisonment and antidiscrimination measure, but finally born as part of a more conservative law-and-order crime control measure."[53]

Federal sentence guidelines are quite stringent, rigid, and complex, reviled by defense attorneys and resented by many judges as a usurpation of their sentencing authority. Sentences are dictated by guidelines established by the commission, which lists generic offense levels in a vertical column and offender characteristics (mainly criminal histories) horizontally, creating a grid that locates the appropriate sentence range, which is fairly narrow. Judges are not supposed to consider mitigating factors, such as a defendant's family or community ties, employment history, or mental and emotional state. Sentencing becomes a technical task, not a creative or judgmental one. Judges have very limited discretion to depart from the guidelines and fashion individualized sentences.

Complaints about inequities are common and publicized. In July 1994, the *New York Times* ran a front-page story about a bankrupt seventy-year-old Nebraska farmer sentenced to federal prison because he engaged in an illegal financial transaction in order to feed his starving hogs. The judge in this case did not approve of the sentence but was bound by law to impose it. "I'm stuck with these guidelines," he said.[54] Fifty-six percent of federal judges surveyed in 1993 by the *American Bar Association Journal* said that the guidelines worked poorly or not at all.[55]

The "best" that can be said about the sentencing guidelines based on this poll, the *Journal* reports, is that "they are less unpopular than the mandatory minimum sentences." Sentence guidelines don't eliminate all judicial discretion from sentencing, as mandatory minimums do. The guidelines have been controversial, but if Congress had stopped at establishing the Sentencing Commission in 1984 and not gone on to enact so many new mandatory minimums, it could have avoided much of the uproar over sentencing today.

The establishment of a sentencing commission, however, isn't nearly as dramatic an anticrime measure as passage of five- or ten- or twenty-year mandatory minimum sentences. So, in the same year that Congress empowered the commission to create sentencing guidelines it enacted new mandatory minimums for drug offenses. This wasn't quite a revolution in sentencing. Federal mandatory minimums date back to 1790. Today, the Sentencing Commission points out, federal penal law comprises a patchwork of about 100 mandatory minimum provisions contained in about 60 statutes, which provide a little social history of crime. Like the federalization of local crimes, the enactment of mandatory minimums is a congressional show of concern for the crimes of the times. In 1790, piracy carried a mandatory life sentence; causing a vessel to run aground carried ten years. In 1888, bribery of a harbor inspector in Baltimore or New York was made punishable by a mandatory term of six months. In 1913, a mandatory prison sentence or fine was imposed on price fixing. In 1934, homicide or kidnapping committed during a bank robbery or larceny was made punishable by a mandatory ten-year sentence. In 1965, the murder of a president or staff member was made punishable by life imprisonment. In the 1980s Congress turned its attention to drug offenses.[56]

All these laws are still on the books; few are enforced. According to the Sentencing Commission, nearly 60,000 cases were sentenced under mandatory minimums between 1984 and 1990; only four out of the sixty mandatory minimum statutes accounted for 94 percent of these cases, all of which involved drug offenses or carrying of a firearm during a drug or violent crime. For fiscal year 1990, 91 percent of the nearly 7,000 defendants sentenced under mandatory minimums were primarily drug offenders.[57]

There are, then, essentially two federal sentencing systems in place. People who are not charged under statutes carrying mandatory sentences are sentenced under the commission guidelines. Since the guidelines are stringent, the mandatory minimums seem, at best, redundant when applied to serious cases; at worst, and quite often, they're more arbitrary than the guidelines and absurdly harsh.

"Pathetic cases come along," Supreme Court Justice Stephen Breyer remarked in a speech to the American Bar Association in New York City in August 1993. "No one will ever formulate a system of law for which you don't have to have exceptions." Breyer is an advocate of the sentence guidelines, which he helped design, and it irritates some defense attorneys to hear him criticize the mandatory statutes for their inflexibility, when, in their view, the guidelines are quite inflexible, too. Breyer defends them because they afford at least a little sentencing discretion to judges, while the mandatory minimums provide none, particularly for the "pathetic cases." He tells the story of a bank robbery case involving "a guy with the IQ of a 7-year-old who got a toy gun, went to a bank, got $70 to get an operation for his dog, his best friend in the world, turned himself in to the FBI and the dog died anyway. What should we do? Give him life?"

As Judge Breyer's story suggests, mandatory minimum sentences hold people strictly liable for their acts, regardless of any mitigating circumstances, which is another way of saying that mandatory minimums preclude individualized determinations of accountability, which is another way of saying they're un-American.

Virtually all of us act immorally, if not illegally, at least on occasion. We'd like to believe that if we ever get caught or feel compelled to confess, we'll be judged not simply by what we've done but by why we did it and who we are. In other words, we want our acts to be judged in the context of our motivation and personal history, and a concept of character that comprises more than our worst offenses. People do sometimes commit bad acts for good reasons, which means that guilt—and especially sentence—ought to be determined by considering the actor as well as the act. Two people may behave similarly but with different degrees of guilt: a retarded man who holds up a bank with a toy gun in order to save his dog seems essentially innocent, unlike, say, a college student who holds up a bank with a toy gun in order to buy a new car. Even in hard cases involving felony assaults or homicides, motive or character ought to play a role in sentencing: a woman who shoots her husband because he had been beating her and her children for years seems less culpable than a woman who shoots her husband for money. Imposing the same sentence in both cases would be imposing punishment without regard to guilt.

So, people who bring a sense of justice to the system of mandatory minimums often find themselves at odds with the law. Justice Breyer observes that mandatory minimum sentencing schemes encourage disrespect and disregard for the law among people charged with enforcing it. "You cannot tell human beings to do things they think are totally unfair . . . they won't do it. They'll figure a way out." The judge may be constrained from imposing a lesser sentence, but "the prosecutor won't prosecute, the juries won't convict." In fact, according to Breyer, 40 percent to 50 percent of federal prosecutors are not prosecuting under mandatory minimums. Mandatory minimum statutes do not eliminate discretion or disparities in sentencing. They shift discretion from judges to prosecutors.

Pursuant to mandatory minimum sentencing laws, prosecutors essentially decide how defendants will be sentenced when they decide how defendants will be charged. This clear usurpation of judicial authority is justified as a way of providing prosecutors with an important bargaining tool: they use the threat of an indictment under a mandatory minimum statute to persuade defendants to cooperate and inform.

But, as a practical matter, the defendants most likely to have information for which prosecutors will bargain tend to be more rather than less culpable participants in the criminal enterprise: the lower you are in a drug deal, the less you're likely to know—the less bargaining power you have to stave off an indictment. Federal law also allows judges to depart from the mandatory minimums after conviction and impose lesser sentences, if the prosecutors request them, based in claims that defendants have provided "substantial assistance," which, once again, tends to reward higher-level defendants and penalize the lowly.

Under this system, sentence disparities abound. In a one-year period from 1989 to 1990, about 40 percent of defendants who appeared eligible for mandatory minimums received lesser sentences. In addition to disparate treatment of higher- and lower-level defendants, there are regional differences in sentencing practices and racial differences.[58]

Racial disparities in sentencing are partly due to the disparate sentences imposed on possession of crack cocaine, which tends to be used by blacks, and possession of powder cocaine, which tends to be used by whites. The 1988 Anti-Drug Abuse Act imposed a mandatory minimum sentence of five years for possession of more than 5 grams of crack, by a first offender—the maximum sentence is twenty years. There is no mandatory minimum prison sentence for possession of the same amount of powder cocaine, for which you can receive probation. You'd have to possess 100 times the amount of powder cocaine—500 grams—to receive the sentence imposed on possession of 5 grams of crack.[59]

Defenders of these laws argue that crack is simply more harmful than powder cocaine, particularly in African American communities. (In this view, harsher treatment of crack offenders is an attempt to protect African Americans, not penalize them.) Crack is commonly associated with more violence than powder cocaine and it's said to be more addictive. Critics of the sentencing laws counter that powder cocaine is easily transformed into crack; they question the scientific evidence that crack is more addictive, and they point out that violence in impoverished African American communities has no simple, single cause. In any case, differential treatment of crack has done nothing to stem violence or drug use; its primary effect, indeed, its only identifiable effect, has been to increase the proportion of African Americans serving long federal prison sentences for drug offenses.

Blacks have always tended to receive longer prison sentences than whites, a report by the Federal Judicial Center notes, but sentence disparities increased with the introduction of new mandatory minimums in the 1980s.[60] Examining data from 1989 to 1990, the Sentencing Commission found that 68 percent of blacks received sentences at or above the minimum, as opposed to 57 percent of Hispanics and 54 percent of whites. Significant racial differences in sentencing remained when the commission factored out the nature of the underlying offenses. (In contrast to this, the commission found that the nature of their offenses did seem to account for differences in the sentencing of males and females.) Calling for further research into the question or racial discrimination, the commission nevertheless reported that its findings imply that race plays a role in sentence disparities, which has yet to be acknowledged, much less addressed by Congress.[61]

If Congress were genuinely interested in truth in sentencing, it would make clear to the public how erratically and arbitrarily mandatory minimums are enforced. It would point out that pursuant to federal sentence guidelines, serious crimes are subject to very tough sentences. It would explain that criminal defendants are not faceless or fungible: defendants vary and their circumstances vary, even when they are charged with the same crime, and judges must have at least limited discretion to vary their sentences.

But there are so few ways for Congress to demonstrate toughness on crime. The Senate passed new mandatory minimums in November 1993, with no apparent opposition from the Clinton administration. "Mandatory minimums are a political response to violent crime," Orrin Hatch conceded. "Let's be honest about it. It's awfully difficult for politicians to vote against them."

◥ | It's equally difficult to address rationally the problems of prison overcrowding without rational sentence policies. But the Congress voted to build new prisons anyway. It allocated $9.8 billion for prisons, including about $8 billion for state prisons; half of this money is reserved for states that adopt mandatory sentencing schemes requiring violent offenders to serve at least 85 percent of their sentences. New prison construction is popular not only with the prison industry but the public at large. Some 60 percent of people polled by Time/CNN in 1993 said they favored building new prisons at the cost of a significant tax rise. More striking is public dissatisfaction with the courts, based on the belief that judges are soft on crime: 81 percent of people surveyed by Time/CNN agreed that "courts do not deal harshly enough with criminals." In fact, most public anger at the criminal justice system seems to be anger at the courts, not legislators, police, or corrections officials. The perception that a great many violent felons are serving very little prison time is driving the crime debate.

It's a perception based primarily on anecdotes, which doesn't mean it's not true. But periodic stories about people on probation or parole or awaiting trial who commit horrific crimes mostly provide political pressure to build more prisons, not empirical evidence that more prisons will make us safe.

It's true that prisons are overcrowded. Barney Frank observes that in some circumstances liberals should support new prison construction in order to make prisons more humane. The trouble is that prisons are a bit like highways: build them and a great many people will come. It's also true that the majority of prisoners do not serve out their full terms; in

Texas, for example, people in noncapital cases reportedly only serve about 20 percent of their sentences.[62] And, it's true that the majority of people convicted by the states—two out of three—are not imprisoned at all.[63]

These are dramatic statistics, but by themselves, they're not terribly informative. We don't know what it means to say that convicted felons serve only a fraction of their sentences unless we know the length of their sentences. Judges are likely to take early release systems into account when they impose sentence, so that, for example, if they want someone to serve six years, they may sentence him to ten. And, the fact that two out of three people convicted of crimes are not incarcerated may be an argument for improving probationary supervision, not increasing the prison population, which already stands at 1 million nationwide (about three-quarters of all prisoners are in state custody; the remainder are in the federal system).

"What's most scarce today aren't prison cells but non-prison supervisory programs," according to Mark Kleiman, professor of public policy at the Kennedy School. With three times as many people on probation or parole as there are in prison, "we're spending too much on the in-patients and not enough on the out-patients," Kleiman says. He believes that except for the relatively small proportion of people who commit single crimes that shock the conscience of the community and the people who repeatedly commit violent crimes, a great many convicted felons should be subject to heavily supervised probation and alternative sentences that stress mandatory, enforceable drug abstinence. "The trouble with most non-prison programs today is that they're not backed up with the threat of imprisonment. I'd be happy to spend $3 billion for more prison cells to use as a back-up to sanction people who don't comply with the terms of their probation or parole. They don't need to be imprisoned for a long time, but they need to be imprisoned every time they don't comply."[64]

Common sense suggests that prescribing long prison sentences for relatively small proportions of offenders (which is all we can reasonably expect to do without a huge investment in new prisons) will not deter potential offenders who have no expectation of ever being imprisoned at all. A 1993 report by the National Research Council (NRC) estimates that "a 50% increase in the *probability of incarceration* would prevent twice as much violent crime as a 50% increase in the average term in incarceration."[65] Of course, increasing the probability of incarceration would require increasing the probability of arrest and prosecution, not merely the re-allocation of prison space. But Mark Kleiman's proposal to use new prisons as back-up sanctions for probationers and parolees would, at least, increase the probability of imprisonment for the great number of "out-patients" already caught up in the criminal justice system. The 1994 crime bill, conditioning the allocation of prison funding partly on the states' adoption of long, minimum sentences focuses, instead, on further increases in the length of incarceration.

Lengthening prison terms is hardly a new idea or one that has proven effective. Between 1975 and 1989, average prison time served per violent crime tripled, according to the NRC. The prison population nearly tripled during that same period—because of an increase in sentence length (reflecting, in part, the increased use of mandatory minimums), not an increase in the chance of arrest, which remained fairly constant. Increases in the chance of incarceration were also less common then increases in the average prison term. (In other words, the rise in the prison population did not mean that more offenders were being caught, it meant that people who were caught, especially for drug crimes, were being put away for longer periods.) Violent crime declined in the early 1980s but rose in the latter half of the decade. The NRC suggests that the increased prison terms of the 1980s had little effect on violent crime and that further increases would have little effect as well.[66] Liberals agree, sometimes pointing out that violent felons, like athletes, peak early and become less violent as they age, negating the need for long sentences. Conservatives, however, argue that violent crime rates would have soared during the 1980s had the prison population remained stable. "America would have been a much more dangerous place today if we hadn't built the prisons we built in the 1980s," Paul McNulty, executive director of the First Freedom Coalition, a conservative lobbying group, asserts, conceding that this claim is impossible to prove, as is the liberal claim that increased incarceration has had no effect or a negative effect on crime.[67]

The prison debate is driven more by ideology than science. Cost benefit analyses of increasing prison terms are suspect, because the secondary costs and benefits of both victimization and imprisonment are very difficult to quantify. As the NRC notes, we have only "imprecise" estimates of prison's effect on crime.[68] We also have no rational system for identifying people who aren't dangerous, or potentially dangerous, and diverting them to alternative sentence programs.

No more than 20 to 25 percent of all people in prison are "dangerous street criminals," according to the National Council on Crime and Delinquency.[69] Does this mean we're imprisoning too many people as the NCCD suggests? Not necessarily. Dangerousness is notoriously difficult to predict and, according to the NRC, most violent crimes are not committed by repeat violent offenders ("dangerous career criminals"); violent crimes tend to be occasional events in long histories of property crimes.[70]

It is this problem of recidivism that bedevils debates about prison policy. Conservative and liberals agree, in principle, that some people in prison would have been more appropriately sentenced to some alternative corrections program. Between political campaigns they can even agree that a number of first time nonviolent offenders, particularly low-level drug offenders, should not be serving long mandatory minimum sentences. But they disagree about the need to imprison nonviolent offenders. The consensus breaks down over recidivism, Paul McNulty confirms. He believes that, in general, people should have only one opportunity to enjoy an alternative sentence. "If they waste that opportunity to obey the law," they should not, in most cases, receive another. "We wouldn't raise children this way," with empty threats, he suggests.

If you believe in imprisoning recidivists, violent or not, McNulty adds, "You win the argument about building more prisons every time. Surveys of state prisoners show that 93% of them are either violent criminals or recidivists. The number of people who ought to be released will never be larger than the number of people who are out on the streets and ought to be incarcerated."

But your view of who ought to be incarcerated depends on your ideology and your instincts about the dangers of nonviolent recidivists. In fact, no one, liberal or conservative, can accurately say how many people in prison today would pose a danger to the community if they were released to strictly supervised parole, or how many would have posed less of a danger if they had been sentenced to strictly supervised probation, including mandatory drug treatment and job training. The difficulty of identifying violent offenders is one reason that three time loser laws may have little overall effect on violent crime. Advocates argue that they will decrease violence even if only applied to a small percentage of offenders, because only a small percentage are responsible for the nation's violent crime. The trouble is, no one can say precisely which offenders compose that percentage.

The unpredictability of dangerousness can, in the end, be used as an argument for imprisoning practically everyone or practically no one, depending on how the due process rights of offenders are balanced with the safety interests of the community that are served by incapacitating offenders (putting aside questions about deterrence or retribution). In recent years, majorities have erred on what looks like the side of safety, demanding more rather than less imprisonment. But in addition to the 1 million people already in prison, there are some 3 million on probation or parole. At some point, ideology and speculation about recidivism become academic: We're not going to imprison 4 million people forever.

Occasionally, Congress lapses into recognition of this—that there are limits to how many people we can incarcerate and for how long, just as there are limits to what imprisonment and other traditional law enforcement measures can accomplish. The $6.9 billion allocated for prevention programs by the 1994 crime bill include grants for drug courts (for the placement of nonviolent drug offenders) and drug treatment for state and federal prisoners. The nearly $10 billion allocated for prisons include $150 million for alternative sentencing programs for youthful offenders—community service, weekend incarceration, and boot camps, one of the trendiest of alternative sentencing proposals.

Boot camps combine the toughness on crime traditionally demanded by conservatives with liberal expressions of compassion and all-American belief in self-improvement through discipline and work. Historically, work has been considered character building; it also symbolizes repentance and restitution to the community. Because they provide alternatives to prison, boot camps are popularly considered progressive; progressives, however, along with researchers, tend to be skeptical about their prospects.

Boot camps work in the military, police officer Ronald Hampton observes, because people graduate from them into the military, with jobs to perform, rules to obey, and a disciplinary system to fear. Inmates of boot camps will generally graduate into anarchy. Nor do boot camps work for everyone in the military, Hampton adds. Some people don't prosper in the service. "That doesn't mean they're not good citizens; it just means they're not good soldiers."

Outcome studies of boot camps have been discouraging. Recidivism rates for people sentenced to boot camps are no better than the rates for prison inmates.[71] Boot camps may also pose particular problems for the juveniles they're intended to help, if they allow mingling of juvenile and adult offenders. There is also a common concern that the quasi-abusive environment of boot camps may be counterproductive for young offenders with histories of familial abuse. As Mark Kleiman observes, "If pushing these people around and screaming at them were therapeutic they wouldn't be in boot camp."

Misgivings about boot camps expressed by people who study them and others who work with young offenders, however, are dismissed by the politicians who establish them. For John Laub, professor of criminal justice at Northeastern University, political enthusiasm for boot camps exemplifies the futility of research on criminal justice. Knowledge isn't power in criminal justice debates; knowledge is irrelevant. Politicians rely on "gut instincts" or "intuition" or fond memories of their own military experiences in supporting boot camps.

"This is why what we do doesn't matter," criminologist Laub says, pointing to a remark by Georgia Governor Zell Miller, proudly proclaiming his intention to ignore research on boot camps. "Nobody can tell me from some ivory tower that you take a kid, you kick him in the rear end, and it doesn't do any good," Governor Miller told the *New York Times.* "I don't give a damn what they say."[72]

Still, a commitment to boot camps, however misguided, does reflect a belated search for alternatives, born of desperation. Public desperation over crime that drives passage of many traditional law enforcement measures, like harsher sentencing, also drove home some long-fought-for reforms— modest attempts to control the distribution of firearms.

◀ | Violent crime overall declined slightly in 1993 and has, in general, remained relatively stable in recent years (leading some commentators to suggest that intense public anxiety about crime borders on hysteria).[73] But if the level of crime has not increased, the nature of crime has changed. Along with juvenile crime, gun violence has risen (it almost seems commonplace), and gun violence holds particular terrors; like an airplane crash, it's sudden, often unexpected, and practically impossible to survive intact.[74]

It's becoming equally impossible for politicians to ignore, and Congress has slowly and painfully begun to change its approach to gun play. In recent years, Congress simply imposed mandatory minimum sentences on some crimes involving the use of firearms; or, in an early version of the 1994 crime bill, the Senate voted to federalize a range of state crimes involving guns. But whatever salutary effect the imposition of longer sentences on gun crimes has had on gun violence has been too subtle to quantify. Liberals have long argued that instead of increasing penalties for the illegal use of guns, the federal government should restrict sales of guns to the public. Congress took a small practical step, or a great symbolic leap, in this direction when it passed the Brady Bill, imposing a waiting period on handgun buyers. (This bill was signed into law at the end of 1993, some seven years after it was first proposed.) The 1994 crime bill also included a prospective ban on certain semi-automatic rifles, labelled assault weapons—a provision that will save few lives (the banned guns are responsible for very few homicides) but very nearly killed the entire bill.

These were not exactly controversial measures, although,

because of National Rifle Association opposition, they were quite difficult to pass. There is strong majority support for some form of gun control: 70 percent of Americans want stricter gun laws, according to a 1993 Gallup Poll; nearly 90 percent of the public favored the Brady Bill. (It's difficult to oppose a bill that simply makes it a little harder for felons and lunatics to buy guns.) But even supporters of the Brady Bill are apt to concede that it will probably have little effect over-all on gun violence. Colin Ferguson, who opened fire on a crowded Long Island commuter train, killing six people and wounding nineteen, bought his gun in California, after complying with a two-week waiting period. And there's no persuasive evidence that waiting periods have decreased violent crime in the twenty-two states that already mandate them.[75] A federally mandated waiting period may well save a few lives, people say, and the Brady Bill represented an important symbolic defeat for the NRA. It could also lead to more stringent gun laws (like the ban on assault weapons), as advocates hope and the NRA fears. But, with some 200 million firearms already at large, including 60 million handguns, there's no reason to have high expectations of traditional point of purchase restrictions or bans on possession. Once an initial battle for gun control had been won, it seemed nearly irrelevant to the war against gun violence.

Because gun control debates have been defined by efforts to restrict the sale of firearms, in the face of NRA opposition, alternative strategies for regulating the nation's enormous stockpile of weapons have only recently begun to be considered. The 1993 report by the National Research Council suggested adopting some of the tactics used against drugs—focusing on illegal transactions and undesirable uses.[76] A shift in focus away from sweeping, hotly contested bans on sale and possession would at least have significant political advantages: the NRA could hardly object to attacking the black market.

This proposal to concentrate on illegal gun markets does not equate drugs and guns or the drug and gun markets, which significantly differ; nor does it necessarily imply that we should focus exclusively on the illegal supply of guns, as we have traditionally focused on the supply of drugs, ignoring conditions that create a demand. But this is an acknowledgment that effective, near total prohibitions of guns are as unrealistic as prohibitions of drugs and alcohol. Given the staggering number of guns already in circulation, the increasing desire for guns by more or less law-abiding citizens concerned with self-defense, and the American tradition of violent individualism, the belief that this might someday be a gun-free country seems more and more utopian.

The failure to enact meaningful gun control measures twenty-five or thirty years ago has made the slogan "When guns are outlawed only outlaws will have guns" seem almost true. So far the explosion of gun violence seems to have increased the desire for moderate gun control more than the desire to own a gun. (Reported ownership of firearms has remained fairly stable during the past ten years, according to Gallup, while support for incremental controls, like the Brady Bill, has increased.) But the balance could shift if the violence continues; if people lose all faith in the government's capacity to protect them, they will take drastic steps to protect themselves. Even if they are presumed accurate, studies demonstrating that keeping a gun at home increases your risk of being killed (often by someone you know) will probably have less effect than studies linking smoking to cancer.[77] Millions of people start smoking and continue to smoke because they don't really believe lung cancer will happen to them. Frightened people will buy guns in the belief that they will never turn them against each other. For many middle-class people who live and work in low-crime areas, fear of crime is often fear of strangers.

Recent polls indicate that the public is wavering between permissive and restrictive laws, as it wavers between self-reliance and reliance on government in its vision of crime control. While a March 1993 Gallup Poll found strong majority support for stricter gun laws in general, it also found a slim majority (54 percent) opposed to a complete ban on handguns. (Stricter gun laws may mean waiting periods or gun licensing or even bans on some semi-automatic rifles.) A December 1993 Gallup Poll on crime found majority support (over 60 percent) for the proposition that stricter gun laws would save lives by cutting down on accidental deaths, suicides, and fatal domestic disputes; but a slim majority (52 percent) also agreed that "stricter gun laws would give too much power to the government over average citizens." This poll found that 54 percent of Americans felt that the police could not protect them from violent crime, 51 percent admitted having a gun in the house, and six out of ten opposed a ban on handgun possession.

"Self-defense replacing reliance on law enforcement," was the lesson the *National Law Journal* drew from its 1994 survey on public attitudes toward crime. The *NLJ* poll found that only 22 percent of respondents supported "greatly restricting gun sales," while 62 percent said that the "need for guns for personal protection is increasing." A 1993 Times Mirror Poll showed a slight public preference for gun ownership over gun control: 51 percent of respondents opposed a law to ban the sale of handguns; 45 percent supported it. Yet, 57 percent of respondents in the same poll said that controlling guns was more important than protecting the right to own guns. The public does seem torn.

Further complicating the campaign for gun control is public resistance to expanding police authority to conduct the kind of searches that might be required to seize guns illegally carried on the street and possessed in the home. According to the *NLJ* poll, an impressive 84 percent of people surveyed believed that the police should not be allowed to conduct searches without probable cause. Civil libertarians will take heart from this finding, but it may be a bit deceptive. People who profess support for constitutional restrictions on search and seizure, in principle, may in practice support arguably unconstitutional searches that appear to offer some protection from crime, particularly if they don't expect to be targets of the searches. And we don't know what people mean when they say they oppose searches without probable cause unless we know how probable cause is defined for them. An expansive definition of what constitutes probable cause would expand police authority to conduct random searches; only a restrictive definition would limit it. Still, it's hard to imagine a majority of Americans granting the police broad power to conduct random, unannounced searches of their own houses, automobiles, and persons (and the 1993 Gallup Poll does show that four out of five people oppose warrantless home searches).

Perhaps the greatest bar to effective gun control is not the arguable Second Amendment right to bear arms, but the well-established Fourth Amendment right to be secure in your own home and person. Most of the 200 million firearms in circulation are not likely to be surrendered voluntarily (particularly with the perceived need for self-defense increasing). They would have to be confiscated by police, who would have to search millions of homes and people, without probable cause, to find them. As long as the Fourth Amendment remains intact, Americans will retain their private stores of firearms.

The tension between Fourth Amendment rights and the desire to stem gun violence has been best exemplified by controversies over warrantless searches of housing projects. The first warrantless housing project sweep occurred in 1988, under the auspices of the Chicago Housing Authority. Without warning, police sealed off one of the more dangerous project buildings and searched every apartment. (The search is described by Steve Yarosh, in an article in the *Responsive Community*.)[78] Project residents generally supported the searches, which made the projects safer, according to Yarosh. In 1993, another similar sweep of a Chicago housing project (the Robert Taylor Homes) made the news. Once again, reports suggested that there was considerable support for the searches from project residents, and civil libertarians who opposed the searches were likely to be labeled "elitist," accused of sacrificing the everyday safety rights of the residents for more abstract concepts of Fourth Amendment law—as if there were anything abstract about a warrantless police search of your home. And it is hardly elitist to advocate extending the same Fourth Amendment rights to rich and poor. Instead of subjecting housing project residents to searches that would not be tolerated in more affluent urban high rises, why not provide people in the projects with the same quality of daily security enjoyed in more affluent neighborhoods? Some projects may already be more heavily policed than upper-middle-class apartment complexes, but they may not be well policed, and security needs are relative. An upscale high rise may not require security patrols or weapons detectors, while some housing projects do. If many project residents in Chicago supported the warrantless searches out of desperation, some reported that security in the projects was inadequate—metal detectors weren't used and security officers weren't deployed properly.[79]

But arguments opposing warrantless searches advanced by civil libertarians probably weren't as persuasive as stories about people living in terror, held hostage in their apartments by stray bullets. Talk about the Fourth Amendment right not to be subject to random searches was met with talk about the right not to be subject to random gunfire. "We are not infringing on rights; we are restoring rights," Chicago Housing

Authority Director Vincent Lane said in defense of the warrantless sweeps. "We are restoring our residents' rights to a safe and decent environment."[80] The right to be secure in your home was put in conflict with the right to be safe in the streets, which, strictly speaking, may not be a constitutional right, but it is surely a basic liberty. President Clinton offered a legalistic compromise, aimed at erasing the appearance of a Fourth Amendment violation: require project residents to "waive" their Fourth Amendment rights as a condition of obtaining an apartment—as if they'd have a choice, as if middle-class Americans would sign away their rights not to have their homes summarily invaded by police. Still, in asking people to choose between a right against police intrusion and protection against violent crime, the president was conceding that government was unable to provide both.

Advocates of gun possession have seized upon the acknowledged failures of government to control violence, using it as an argument to arm, not disarm, individuals. The NRA has championed the rights of housing project tenants to bear arms, and it has generally appealed to fear of violence in promoting gun ownership. In recent years it began targeting women, who generally feel more vulnerable than men. Using the rhetoric of choice, NRA ads promoted handguns as the best defense against rape: "How to Choose to Refuse to Be a Victim," the ads say, showing a mother and young daughter approaching their car at night in an isolated parking lot. The success of appeals like this is difficult to gauge. According to the NRA, female membership has increased 15 percent since the late 1980s. The percentage of women owning firearms, however, has been relatively stable.[81]

In addition to fear of crime, loathing of government fuels support for permissive gun laws. Although the NRA and pro-gun forces, in general, tend to support harsh sentencing and pretrial detention laws and government crackdowns on crime that afford little respect for the rights of criminal suspects, they oppose government interference with the rights of "law-abiding" citizens. How we might sort out the criminals from the law-abiding folks preemptively, without affording everyone the same constitutional rights, like the presumption of innocence, for example, is never made clear. Opponents of gun control seem to assume that there are two easily identifiable classes of people—bad criminal offenders and good Americans, who may occasionally commit crimes, like illegally possessing firearms, but only for good reasons.

Appealing to its constituency of presumptively good people who can be trusted with guns, the pro-gun lobbyists rely on the kind of strident antigovernment rhetoric that hasn't been fashionable since the 1960s. It raises the specter of storm troopers invading your home and presents private gun ownership as the only sure protection against a hostile government. "Gun prohibition is the invisible harbinger of oppression," NRA Executive Vice President Harlon Carter said back in 1980. "It can only be pursued by 'no knock' laws under which jack-booted minions of government invade the home of citizens." The Chinese government's massacre of pro-democracy demonstrators in Tiananmen Square might never have occurred, a 1989 NRA ad implied, if the students had been armed. "The students of Beijing did not have a Second Amendment right to defend themselves when the soldiers came. The right to own a firearm is a statement about freedom."[82]

The rhetoric is, no doubt, inspiring to some, but it reflects a tenuous grip on reality. The right to own a firearm hardly guarantees freedom from a hostile government with state-of-the-art weaponry (the right to a good lawyer might make a more powerful "statement about freedom"). The students in Beijing could not have outgunned the Chinese government if they had been armed, just as David Koresh and his followers could not outgun the U.S. government in Waco, despite their stockpile of weapons and explosives. Yet, one gun possession advocate points out, in 1992, the rioters in Los Angeles kept police out of their neighborhoods for several days. When the riots "erupted, the police fled to avoid being overrun by mobs of looters," Jay Simkin writes in the March 1994 issue of *Guns and Ammo*. He notes approvingly that in urban uprisings, even primitive weapons can be quite effective: "A tank crew on city streets is in peril from a single handmade weapon: a Molotov cocktail." Simkin goes on to explain that a Molotov cocktail is a "gasoline-filled bottle with a wick on the top, lit just before use"—in case you didn't know how to make one.[83]

The image of pro-gun forces embracing "looters" in L.A. as comrades in arms might unsettle supporters of the NRA's "CrimeStrike" campaign, which advocates the usual list of traditional tough on crime measures, aimed at imprisoning and executing the criminals who are "raping your rights." It's doubtful that a great many NRA members are among the advocates of racial justice who considered the mob violence in L.A. an uprising instead of a riot. But the NRA is quite friendly to the notion of citizen uprisings. The attachment of gun possession advocates to statist approaches to crime control (such as three time loser laws) is matched by their attachment to individual rights of self-defense, not just against crime but against the state.

Gun control causes genocide, Jay Simkin argues in his *Guns and Ammo* article. Simkin, who is identified with Jews for the Preservation of Firearms, lists seven "major 20th century genocides" that could have been avoided by permissive gun laws. He deduces this from the fact that each "major genocide"—from the Turkish massacre of Armenians in 1915 to Pol Pot's slaughter of Cambodians in the late 1970s—was preceded by a gun control law. "Every government can become genocidal," Simpkin writes, preying on the fears of African

Americans and Jews and other groups with histories of persecution. "But," he assures them, "an armed citizenry is close to being genocide proof."[84]

It's tempting to dismiss this linkage of gun control to genocide as the ravings of a marginalized minority in a gun magazine. (How large an organization is Jews for the Preservation of Firearms anyway?) But *outré* arguments against gun control appear in the stodgiest places. In its Fall 1993 issue, the *Public Interest* published an article by Jeffrey Snyder that describes gun possession as an obligation, not merely a right—an obligation that's divinely ordained. Not to own a gun is to risk not protecting yourself or your family from attack, Snyder writes; and failing to defend yourself or your loved ones is failing to respect the life that God has given you. "In truth, one who believes it is wrong to arm himself against criminal violence shows contempt of God's gift of life . . . does not live up to his responsibilities to his family and community, and proclaims himself mentally and morally deficient, because he does not trust himself to behave responsibly." Snyder implicitly endorses armed insurrection as the last answer to gun control laws. "A government that abrogates any of the Bill of Rights, with or without majoritarian approval, forever acts illegitimately, becomes tyrannical, and loses the moral right to govern. This is the uncompromising understanding reflected in the warning that America's gun owners will not go gently into that good, utopian night: 'You can have my gun when you pry it from my cold, dead hands.' "[85]

Meanwhile, back in the real world of crime-ridden urban communities, the easy availability of guns seems less defiant than self-destructive; escalating gun violence seems more a function of fear than religion or ideology.

Fear appears to play an important role in the proliferation of guns among juveniles, particularly urban minorities, according to Kennedy School Research Fellow David Kennedy. In 1993,

30 percent of black adults surveyed nationally said that they knew a child who got a gun for self-protection.[86] A 1993 National Institute of Justice study of male juvenile offenders and male students in inner city high schools found that "self-protection in a hostile and violent world was the chief reason to own and carry a gun." Some 22 percent of the students reported owning a gun, and 35 percent reported carrying a gun regularly or on occasion; family, friends, and illegal markets were their primary sources. A majority of students (69 percent) came from families in which men owned guns, and nearly half (45 percent) reported having been "threatened or shot at on the way to or from school."[87] David Kennedy observes that youth culture in the inner city is akin to prison culture: "captive, lawless, dangerous, self-regulated." Depressing as this is, he adds, it does suggest that the demand for guns among juveniles may be malleable: police juvenile gun markets and limit the availability of guns and you begin to control the fear that fuels the desire for guns: control the market, control the fear, control the guns. Gun violence among juveniles may spiral down as it has spiraled up.[88]

"Good kids have guns," John Silva, director of safety and security for the Cambridge Public Schools, in Massachusetts, remarks. "From a district attorney's perspective, a good kid would never carry a gun, but the D.A.'s don't live in the projects. There's so much fear. Good kids who want to go to school and do the right thing—they're afraid of the gangs and the drug dealers; they want to protect themselves and their families. Good kids, bad kids; the categories don't apply anymore."[89]

◀ | If good kids use guns, then crime is not simply a failure of character, as Ronald Reagan claimed. Nor is it merely a failure of government—to reduce poverty and en-able good people to grow. If good kids use guns, then crime is partly a failure of community. That, at least, is one relatively progressive view of violent crime.

Talk about community and idealized notions of community have begun to infiltrate criminal justice debates. Community policing, community defender services, community courts, and community "empowerment" efforts are praised for their "holistic" approach to crime. ("Holistic" may be another coming word in progressive crime control.) The concept of community is one both liberals and conservatives can embrace. The community is a private and a public place, located somewhere between the individual and big government. It combines conservative belief in individual responsibility with liberal faith in collective, civic solutions to individual concerns.

For a brief period during the first two years of the Clinton administration, politicians who wanted to sound progressive sometimes claimed that partisan approaches to crime were giving way to a new, bipartisan pragmatism. And it's true that liberals and conservatives seemed to be staking out some common ground on crime control, at least rhetorically, although the neat divisions between liberal and conservative approaches to crime have always been a little facile. Liberals focus on root causes, while conservatives focus on controlling the effects of crime, we always say. But, in fact, liberals have never advocated disbanding police department, burning down prisons, and doing nothing to address the problem of crime, in the meantime, while we await its cure. Conservatives have never ignored root causes; they've just defined them differently. If liberals cite poverty as a cause of crime, conservatives cite welfare. Every time conservative preachers and politicians rail against pornography, as well as the media's attack on family values, the legitimation of homosexuality, or the extension of welfare benefits to teenage mothers, they're addressing what they see as the root causes of crime. There have even been exceptions to the liberal attachment to individual rights and the conservative attachment to authority. In the gun control debate, conservatives defend the rights of individual gun owners against liberal assertions of the need for social order.

The establishment of community as a primary political value greatly facilitates liberal appeals for order—by finessing the conflict for liberals between individual rights and social control. Liberal advocates of community use the concept of communal "rights" to peace and security as a limit on individual rights to engage in deviant behavior. The concept is misleading—communities don't have rights under our constitution; communities have interests and a prerogative for majority rule, which they're required to exercise with respect for individual rights. But the language of communal rights is politically effective; it provides liberals with a language of values—a way of positing social order as a primary liberal value.

Is this common ground or merely common language? Liberals and conservatives maintain very different notions of government's role in facilitating community development and instilling values in citizens. Orrin Hatch thinks that the federal government should allow each of the fifty states to develop values curriculum for public schools, without worrying so much about strict separations of church and state; some religious values are "generic values that help people realize there is a better way." Janet Reno talked about providing social services to families that will help ensure that every child is raised with a conscience. She talked about the need for community advocates who help individual citizens obtain the services of their government and mediate disputes with landlords. She talked about *pro bono* lawyering. Under the general rubric of community, Janet Reno could call for a return to the legal service ethic of the early 1970s, while Orrin

Hatch called for government vouchers to ensure school choice, getting values into schools, and "cleaning up" television and movies. Reno did seem ready to provide the broom. It is one of the ironies of the crime debate that liberals and conservatives can come together over the need to censor violence in the media, while they argue over the ways to address violence in real life.

It is fitting, however, that the media emerge as a battleground for crime prevention. Crime control debates have always been driven by imagery. Members of Congress are used to gesturing on crime, passing laws that are less effective than expressive of an attitude toward crime (they're against it). Crime also undermines the image of America that politicians celebrate: "The American people are fundamentally decent," they intone, as if criminals were of some other species.

Violent crime became a preeminent problem in the 1990s not because fundamentally decent middle-class people, who set the political agenda, had an awakening of conscience; they were awakened by fear. Crime began to seem less contained in the inner cities as it spilled out on rare occasion onto highways, shopping centers, and suburban schools. Violence in impoverished, urban communities had been more or less ignored for many years because middle-class people didn't feel threatened by it, just as they didn't feel threatened by the lack of health care for the poor. Health care became a national priority when middle-class voters began worrying about losing their jobs and their insurance; crime became a priority when middle-class people began living in fear of it. Somehow, it seemed to take them by surprise. "How did this happen?" people ask, surveying the wreckage.

⍣ 8 | Virtue Talk

Blame it on welfare's culture of dependency and out-of-wedlock births. Blame it on the cutthroat individualism of a free market system. Blame it on unemployment, consumerism, and low self-esteem, or no self-control. Blame it on drugs. Blame it on secularism, the abolition of prayer in school, the sexual revolution, feminism, or pornography. Blame it on Rock and Roll.

We suffer from no dearth of explanations for violence and disorder, and today, right and left, the most popular critiques of culture are rather moralistic. Single motherhood has been singled out for its destructive effect on character development and community life, and even liberals may find it difficult to discuss the problem of single motherhood without passing judgment on the women and girls who choose it, however unwittingly. "I don't like to put this in moral terms, but I do believe that having children out of wedlock is just wrong," Donna Shalala, secretary of Health and Human Services, declared in a widely quoted statement to *Newsweek*.[1]

Public policy discourse has turned into a kind of morals

discourse, political theorist Nancy Rosenblum remarks. "The transformation has been stunning." Twenty-five years ago, social science reflected the effort to make factual determinations unaffected by value judgments. Like Data on *Star Trek*, the ideal social scientist was detached and unbiased. Today, instead of struggling to excise values from the study of facts, social scientists are striving to include them, Rosenblum suggests. In discussions of social problems today, "no one will stand up and offer a non-normative analysis"—a straightforward analysis of economic problems, for example, that does not focus on notions of good or bad character or virtue.[2] "At root, in almost every area of important public concern, we are seeking to induce people to act virtuously," James Q. Wilson wrote in 1985. "In the long run, the public interest depends on private virtue."[3]

Lately, in their efforts to unearth the root causes of crime, both liberals and conservatives have seized upon this discussion of virtue. With his bestselling "book of virtues," a collection of moral tales, William Bennett became the leading popular exponent of virtue in 1994, but, along with James Q. Wilson, he was joined on his left by politicians and academicians including sociologist Amitai Etzioni, a leader in the communitarian movement; Yale law professor Stephen Carter, best known for his book lamenting the denigration of religion in public life; and political scientist William Galston, domestic policy advisor to the president. Both President and Mrs. Clinton too have relied on moralism and notions of virtue in promoting welfare reform as well as the aborted politics of meaning.

Virtue talk only recently became a national pastime (*Newsweek* devoted a cover story to it in June 1994), but in its current incarnation, it dates back to the early 1980s, when the then ascendant New Right exemplified by Jerry Falwell's Moral Majority was bemoaning the decline of traditional values, while promoting a fiercely sectarian political agenda. Virtue seemed a less divisive, more pluralistic concept than "values," and eventually some liberals saw it as an opportunity to talk about morality without abandoning their attachment to tolerance.

"We've lost something at the core of our national character, that once acted to shape our behavior. We've lost our sense of virtue," Kathleen Kennedy Townsend wrote in 1982.[4] Townsend stressed that the Moral Majority might be "on to something." But, "it's on to it too narrowly," she asserted, because it used the language of virtue to denote particular conservative, political positions exclusively. Liberal democrats should lead an ecumenical moral and spiritual revival, she suggested, offering vague references to the joys of service and faith and more pointed reminders about the traditional religiosity of African Americans (part of the Democrats' core constituency), whose faith had fueled the civil rights movement.

This call for a liberal politics of virtue helped shape the communitarian movement that emerged in the mid-1980s. It was indeed a more or less liberal democratic counterpart to conservative moral reform campaigns. Communitarians focused on the need to "rebuild America's moral foundation," issuing vague but heartfelt appeals to the spirit of community, preaching connectedness instead of the isolation said to be fostered by an ethic of individualism, and calling for assumptions of social responsibilities as a counterpart to assertions of individual rights. Perhaps even more than they targeted free market conservativism, communitarians took aim at liberal individualism (exemplified by the ACLU) which was condemned as selfish and blamed for an array of fashionable social ills—alienation, anomie, and rampant moral relativism.[5]

It is conventional wisdom that we live in an "age of moral relativism," as Kenneth L. Woodward wrote in *Newsweek*, meaning that we have "reduced all ideas of right and wrong to matters of personal taste and emotional preference or cultural choice"—different strokes for different folks.[6] Often this is described as a legacy of the 1960s—that notoriously permissive, anti-authoritarian decade commonly blamed by conservatives for the moral disarmament of America's children (and a consequent rise in violent crime). Vehement public dislike of Bill and Hillary Clinton partly reflected their dubious status as symbols of the 1960s. Despite the moralistic speeches he made in church, despite her calls for a politics of meaning, they were unable to assume the roles of moral exemplars, partly because of his reputation for womanizing but also because of their association with '60s liberalism. (Clinton's reputation for indecisiveness and his penchant for compromise were reminders of the moral "softness" popularly linked to the 1960s.) The president was unable to provide moral leadership, then prospective House Speaker Newt Gingrich charged the day after the 1994 election, because he was a counterculture McGovernik.

In fact, the counterculture and the movement to elect George McGovern president in 1972 were quite moralistic. The 1960s were in part a decade of moral absolutism, which was partly why it was a decade of political protests. The student movement was infused with a Manichean world view and an unassailable belief in the evils of the Vietnam War, the military industrial complex in general, and, to a lesser extent, a free market economy. Put more positively, it was a movement infused with a passion for peace, and for racial and social justice—absolute, not relative moral values. In any case, we can hardly call this decade morally relativistic when it included so much self-righteous political violence—the occasional bombing or bank robbery or campus riot aimed at ending the war, the police attack on demonstrators in Chicago during the 1968 Democratic Convention, the killing of student protesters at Kent State. The hedonistic relativism commonly associated with the 1960s—the belief that whatever feels good is good—was limited to the personal sphere, and even there a fair amount of moral dogmatism prevailed: sexual promiscuity was healthier than chastity; marijuana was better than booze. Personal career choices were also apt to be evaluated by a communal moral code: a job with VISTA or the Peace Corps was a social good and a job with the CIA a social evil. There was as much moral dogmatism in the student movement of the 1960s as there is among social issue conservatives today.

The image of America as awash with moral relativism in the 1990s is about as accurate as the popular image of the nonjudgmental 1960s. There are surely strains in the culture of what is commonly derided as the selfism of personal development movements, evident in much of the rhetoric about self-esteem and the popular view that feeling good about yourself is not just a developmental goal but a moral imperative. Yet there is nothing new about the American absorption in self-improvement (it dates back to the beginnings of the republic), and in its various forms self-improvement has appealed to people of various political persuasions. Today, popular therapies tend to be scorned by conservatives, for their "whining" and "victimism," and our focus on personal development, in general, is often blamed on the 1960s and the generation of Baby Boomers raised by Dr. Spock. But, in the 1950s, Norman Vincent Peale was preaching the gospel of self-centered personal development and professional advancement to Republican middle managers (and their wives). *The Power of Positive Thinking*, a landmark bestseller, was a book about how to enhance your self-esteem, your income, and status; it focused on how to improve your own life, not the life of your community.

The moral relativism that follows from self-centeredness has always been present in American culture, right and left, but so has a conflicting tradition of moral dogmatism, which follows from self-righteousness. (And the conflict between individual and universal moral codes is hardly uniquely American.) Some people are content with subjective moral codes; others require the assurance that their own subjective preferences accord with a transcendent, universal truth. Indeed, even people who claim to be moral relativists are likely to harbor suspicions that what is right for them is simply right, and what they believe is simply true. (Although people who consider themselves relativists will probably forbear from imposing their beliefs on others.)

In American history, moral absolutism has been a potent political force. The great nineteenth- and twentieth-century social reform movements have been moral crusades, often imbued with a Christian religiosity. The abolition of slavery, and Prohibition, feminism, and the civil rights movement derived power from the conviction that they were morally compelled, or even divinely ordained. Of course, there were practical interests served by all these movements, and some of their successes can be attributed to an unenlightened self-interest more than a desire to do good. (Around the turn of the century, women's suffrage was advanced, in part, as a way of neutralizing the votes of African American and immigrant men.) Still, on balance, moralism has often been at least as powerful as pragmatism in effecting America's landmark social reforms.

A preoccupation with virtue is also part of our history. Like the romance with self-improvement, it's as American as Ben Franklin, who advocated virtues such as punctuality and frugality—virtues that would make people economically productive. There was a natural concern with republican virtues when the country was founded, and today, democratic theorists focus as well on the classic civic virtues—the willingness to subordinate private interests to the public good and to participate actively in community life and the formulation of political priorities. This means, in everyday terms, that coaching Little League and attending town meetings are virtuous uses of leisure time; networking on the golf course of an exclusive country club or spending weekends at the spa with your support group are virtueless.

For at least two decades, according to many virtue theorists, Americans have spent too much time with their golf clubs and therapists pursuing wealth, physical fitness, and emotional fulfillment. In part, liberal virtue talk is a critique of consumerism (which is particularly destructive to lower-income people who can least afford it). Consumerism represents self-interest in one of its least productive and most insatiable forms. Conservative virtue talk focuses more on moral relativism and the self-centered "feel good," "different strokes" ethos associated with the 1960s.

What unites virtue theorists, both liberal and conservative, is a concern about character, which is what distinguishes them from traditional moral reformers. Historic political reform movements have often focused on questions of justice and principle, Nancy Rosenblum observes; they would make the world a better place by elevating its underlying principles. (Civil rights activists, for example, targeted America's failure to practice the principles of equality it preached; they sought to change the rules of the game more than the hearts of the players.) Virtue theorists focus on questions of character. They're not moral reformers; they're character reformers. They ask, "How do we make people good?"

Answers to this question are as diverse and as vague as you might expect (virtue talk can be platitudinous), but nearly everyone agrees that idleness is a vice; it corrodes character—which is one reason welfare recipients are regarded with particular horror. Less horror but some disdain is sometimes directed toward rich idlers—coupon clippers who don't even engage in charity work. Nor are middle-class idlers spared (though their numbers have dwindled). Yuppies were ridiculed for spending too much of their leisure time and disposable income on satisfying themselves instead of serving their communities.

Historically, character reformers have generally extolled the virtues of an ideal middle class—a strong work ethic, and a spirit of voluntarism, honesty, godliness, loyalty, and perseverance—and, perhaps most of all, moderation.[7] Taken to extremes, even virtues can be socially disruptive: religious belief becomes religious fanaticism, which threatens the established churches with cults. The work ethic becomes "workaholism" which threatens family life, not to mention the vacation industry.

Practically all virtue theorists agree, as well, that the effort to inculcate virtue and build character must start early on, in childhood. "For most social problems that deeply trouble us," James Q. Wilson wrote in 1985, "the need is to explore, carefully and experimentally, ways of strengthening the formation of character among the very young."[8] As a society, we have given up most hope of redeeming bad characters in adulthood (and we know relatively little about the moral development of adults; developmental psychologists have traditionally focused on children.) As a society we have decided that a large proportion of criminal offenders are unredeemable and ought to be imprisoned forever, if not killed. Today the rise in violent juvenile crime has fostered the belief that the worst characters may be unredeemable by an early age, fifteen, sixteen, or in some cases even younger. We give up on people early these days. The question "How do we make good people?" becomes "How do we make good preschool and grade school children?"

By restoring the family, virtue theorists on all sides assert. They single out the family as the most important incubator of good character. They look next to the usual institutions—schools and churches, paying less attention to voluntary associations, which have long played a role in character building, (think of the Boy Scouts).[9] Conservatives, especially social issue conservatives, are more likely to dictate the proper form for virtuous institutions and the ideas the institutions should espouse. A nagging concern for pluralism makes liberals more tentative architects of virtue. They shy away from coercive methods of promoting virtue (such as nominally voluntary school prayers, which many young children would feel pressured to recite). Because diversity is a primary liberal value, William Galston has observed, tolerance is a liberal virtue—one that is often wrongly equated with moral relativism. "Tolerance is fully compatible with the proposition that some ways of life can be known to be superior to others," Galston notes. "It rests on the conviction that the pursuit of the better course should be . . . the consequence of education to persuasion rather than coercion."[10]

But whether liberal or conservative, government is in the business of coercion, either imposing punishment for proscribed behavior through criminal laws or providing incentives for preferred behavior, through tax laws, domestic relations laws, or laws governing health care plans that deny benefits to homosexual partners and offer them to married heterosexuals. Welfare policies arouse great wrath precisely because they're said to provide incentives for behavior that many believe ought to be proscribed or at least actively discouraged—idleness and out-of-wedlock childbearing. (Although, as Christopher Jencks has pointed out, the belief that welfare causes out-of-wedlock births is generally unsupported by the evidence.)[11]

Two married parents are better at promoting virtue than any single one, virtue theorists on all sides agree, or, as a celebrated 1993 article in the *Atlantic Monthly* put it, "Dan

Quayle Was Right."[12] (According to the polls, the general public has also singled out family breakdown as a primary cause of crime.) Relatively liberal virtue theorists sometimes abandon their commitment to pluralism when the family is at stake, asserting, however reluctantly, that traditional families provide healthier, more virtuous environments for children. Communitarians tend to favor coercive policies aimed at restoring the nuclear family, such as limiting or even prohibiting divorce in families with minor children and restricting abortion rights, with spousal consent and parental notification requirements.

The effect of divorce on children is not nearly as clear as the Dan Quayle Is Right chorus claims. Children living in conflict may fare worse than children living with divorce.[13] But there is persuasive evidence that children raised by single parents (who tend to be women) are at a relative disadvantage, Sara McLanahan points out in the *American Prospect*. They're more at risk of dropping out of school, remaining unemployed, and becoming single parents themselves in adolescence.[14] What does this prove? The debate about single parenthood is a bit like the debate about media violence. You can show a correlation between single parent families and various social pathologies just as you can show a correlation between media violence and aggressive behavior; but you can't prove causation. Single parenthood itself may correlate to other problems that disadvantage children—unemployment, for example. At this point, the debate becomes driven almost purely by ideology, not statistics. Critics right and center who instinctively favor the nuclear family will infer causation from the correlations between single parent families and, say, the high school drop-out rate. Critics on the left who favor alternative family structures will not.

Even so, few people dispute that children with two parents in a relatively peaceful, not unhappy home are better off than children with one parent (the parents are surely better off as well). Few people would dispute that children suffer from familial disruption. The debate about the deleterious effects of single motherhood is, in some ways, secondary to the debate about its causes. Centrists and critics on the right blame welfare for the rise of lower-income female-headed families and a host of attendant pathologies; they blame feminism, especially careerism for women, for the smaller rise in middle- and upper-income female-headed families. On the left, defenders of welfare and feminism blame unemployment and the decline in jobs paying liveable wages. They seem, however, a small minority. Moral explanations—for crime or single motherhood—are much more in vogue than economic analyses, partly because morality is easier to understand than economics and because traditional family life, like religion, has always been deemed essential to moral development; its decline feels like a moral lapse.

It's no coincidence that nostalgia for the traditional family followed a fierce assault on pervasive familial dysfunctions. (Under siege, the family always finds defenders.) Reinforcing a longstanding feminist critique of traditional family life, popular therapies have demonized the family (96 percent of all American families are dysfunctional, according to recovery experts, meaning that they're rife with addiction and abuse).

For better and worse, an indeterminate number of Americans who read self-help books and watch TV have recently gone on the alert for the ravages of family life. Some instances of incest were discovered; others were invented. We'll never know the ratio of true to false claims of abuse, because the truth in these cases can be hard to discern, particularly when they involve allegedly recovered memories. Again, ideology prevails. People who mistrust the family as an institution are more likely to believe claims of abuse; people who mourn the passing of the traditional family are more likely to question them.

Apart from generating a highly charged debate about the incidence of incest, the focus on familial dysfunction raised public awareness of the damage done to children by early neglect and abuse. While that contributed to disenchantment with traditional family life, it also focused discussion of social ills on problems of individual character development—which animated the politics of virtue.

Terms like "virtue" and "vice" are not part of the therapeutic vocabulary, but they are mirrored in concepts of health and disease. To the extent that popular therapies strive to make us healthy (one by one) they strive to make us virtuous. Personal development experts rarely offer social or political explanations for social and political problems; they're apt to blame everything—from global pollution to white-collar crime to violence—on individual dysfunctions spawned by bad parenting. Virtue theorists, in general, are not as simpleminded as mass market self-help authors, and they promote different values (inhibition instead of untrammeled self-expression), but they do share this preoccupation with individual character and the concern about good parenting, along with a tendency to diagnose public problems as cumulative failures of character. They rely on moralistic instead of therapeutic rhetoric, and virtue theorists, particularly on the right, generally disparage popular psychology as narcissistic; but they owe it much.

◆ | What separates character reformers, like William Bennett, from personal development experts, like John Bradshaw, most decisively are the values they preach. Character reformers advocate self-control; it is the primary virtue. Personal development experts pathologize self-control, labeling it a symptom of disease (codependency), which is the therapeutic equivalent of a vice. Personal development experts advocate self-expression, which is why their messages are derided as narcissistic. Virtue theorists in general, conservative and liberal, lament the elevation of self-expression over self-control, blaming it, in part, for violent crime, although conservatives do so with particular enthusiasm, associating it with liberalism and the ethos of individual rights.

The "machinery of society" has broken down because of the exaltation of individuality that took hold in the 1960s, John Howard declared in 1991. Referring to his experience serving on a Presidential Task Force on Higher Education, in 1969, Howard attacked "the me-generation and the do your own thing mind set" of the counterculture. "The new pattern of ideas" that emerged in the 1960s and haunts us still, he explained, "insists upon the right of each person to live according to self-determined goals and rules. It acknowledges only one small category of virtue, variously described as tolerance, non-judgmentalism, inclusiveness, diversity, and pluralism . . . it is forbidden to forbid . . . anything goes." As a result, Howard asserted, "the courts, the families, the schools, the government, the businesses are having more and more trouble performing their functions successfully, as an increasing number of their participants are bent on pursuing their own ends, unrestrained by a sense of obligation to the common well-being."[15]

This jeremiad against self-interest unrestrained by a "sense of obligation" to the public good might apply to cigarette manufacturers, any number of investment bankers, and white-collar criminals, as well as violent offenders and a few aging hippies. But never mind. Howard's speech is a classic right-wing caricature of the counterculture, which captures some of the concerns expressed less simplistically by leading virtue theorists today. James Q. Wilson offered a related critique of individualism in the 1975 classic, *Thinking About Crime.*

Wilson acknowledged that self-expression is not simply a vice: "It can lead to creativity and innovation that entail substantial personal sacrifices." Still, he argued, in American culture, the ethos of self-expression was linked to an elevation of rights over duties. "A commitment to rights implies a preference for spontaneity over loyalty, conscience over honor, tolerance over conformity, self-expression over self-restraint." (If you have to stop and think about why honor is preferable to conscience and conformity preferable to tolerance, you're probably doomed to individualism.) Wilson also lamented the decline of Victorian morality, which placed the highest value on self-control (the transcendent goal of the temperance and social purity movements) and on "the management of social relations on the basis of mutual restraint."[16]

This familiar attack on individualism for promoting intemperate self-centeredness that threatens the social order and promotes the permissiveness that makes crime pay is offered in diluted form by communitarians when they stress the need to balance rights with responsibilities and to locate individuals in their community. As one communitarian platform statement declares, "American men, women, and children are members of many communities—families, neighborhoods; innumerable social, religious, ethnic, work place, and professional associations; and the body politic itself. . . . The exclusive pursuit of private interests erodes the network of social environments on which we all depend, and is destructive to our shared experiment in democratic self-government."[17]

Statements like this are hard to dispute (not even a radical individualist member of the ACLU, like me, would deny that social relations matter and that people should be nice to each other). That's the trouble with the usual critique of the liberal attachment to rights. It misconstrues the liberal attitude toward community. Civil libertarianism protects self-expression and yet requires self-control. The corollary to asserting your own rights is respecting the rights of others. That much should be clear whenever First Amendment devotees defend whatever they consider loathsome speech. Tolerance itself is not self-indulgence but the self-restraint not to impose your beliefs on others, as political theorist Judith Shklar pointed out: "Far from being an amoral free for all, liberalism is, in fact, extremely difficult and constraining. . . . The refusal to use public coercion to impose creedal unanimity and uniform standards of behavior demands an enormous degree of self-control." Tolerance is an alternative to cruelty, Shklar suggested, describing the birth of liberalism as a reaction to the "cruelties of the religious civil wars."[18] Tolerance, then, rests partly on the cultivation of empathy, which is surely essential to community and the cessation of violence. Without the liberal values of tolerance, respect for diverse individuals, communities devolve into lynch mobs, or tribes, and sometimes engage in civil war. Without tolerance, a sense of community is not such a wonderful thing.

Of course, liberalism values self-expression, but it values self-expression mitigated by tolerance, civility, and some concern for social order. (It tells you that if you have the urge to yell fire in a crowded subway station you should probably repress it.) The tendency of character reformers to associate liberalism with the vice of self-expression (and crime) while associating conservatism with the virtue of self-control (and punishment) is misleading and much too simplistic.

Liberals tend to value self-expression to the extent that they value political dissent and individual privacy and autonomy, particularly with regard to matters such as religious belief, reproductive behavior, and sexual orientation. But they tend to demand self-control in the commercial sphere—advocating restrictions on the liberty of employers to discriminate against their workers or pay them less than living wages and restrictions on the liberty of producers to price-gouge. Liberals who advocate government control of the market, through antitrust laws, consumer protection agencies, and civil rights laws can't simply be characterized as individualistic, particularly by conservatives who favor free markets.

Conservatives tend to focus on the need for self-control in social and sexual relations, favoring at least some restrictions on sexual and reproductive behavior and adherence to a presumptively universal Judeo-Christian code (nowadays, some might refer to a Judeo-Christian-Muslim code). Others unabashedly call for a sectarian Christian state. At the same time, they defend untempered self-expression in the commercial sphere, for employers and producers. They tend to oppose government restrictions on employment or pricing practices or sales to the Third World of dangerous products, like pesticides, banned in the United States. In the marketplace, conservatives value the liberty of employers and producers over their social obligations. Or, they eschew the concept of social obligations, preferring to focus on good works that people are encouraged to perform voluntarily. Conservatives prefer a noncoercive approach to social responsibilities in the public sphere, just as liberals prefer a noncoercive approach to the cultivation of private virtue.

It's worth noting that the moralism that dominates so many of our policy debates about social issues plays a minimal role in debates about business policy. People who protest the activities of American companies abroad, for example, seem like a minority of bleeding hearts. Occasionally morality intrudes: cigarette companies are subject to some moral disapprobation, but the debate about regulating or not regulating tobacco has focused on the conflict of rights between smokers and nonsmokers, not on the moral obligations of producers. Self-interest in the business world is no vice: either it's praised

as entrepreneurialism or equated with the public good—
"What's good for General Motors is good for the U.S.A."

Moralism also plays an incidental role in foreign policy debates. Moral justifications for war—such as the salvaging of
democracy in Kuwait in 1991—are rarely as effective as pragmatic ones—the salvaging of the oil fields in Kuwait. As the
hesitancy to intervene in Bosnia, Rwanda, or Haiti has
shown, self-interest is considered more of a virtue than a vice
in the conduct of foreign affairs.

     ❧ | Virtue talk is not, then, universally applied,
although it's presented as a search for universal truths. It focuses on a particular set of domestic problems—crime, welfare, and disorder. It is when considering these problems that
self-interest (mainly in the form of self-expression) is considered a primary vice, at least by implication. James Q. Wilson
has defined virtue as "acting with due restraint in one's impulses, due regard for the rights of others, and reasonable
concern for distant consequences."[19]

It is no coincidence that these are precisely the virtues that
criminal offenders often lack. They have little, if any, self-
control and act on their impulses compulsively, without regard for the rights of others, or even the distant consequences
to themselves. Wilson's emblematic definition of virtue
blames crime, in part, on vice, or in other words, on bad
character.

For virtue theorists, character is fate, although fate, in the
form of genetics at least, doesn't necessarily determine character. Virtue theory is not deterministic; it attributes bad character not to biological but social pathologies, as did reformers in
Jacksonian America. Virtue theorists share some of the essential optimism of mid-nineteenth-century reformers—a belief in
the efficacy of human endeavors, the sense that many people

are not born to be bad and can be made to be good. But the optimism of virtue theorists is tempered by historic failures of the prison system. While Jacksonian reformers hoped to rehabilitate offenders, virtue theorists focus almost exclusively on instilling virtues in children. They're less interested in rehabilitating bad characters than in fashioning good ones, which makes them receptive to harsh sentencing laws for adult offenders and juveniles presumed incorrigible. For all their talk about character, they may support three strikes you're out laws and other mandatory minimum sentences that preclude judges from even thinking about the characters of the offenders before them. Mandatory minimum sentences simply assume the unredeemably bad characters of offenders, reflecting public impatience with those who claim to be victims of circumstance. Virtue talk is easily reconciled with this demand for toughness on crime; by focusing on children, it seeks the preservation of the innocent, not the salvaging of the guilty.

It also implies that government has a limited role to play in crime prevention. The premise that character is mutable, malleable in early childhood, makes crime prevention an essentially private matter, because the family is seen as the primary arena for character building. Liberals and conservatives often disagree about precisely how the government should support character-building institutions—schools, churches, and families. (Conservatives want more support for churches and less for public schools.) But they tend to agree that government plays only a supporting role, particularly with regard to family life. Government has an attenuated, indirect relationship to character reformation. It encourages the formation of what are regarded as virtuous families (traditional two-parent families) and discourages "virtue-less" families (single female or homosexual parenting). This implies that crime prevention is more a matter of formulating virtuous welfare and tax policies and domestic relations laws than funding after-school programs for troubled teens. Liberals are still likely to favor direct government intervention when families break down (the debate about midnight basketball was partly a debate about the government's role in raising children who lack stable families); but the logic of virtue talk implies that punishment, not prevention, is the primary business of government.

In an ideal world, however, punishment would only be needed to catch the minority of people who fall from virtue, to spirit them away from the rest of us. The goal of character reformers is to imbue children with the internal controls that will make the external control of criminal law redundant. In a democratic society, after all, laws are only effective if they reflect a general consensus about moral and ethical behavior. Virtue talk is, in part, a reaction to the breakdown of consensus over the evils of what were once commonly acknowledged vices—single motherhood and drug use, in particular. As Democratic Senator Daniel Moynihan asserted in a frequently cited article, we have normalized these behaviors; we've "defined deviancy down."[20] Virtue talk is, in part, an attempt to resurrect traditional standards of behavior and define deviancy back up.

Reasonable people may disagree about whether the increase in single motherhood, particularly among adolescents, is purely pathological or reflects a loss of virtue. (In my own view, it often reflects poor judgment; it is rarely in the best interests of mother or child or the community at large; but I have a hard time calling childbearing immoral.) There is less disagreement about the "scourge" of drug abuse, even among people who oppose the war on drugs. (Arguments in favor of legalization don't generally involve the endorsement of drug use but a belief that legalization would cause less violent crime and disease than prohibition.) There is little disagreement about the horrors of violence—although people often find personal and political justifications for particular violent acts.

But consensus about the immorality of drug use or even violence sometimes seems more rhetorical than real, considering how much both violence and drug use have been normalized (that was, in part, Senator Moynihan's point). If the great majority of Americans profess sincere dismay about violence, they are learning to live with it; senseless murder has come to seem horribly routine when it was once extraordinary.

In the 1920s, Clarence Darrow successfully argued that Leopold and Loeb were clearly insane because they killed with no motive or apparent emotion. In his plea for mercy (life imprisonment over death), Darrow dwelled on the senselessness of their crime (the murder of an eight-year-old boy) and the randomness with which their victim was chosen:

> Without any excuse, without the slightest motive, not moved by money, not moved by passion or hatred, by nothing except the vague wanderings of children, they rented a car and about 4 o'clock in the afternoon started to find somebody to kill. For nothing. . . . They picked up a little boy right in sight of their own homes, and surrounded by their neighbors. . . . They hit him over the head with a chisel and go about their business. . . . They stop at the forks of the road and leave little Bobby Franks soaked with blood, in the machine, and get their dinner, and eat it without an emotion or qualm.[21]

In Darrow's day, one could argue that "there is not a sane thing in all of this from the beginning to the end." Today, senseless, random crimes committed by emotionally numbed young men, "for nothing," seem all too normal. Darrow wouldn't have had a prayer.

How do we resurrect a common morality that will make cases like this extraordinary once again and ensure that most people obey criminal laws instinctively? That is the formidable task chosen by virtue theorists. Sometimes it seems we don't even have enough consensus on the desirability or feasibility of a common moral code, or on the virtue of virtue. Among some self-proclaimed radical academics, it has become conventional wisdom that there are no objective realities or truths; there are only subjective perceptions. Virtue theorists are susceptible to the charge that they are "privileging" their own moral biases. Some advocates of multiculturalism will agree that virtue theory is a kind of cultural imperialism that represents the preferences of a mostly white, male ruling class.

Nor do we have strong consensus on the nature of virtue. If virtue theorists right and center associate it with education and hard work, others, on the left and in the personal development culture, posit virtue as a matter of circumstance, or history: virtue accrues naturally to people who have been oppressed—by their families or society at large—just as vice accrues naturally to their oppressors. A sense of virtue or righteousness is one of the perquisites of victimhood, and to the extent that victimhood is a matter of perspective, so is virtue.

The denigration of objectivity and universal truth does promote a kind of moral relativism on the left, but it's coupled paradoxically with a strong, universalized moral code: racism, sexism, and homophobia are evils, which pervade society, which government, business, and academic institutions have an obligation to eradicate (even at the expense of free speech). Any movement known for its orthodoxies and intolerance for the politically incorrect is not exactly relativistic.

Leftist academics and advocates of multiculturalism are essentially moral reformers, unlike the character reformers engaged in virtue talk. Instead of focusing on virtue and questions of individual character, they focus on moral principles—notably racial and sexual equality—and questions of justice.

Putting aside some of the silliness associated with their political orthodoxies (what orthodoxies aren't occasionally silly?), left-wing reformers offer a valuable perspective on violence and disorder: it is rooted, in part, in a sense of injustice. Whether or not you believe that the claims of injustice are true, you have to acknowledge their power to affect both character and behavior. Experiencing injustice, or perceiving themselves the victims of it, can make people empathetic, arousing compassion and a sense of identity with other victims, or it can make them cruel. (The occasional competition between blacks and Jews over the respective horrors of slavery and the Holocaust testify to the mean self-absorption that extreme suffering, even when experienced vicariously, can create.)

Sometimes when people feel themselves to be the victims of injustice, instead of feeling guilty about their worst behaviors, they feel entitled to them. The acquittal in the first trial of the officers who assaulted Rodney King imbued some residents of Los Angeles with a sense of entitlement to riot, just as the belief that they are under siege because the courts are soft on crime imbues some police officers with a sense of entitlement to beat the people they arrest. We can't fully understand violence unless we understand the pervasive sense of injustice that crosses racial and class lines.

Who are the real victims? Who is to blame? Assigning blame has always been the job of the criminal justice system. It's a particularly daunting one today because there's too much blame to go around. How do we make sense of the constant interchange of accusations and justifications for bad behavior? What's remarkable about much of the violence that plagues us today is not just its apparent senselessness but the righteousness with which people engage in it. To people who feel like they're fighting back, violence doesn't seem so sense-less after all.

Striking out violently against perceived injustice expresses a feeling of helplessness but also assuages it, at least tempo-rarily. The rampant victimism that has drawn so much atten-tion in recent years reflects a loss of faith in our own moral agency, the sense that we're at the mercy of forces we cannot control. Violent behavior is an attempt to reassert control and self-determination, which is why vigilantism, in its various forms, makes people feel so virtuous. Urban rioters, riotous police officers, and citizen avengers generally exhibit much more pride than remorse. Pro-gun advocates take pride in their preparedness, exhorting people to do the right thing by arming themselves.

Crime is "an act of enslavement," Jeffrey Snyder observed in the *Public Interest*. In his view, failure to resist it, even when our wallets and not our lives are threatened, is a kind of vice—an act of cowardice, a defect of character:

> It is impossible to address the problem of rampant crime with-out talking about the moral responsibility of the intended vic-tim. Crime is rampant because the law-abiding, each of us, condone it, excuse it, permit it, submit to it. We permit and encourage it because we do not fight back, immediately, then and there, where it happens. Crime is not rampant because we do not have enough prisons, because judges and prosecutors are too soft, because the police are hamstrung with absurd technicalities. The defect is there, in our character. We are a nation of cowards and shirkers.[22]

The willingness to act violently to protect yourself or your community is a historic American virtue, particularly for men (remember Gary Cooper in *High Noon*). Respect for self-defense is nothing new, but as we become increasingly anx-ious about threats to our safety, dignity, and entitlements, our definition of self-defense expands, and, in the therapeutic culture, it becomes increasingly subjective. How do we distinguish between an actual and imagined injustice in a culture that defines reality as a matter of perception? How do we decide whether a perception of danger is unreasonable when so many people live with fear of crime or a sense of oppression? Nowadays, many jurors are bound to feel sympathy for homeowners, like Louisianian Rodney Peairs, who answer the door with a gun. Sometimes, watching the crime news, and the public response to it, you do feel as if you're watching a Western, in which it's hard to tell violence from virtue.

The association of violence with courage and good character affects our view of public as well as private justice. Capital punishment is sometimes described as a moral obligation, like gun ownership. The willingness to carry out an execution is equated with strength of character (Bill Clinton had to authorize an execution during the 1992 presidential campaign to prove his toughness, not just on crime, but in general). "Many disagreeable duties are the price of maintaining a civil society," John Hanna, an advocate for the death penalty, asserted in testimony before the Massachusetts legislature. "Neglecting those duties is moral cowardice."[23]

This is the notion of virtue, or moral courage, that is generally invoked during wartime. It was invoked as well during the Cold War, to arouse support for the arms race. If people opposed to capital punishment had prevailed historically, Hanna noted in his plea for the death penalty, "we'd be under some Communist command today." Fear of crime has indeed supplanted fear of communists, although, at least, it's not utterly irrational for Americans to fear finding burglars under the bed; unlike fear of Commies, fear of crime is grounded in reality, however exaggerated. Still, there are striking similarities between the war on crime and the war on communism (not the least of which are the benefits derived from both by defense contractors who are now developing law enforcement technologies). In general, Americans are being exhorted to protect themselves against criminals, with guns and home security systems, as they were once exhorted to prepare for nuclear war. The household arsenal of the 1990s, envisioned by the NRA, recalls nothing so much as the fallout shelters of the 1960s. Barricaded, in their basements or behind elaborate security systems, the virtuous American is on guard, a well-defended American.

These are not the virtues extolled by virtue theorists who want increased participation in the body politic, not withdrawal behind locked doors. Nor is this vision of America as a collection of disparate individuals and families, connected only by mistrust, conducive to the formation of community, much less good character. Fear of crime is much more destructive of community than any ethos of individual rights.

◺ | The contradictions in cultural and political response to violent crime are legion. Calls for community are countered by calls for self-reliance. The politics of virtue confronts the policies of fear. A historic belief in the reformative powers of discipline, reflected in the penitentiary movement, conflicts with a belief in the therapeutic power of self-expression, just as authoritarian notions of child rearing, reflected in resurgent demands for corporal punishment, conflict with concern about abuse. On all sides, the rhetoric is moralistic, but how could it be otherwise? Criminal law is supposed to enshrine a moral code, whether based in natural, moral law or a cultural consensus on moral behavior.

The justice system has some of the power and appeal of religion. It doesn't promise to save offenders' souls, but it does address the state of them. Determining guilt or innocence, defining accountability, and imposing punishment, the criminal justice system is supposed to play the role on earth that some believe God plays in heaven.

You may play this role well if you realize that you are only capable of playing it badly. It requires both a willingness to make decisions and an awareness that you will sometimes make mistakes. This is not moral relativism but moral modesty; it assumes the existence of right and wrong but questions our capacity to choose with unerring accuracy between them. At best, the criminal law renders relative justice by the fair balancing of injustices. The harm that defendants have suffered is weighed against the harm they inflict.

This is not a satisfying notion of justice for people who want pragmatic delineations of guilt and innocence to reflect existential divisions between good and evil. Today, in decline, but more in demand than ever, the criminal justice system is beset with expectations that it will restore an uncomplicated moral order and surely resolve the conflicting claims of victimization that rationalize violence. The more confidently we can assign blame, the more control we assert, the less we feel at the mercy of circumstance, or evil. God has given us the responsibility to impose order on the world, to have such faith in our own judgment that we enforce it to the death, some say. (In trying to pass the 1994 crime bill, President Clinton declared that he was doing God's work.) If there is no God, who will save us from such moral certainty?

Virtue theorists extol moderation. Voters tend to favor moderation in elected officials, seeking the middle ground between extremes. Yet, hardly anyone rails against our immoderate, immodest notions of criminal justice. We want it to go to extremes. Feeling helpless and victimized by criminal offenders, we don't want to regard them as helpless and victimized too. How could we? Many of us want the great majority of criminal offenders to be considered independent actors, absolutely, so that we can punish them absolutely, without qualms, in part because we feel ourselves to have been acted upon.

If only guilt and innocence were absolute, instead of merely relative. It's true that all of us have been subject to accidents of upbringing and birth; none of us set our own lives in motion. Yet at some point, it's necessary that we accept responsibility for their direction. At some point, we must treat ourselves and each other as if our crimes were indeed our fault. Defining that point at which innocence is outweighed by guilt is the burden of the criminal law.

Sometimes we have to pass judgment on each other—that is one of the awful necessities of a civilized society. But we ought to judge with modesty and reluctance, knowing that our judgments are flawed. Today, we tend to alternate between judging too harshly—condemning people to life sentences or death, with an arrogant belief in our own righteousness—and not judging at all. Watch the talk shows, attend some support groups, and then spend a few days in the criminal courts, following the disposition of uncelebrated cases. The conflicts and inconsistencies come clear. We lack a nuanced view of moral agency, an ethic of relative accountability to guide us. There's not much virtue in our confusion and precious little justice.

Notes

Chapter 1: Guilty Victims

1. David Margolick, "Lorena Bobbitt Acquitted in Mutilation of Her Husband," *New York Times,* Jan. 22, 1994, A1.

2. Dominick Dunne, "Menendez Justice," *Vanity Fair,* March 1994, 108.

3. Remarks by Hazel Thorton, NAACP Legal Defense Fund Annual Capital Punishment Conference, Warrenton, Virginia, July 22, 1994.

4. "Sanity on Insanity," *Boston Globe,* April 1, 1994, 18.

5. "Denny Assaulter Unaware of King Verdicts," *San Francisco Examiner,* Dec. 8, 1993, A14.

6. Judith Shklar, *The Face of Injustice* (New Haven: Yale University Press, 1990), 1.

7. Ibid., 2.

8. Arthur Weinberg, ed., *Attorney for the Damned: Clarence Darrow in the Courtroom* (Chicago: University of Chicago Press, 1989), 56.

9. Barbara Ehrenreich, "Feminism Confronts Bobbittry," *Time,* Jan. 24, 1994, 74.

10. Margolick, "Lorena Bobbitt Acquitted in Mutilation of Husband."

11. Remarks by Hazel Thorton.

12. Portions of Goetz's videotaped confession were broadcast on *American Justice*, Arts and Entertainment Network, June 29, 1994. For an account of the Goetz case see also George P. Fletcher, "Goetz on Trial," *New York Review of Books*, March 26, 1987.

13. Eric Pooley, "Frontier Justice: Fed-up New Yorkers Are Taking the Law into Their Own Hands," *New York Magazine*, July 23, 1990, 34.

14. Jeffrey R. Snyder, "A Nation of Cowards," *Public Interest*, Fall 1993, 40, 43.

15. Frank Lynn, "Rinfret Seeks Volunteer Band of 'Vigilantes,' " *New York Times*, Oct. 25, 1990, B1.

16. Pooley, "Frontier Justice."

17. Art Harris, "What Price Vengeance? A Louisiana Town Weighs the Issue in Slaying of Accused Kidnaper," *Washington Post*, March 29, 1984.

18. "Louisiana Jury Clears Man Who Shot Japanese Student," *New York Times*, May 24, 1993, A10.

19. Ibid.

Chapter 2: Voyeurism and Vengeance

1. Jennifer Warren, "Judge Says He'll Defy '3 Strikes' Sentencing Law," *Los Angeles Times*, July 22, 1994, A1.

2. Jane Gross, "Simpson Case Galvanizes U.S. about Domestic Violence," *New York Times*, July 4, 1994, A6.

3. Ronald G. Shafer, "Minor Memos," *Wall Street Journal*, July 29, 1994, A1.

4. "The Bundy Carnival," *Newsweek*, Feb. 6, 1989, 66.

5. "Czar Suggested to Bar TV Crime," *New York Times*, Oct. 20, 1954, 40.

6. Matthew Purdy, "1993 Homicides Fewer and More Clustered in New York City," *New York Times*, Jan. 10, 1994, B1.

7. Jose de Cordoba, "Streets Are Murder, But the Tube Is Safe: Colombia Tames TV," *Wall Street Journal*, May 12, 1993, A1.

8. Brandon S. Centerwall, "Television and Violence: The Scale of the Problem and Where to Go from Here," *Journal of the American Medical Association* 267, no. 22 (June 10, 1992), 3060.

9. Sissela Bok, "TV Violence, Children, and the Press: Eight Rationales Inhibiting Public Policy Debates," Discussion Paper, published by the Joan Shorenstein Barone Center, Press, Politics, Public Policy, John F. Kennedy School of Government, Harvard University, April 1994.

10. Opening remarks of Chairman Robert C. Hendrickson at hearings of the Subcommittee to Investigate Juvenile Delinquency of the Committee on the Judiciary, United States Senate, June 5, 1954.

11. Remarks of Clara Logan before the Subcommittee to Investigate Juvenile Delinquency of the Committee on the Judiciary, United States Senate, October 20, 1954.

12. Remarks of James Bennett and Eleanor Maccoby before the Subcommittee to Investigate Juvenile Delinquency of the Committee on the Judiciary, in accordance with S. Res. 62, United States Senate, April 6, 1955.

13. Remarks of Joseph Heffernan before the Subcommittee to Investigate Juvenile Delinquency of the Committee on the Judiciary, United States Senate, October 19, 1955.

14. Remarks of Al Hodge before the Subcommittee to Investigate Juvenile Delinquency of the Committee on the Judiciary, United States Senate, October 19, 1955.

15. Remarks of Joseph Heffernan, October 19, 1955.

16. Marjorie Heins, "Media Violence and Free Speech," Paper presented at the International Conference on Violence in the Media, New York, October 4, 1994.

17. Charles S. Clark, "TV Violence: Will Hollywood Tone It Down—or Face Regulation?" *Congressional Quarterly Researcher,* March 26, 1993, 169.

18. Bok, "TV Violence, Children and the Press: Eight Rationales Inhibiting Public Policy Debates," 13.

19. Clark, "TV Violence: Will Hollywood Tone It Down—or Face Regulation?" 167.

20. Mitchell Stephens, *A History of News: From the Drum to the Satellite* (New York: Viking, 1988), 113.

21. Ibid., 112–17.

22. Louis P. Masur, *Rites of Execution: Capital Punishment and the Transformation of American Culture, 1776–1865* (New York: Oxford University Press, 1989), 114.

23. For histories of the death penalty, see generally, William Bowers, *Legal Homicide: Death as Punishment in America, 1864–1982* (Boston: Northeastern University Press, 1984); Masur, *Rites of Execution*; Michel Foucault, *Discipline and Punish: The Birth of The Prison* (New York: Vintage Books, 1979).

24. Foucault, *Discipline and Punish*.

25. Daniel Gerould, *Guillotine, Its Legend and Lore* (New York: Blast Books, 1992), 133–34.

26. Ibid., 137–38, 140–41.

27. For an excellent analysis of revenge in law and culture, see Susan Jacoby, *Wild Justice: The Evolution of Revenge* (New York: Harper & Row, 1983).

28. Richard A. Posner, *Law and Literature* (Cambridge: Harvard University Press, 1988), 56.

29. Dennis Hevesi, "Slaying of Girl, 7, Attributed to Unpaid $40 Loan," *New York Times*, Nov. 25, 1992, B3.

30. Quoted in Barbara Carton, "Is the Family Crumbling?" *Boston Globe*, Nov. 12, 1992, 59.

31. Sam Dillon, "Pleading for Life, Student Is Slain," *New York Times*, June 8, 1993, A1; Lynda Richardson, "On a Child's Playground, Death Intrudes in a Game," *New York Times*, April 12, 1993, B3; Sam Dillon, "15 Year Old Dies in Attack in School Hall," *New York Times*, Feb. 25, 1993, B1; Raymond Hernandez, "Rivalry Ends in Death of Queens Boy, 14," *New York Times*, July 8, 1993, B3.

32. Lynette Holloway, "Passenger in Car Wounded in a Queens Shooting," *New York Times*, Dec. 27, 1992, B33; Betsy Q. M. Tong, "Peabody Man Stabbed to Death in Traffic Dispute," *Boston Globe*, Dec. 23, 1992, 17.

33. Joan E. Rigdan, "Companies See More Workplace Violence," *Wall Street Journal,* April 12, 1994, B1.

34. Matthew Purdy, "Workplace Murders Provoke Lawsuits and Better Security," *New York Times,* Feb. 14, 1994, A1.

35. Patricia Nealon, "Fears Voiced on Court Security," *Boston Globe,* Feb. 15, 1993, B17, B20.

36. Anne Driscoll, "Casework Increasingly Dangerous," *Boston Globe,* May 22, 1993, A1.

37. Alison Mitchell, "Utility Workers Fear Violence," *New York Times,* Nov. 22, 1992, 41.

38. Sam Howe Verhovek, "In Killing of Repo Man, Law Shields the Killer," *New York Times,* March 8, 1994, A16.

39. Jim Sleeper, "Psycho-killer," *New Republic,* Jan. 10, 1994, 18.

40. Sheldon Hackney, "Southern Violence," in Hugh Davis Graham and Ted Robert Gurr, eds., *Violence in America: Historical and Comparative Perspectives* (Beverly Hills: Sage, 1979), 407.

41. Bertram Wyatt-Brown, *Southern Honor: Ethics and Behavior in the Old South* (New York: Oxford University Press, 1982), 368.

42. Melody Beattie, *Codependent No More* (New York: Harper & Row, 1989), 114–15.

43. "Law in Singapore," *Wall Street Journal,* May 9, 1994, A14.

44. William Safire, "Crime in Singapore," *New York Times,* April 7, 1994, A27.

45. Remarks of State Senator James Jejuga before the Joint Committe on Criminal Justice of the Legislature of the Commonwealth of Massachusetts, July 1, 1994.

Chapter 3: The Right Victims and Victims Rights

1. Weinberg, *Attorney for the Damned,* 36.

2. John Edgar Wideman, *Brothers and Keepers* (New York: Penguin Books, 1984), 72.

3. Juan Cardenas, "The Crime Victim in the Prosecutorial Process," *Harvard Journal of Law and Public Policy* 9, no. 2 (1986), 357–98.

4. *Mapp v. Ohio,* 367 U.S. 643 (1961). *Miranda v. Arizona,* 384 U.S. 486 (1966). *Escobedo v. Illinois,* 378 U.S. 478 (1964).

5. *Gideon v. Wainwright,* 378 U.S. 335 (1963).

6. *Douglas v. California,* 372 U.S. 353 (1963). *Griffen v. Illinois,* 351 U.S. 12 (1955).

7. *Brady v. Maryland,* 373 U.S. 83 (1963).

8. *Duncan v. Louisiana,* 391 U.S. 145 (1968).

9. Elliot Currie, *Confronting Crime: An American Challenge* (New York: Pantheon, 1985), 65–67.

10. James Q. Wilson, "Just Take Away Their Guns," *New York Times,* March 20, 1994, sec. 6, p. 47.

11. Herbert McClosky and Alida Brill, *Dimensions of Tolerance* (New York: Russell Sage Foundation, 1983), 49, 124.

12. Philip Shenon, "Overlooked Question in Singapore Case," *New York Times,* April 17, 1994, A10.

13. Cardenas, "The Crime Victim in the Prosecutorial Process"; Deborah P. Kelly, "Victims' Perceptions of Criminal Justice," *Pepperdine Law Review* 11, no. 15 (1994), 15–22.

14. "Facing Violence Today: Fewer Victims Tomorrow," Resource Book, Massachusetts Annual Victims Rights Week Conference, Boston, April 26, 1994, B5-B7.

15. *Booth v. Maryland,* 482 U.S. 496 (1987).

16. *South Carolina v. Gathers,* 490 U.S. 805 (1989).

17. *Payne v. Tennessee,* 111 S.Ct. 2597 (1991).

18. Joe Sexton, " 'Testilying,' " *New York Times,* May 7, 1994, B1.

19. Conversation with David Kennedy, Cambridge, Massachusetts, June 1994.

Chapter 4: The Death Penalty—How It's Perceived

1. For an account of the Adams case, see Michael L. Radelet, Hugo Adam Bedau, and Constance E. Putnam, *In Spite of Innocence* (Boston: Northeastern University Press, 1992).

2. Statement of Bryan A. Stevenson before the U.S. Senate Committee on the Judiciary, Innocence and the Death Penalty, April 1, 1993.

3. Radelet's and Bedau's research was published in Radelet, Bedau, and Putnam, *In Spite of Innocence.*

4. Steven J. Markman, Assistant Attorney General, "Response to

Bedau," Memo to Attorney General Edwin Meese, Jan. 13, 1986.

5. *When the State Kills . . . The death penalty: a human rights issue* (New York: Amnesty International USA, 1989), 229.

6. *Penry v. Lynaugh,* 492 U.S. 302 (1989).

7. *When the State Kills . . . ,* 229.

8. For a comprehensive account of the Rector case, see Marshall Frady, "Death in Arkansas," *New Yorker,* Feb. 22, 1993, 105.

9. *Ford v. Wainwright,* 477 U.S. 399 (1986).

10. *When the State Kills . . . ,* 229.

11. *Perry v. Louisiana,* National Legal Aid and Defender Association, Washington, D.C., Capital Report, Sept./Oct. 1992, 1; Brief for the Respondent on Writ of Certiorari to the Supreme Court of Louisiana, *Perry v. Louisiana* no. 89–5120, October Term 1989, 32; Brief for the Respondent on Petition for Writ of Certiorari to the Supreme Court of Louisiana, *Perry v. Louisiana* no. 89–5120, October Term 1989, 54.

12. Mike Allen, "Debate Rages on Executing Inmate in Wheelchair," *New York Times,* October 30, 1992, B16.

13. *Stanford v. Kentucky,* 109 S.Ct. 2969 (1989), and *Wilkins v. Missouri* 109 S.Ct. 2969 (1989).

14. *United States of America: The Death Penalty and Juvenile Offenders* (New York: Amnesty International, October 1991), 1–2, 64–68; "Facts About the Death Penalty," the Death Penalty Information Center, Washington, D.C., June 15, 1994, 3.

15. *United States of America: The Death Penalty and Juvenile Offenders,* 1.

16. Neil Vidmar, Phoebe C. Ellsworth, "Research on Attitudes Toward Capital Punishment," in Hugo Adam Bedau, *The Death Penalty in America* (New York: Oxford University Press, 1982), 74.

17. For a critique of the Erlich study, see Hans Zeisel, "The Deterrent Effect of the Death Penalty: Facts v. Faith," in Bedau, *The Death Penalty in America,* 125–32. See also Bowers, *Legal Homicide,* 303–33.

18. Dick Lehr, "Death Penalty Foes Seek a New Debate, See Stronger Case," *Boston Globe,* Jan. 10, 1993, A1.

19. Hugo Adam Bedau, *The Death Penalty in America* (New York: Oxford University Press, 1982), 98–99.

20. Ibid., 74–79.

21. "Facts About the Death Penalty," 4.

22. Testimony of Gov. William F. Weld before the Joint Committee on Criminal Justice, Massachussetts State Legislature, July 1, 1994.

23. Harold Grasmick and Robert Bursik, Jr., Survey of 353 adults in Oklahoma, conducted on behalf of Amnesty International USA, November 1988, 6.

24. William J. Bowers, Margaret Vandiver, and Patricia H. Dugan, "Punishment Priorities and the Preference for Death Penalty Alternatives Among Citizens and Legislators: A New Look at Public Opinion on Capital Punishment," Northeastern University, Jan. 19, 1994, 4.

25. Bedau, *The Death Penalty in America,* 65–80.

26. Ibid., 83–84.

27. E. J. Dionne, Jr., "Poll on Abortion Finds the Nation Is Sharply Divided," *New York Times,* April 26, 1989, sec. 1, p. 1.

28. Daniel Goleman, "Pollsters Enlist Psychologists in Quest for Unbiased Results," *New York Times,* Sept. 7, 1993, C1.

29. *Gregg v. Georgia,* 428 U.S. 153 (1976).

30. Austin Sarat and Neil Vidmar, "Public Opinion, the Death Penalty, and the Eighth Amendment: Testing the Marshall Hypothesis," *Wisconsin Law Review* 171 (1976), 190–94.

31. Bowers, Vandiver, and Dugan, "Punishment Priorities and the Preference for Death Penalty Alternatives Among Citizens and Legislators," 5.

32. Ibid., 4.

33. Ibid., 6.

34. "Sentencing for Life: Americans Embrace Alternatives to the Death Penalty," the Death Penalty Information Center, April 1993, 4.

35. *Gregg v. Georgia,* 428 U.S. 153 (1976).

36. William J. Bowers, "Capital Punishment and Contemporary Values: People's Misgivings and the Court's Misperceptions," *Law and Society Review* 27, no. 1 (1993), 169.

37. Written testimony of Dr. William J. Bowers prepared for Hearings on Capital Punishment of the Joint Committee on Criminal Justice of the Legislature of the Commonwealth of Massachusetts, July 1, 1994.

38. Ibid.

39. Marcia Coyle, Fred Strasser, and Marianne Lavelle, "Fatal Defense: Trial and Error in the Nation's Death Belt," *National Law Journal*, June 11, 1990, 2.

Chapter 5: The Death Penalty—How It's Applied

1. Interview with Arlen Specter, Washington, D.C., Oct. 1993.

2. "Talking Points on Federal Habeas Corpus," National Legal Aid and Defender Association, Washington, D.C., 1989.

3. Statement of John J. Curtin, Jr., and James Liebman on behalf of the American Bar Association, before the Subcommittee on Civic and Constitutional Rights of the House Judiciary Committee; concerning "Fairness and Efficiency in Habeas Corpus Adjudication," July 17, 1991, 14.

4. For a comprehensive history of recent attempts to restrict habeas corpus, see Richard Faust, Tina J. Rubenstein, Larry W. Yackle, "The Great Writ in Action: Empirical Light on the Federal Habeas Corpus Debate," *Review of Law and Social Change* 18 (1990–91), 637.

5. *McCleskey v. Zant,* 1115 S.Ct. 1454 (1991). *Teague v. Lane,* 109 S.Ct. 1060 (1989).

6. Curtin and Liebman, "Fairness and Efficiency in Habeas Corpus Adjudication," 25–26.

7. Faust, Rubenstein, Yackle, "The Great Writ in Action."

8. Interview with Paul McNulty, Washington, D.C., Oct. 1993.

9. Statement of Robert Stearns to the House Judiciary Committee, May 20, 1993.

10. Statement of Rubin Carter to the House Judiciary Committee, May 20, 1993.

11. Interview with Mary Broderick, Washington, D.C., October 1993.

12. Jane Fritsch and Matthew Purdy, "Lawyers for New York Poor: A Program with No Monitor," *New York Times,* June 11, 1990, A1.

13. Coyle, Strasser, and Lavelle, "Fatal Defense," 2.

14. *Strickland v. Washington,* 466 U.S. 668 (1984).

15. Coyle, Strasser, and Lavelle, "Fatal Defense," 14.

16. *Wainwright v. Sykes,* 433 U.S. 72 (1977).

17. Stephen B. Bright, "Death by Lottery: Procedural Bar of Constitutional Claims in Capital Cases Due to Inadequate Representation of Indigent Defendants," *West Virginia Law Review* 92 (1990), 679, 691–92.

18. Curtin and Liebman, "Fairness and Efficiency in Habeas Corpus Adjudication," 30.

19. Interview with Arlen Specter, Oct. 1993.

20. *Herrera v. Collins,* 113 S.Ct. 853 (1993).

21. *Coleman v. Thompson,* 111 S.Ct. 2546 (1991).

22. Linda Greenhouse, "Death Penalty Is Renounced by Blackmun," *New York Times,* Feb. 24, 1994, A1. (Blackmun made these remarks in his dissent in a Texas death penalty case involving murders committed during a robbery, *Collins v. Collins,* no. 93–7054).

23. *Furman v. Georgia,* 408 U.S. 258 (1972).

24. *McGautha v. California,* 481 U.S. 279 (1971).

25. Franklin E. Zimring and Gordon Hawkins, *Capital Punishment and the American Agenda* (Cambridge: Harvard University Press, 1986), 30.

26. William J. Bowers, *Legal Homicide* (Boston: Northeastern University Press, 1984), 59–60, 70, 98–99.

27. *Furman v. Georgia,* 408 U.S. 238, 364 (1972).

28. Dan T. Carter, *Scottsboro: A Tragedy of The American South* (Baton Rouge: Louisiana State University Press, 1979), 105–6, 135.

29. Ibid., 348.

30. Mark Twain, *Roughing It* (New York: New American Library, 1962), 256–57.

31. *Gregg v. Georgia*, 428 U.S. 153 (1976).

32. *Proffit v. Florida*, 428 U.S. 153 (1976).

33. *Jurek v. Texas*, 428 U.S. 262 (1976).

34. *Furman v. Georgia*, 408 U.S. 238, 239 (1972).

35. The 1977 Harris Survey, cited in Bedau, *The Death Penalty in America*, 67, 92.

36. *Gregg v. Georgia*, 428 U.S. 153, 229 (1976).

37. See generally Ronald Dworkin, *Life's Dominion* (New York: Knopf, 1993), 118–40.

38. Remarks made by Senator Edward Kennedy during floor debate on the Racial Justice Act, Congressional Record, May 6, 1994, S5334.

39. William J. Bowers and Glenn L. Pierce, "Racial Discrimination and Criminal Homocide under Post-Furman Capital Statutes," in Bedau, *The Death Penalty in America*, 210.

40. Leigh B. Bienen, "Selecting Cases for Death," paper presented to the Law and Society Association Annual Meeting, Chicago, May 28, 1993.

41. Randall L. Kennedy, "*McCleskey v. Kemp:* Race, Capital Punishment, and the Supreme Court," *Harvard Law Review* 101 (May 1988), 1388.

42. Bowers, *Legal Homicide*, 228–31.

43. *McCleskey v. Kemp*, 481 U.S. 279 (1987).

44. Remarks made by Republican Senator Alphonse D'Amato during debate of the 1994 Omnibus Crime Bill, Congressional Record, May 6, 1994, S5329.

45. *Woodson v. North Carolina*, 428 U.S. 280, 305 (1976).

46. Funded by the National Science Foundation and directed by William Bowers, at Northeastern University, the Capital Jury Project is conducting in-depth post-trial interviews with capital jurors in fourteen states.

47. James Luginbuhl, North Carolina State University, "Discretion in Capital Sentencing: Guided or Misguided?" paper presented to the Law and Society Association Annual Meeting, Chicago, May 30, 1993.

48. Conversation with Marla Sandys, Indiana University, August

1994, and see "The Capital Jury Project in Progress: Kentucky," presented, in part, at the American Society of Criminology Annual Meeting, Phoenix, May 1993.

49. Marla Sandys, Presentation at The Law and Society Association Annual Meeting, Chicago, May 1993.

50. Leigh B. Bienen, "Helping Jurors Out: Post-Verdict De-briefing for Jurors in Emotionally Disturbing Trials," *Indiana Law Journal* 20, no. 1 (1993). And see Daniel Goleman, "For Many Jurors, Trials Begin After The Verdict," *New York Times,* (May 14, 1991), C1.

51. Joseph Hoffmann, paper presented to the Law and Society Association Annual Meeting, Chicago, May 1993.

52. Bienen, "Helping Jurors Out," 10.

53. "Innocence Lost, the Verdict," *Frontline,* July 21, 1993.

54. "Georgia Rejects Clemency for a Killer Who Says He Is Retarded," *New York Times,* March 31, 1994, 19.

55. Theodore Eisenberg and Martin T. Wells, "Deadly Confusion: Juror Instructions in Capital Cases," *Cornell Law Review* 79, no. 1 (Nov. 1993), 12, 14.

56. *Simmons v. South Carolina,* 62 U.S. Law Week 4509, June 17, 1994.

57. "Sentencing for Life," the Death Penalty Information Center, April 1993.

58. Bowers, "Capital Punishment and Contemporary Values: People's Misgivings and the Court's Misperceptions," 169.

59. Joseph Hoffmann, "Themes of Moral Responsibility in the Sentencing Decisions of Capital Jurors," an informal paper prepared for a faculty workshop at the University of Virginia Law School, 1993. Presented at the Law and Society Association Annual Meeting, Chicago, May 1993.

60. Stephen Trombley, *The Execution Protocol: Inside America's Capital Punishment Industry* (New York: Crown Publishers, 1992), 213.

61. Robert Johnson, *Death Work: A Study of the Modern Execution Process* (Pacific Grove, Cal.: Brooks/Cole, 1990), 28.

Chapter 6: The Prosecutor's Perspective

1. Augustine, *The City of God,* translated by Henry Bettenson (London: Penguin Books), 1984, 860–61.

2. Interview with Doug Pullen, Columbus, Georgia, June 1993.

3. Interview with Susan Bolyn, Atlanta, Georgia, June 1993.

4. Coyle, Strasser, and Lavelle, "Fatal Defense."

5. Ibid.

6. Interview with Mike Bowers, Atlanta, Georgia, June 1993.

7. Interview with Harold Clarke, Atlanta, Georgia, June 1993.

8. Interview with Bob Wilson, Atlanta, Georgia, June 1993.

9. Masur, *Rites of Execution,* 41, 93–110.

10. Albert Camus, "Reflections on the Guillotine," in Albert Camus, *Resistance, Rebellion, and Death* (New York: Vintage Books, 1974), 190–91, 225.

11. Walter Berns, *For Capital Punishment: Crime and the Morality of the Death Penalty* (New York: Basic Books, 1979), 6, 162.

12. Ibid., 168.

13. Ibid.

Chapter 7: Knowledge Is Irrelevant—Federal Crime Control

1. Timothy Egan, "A 3-Strikes Law Shows It's Not as Simple as It Seems," *New York Times,* Feb. 14, 1994, A1.

2. Remarks of Chase Riveland, made on the *MacNeil-Lehrer Newshour,* Jan. 26, 1994.

3. Egan, "A 3-Strikes Law Shows It's Not as Simple as It Seems" and "New Sentencing Law Has Unintended Effect," *New York Times,* Dec. 21, 1994, D22.

4. Edward Felsenthal, "Life Terms Aren't Viewed as Big Deterrent," *Wall Street Journal,* Nov. 11, 1993, B12.

5. Howell Raines, "Reagan Proposes Revision of Laws to Combat Crime," *New York Times,* Sept. 29, 1981, A1.

6. Excerpt of statements on crime and violence made to the Committee on Resolutions, Republican National Convention, as reprinted in the *New York Times,* Aug. 1, 1968, A1.

7. David Rothman, *The Discovery of the Asylum: Social Order and Disorder in the New Republic* (Boston: Little Brown, 1971), 53.

8. Ibid., 101–3.

9. Ibid.

10. Stephen Jay Gould, *The Mismeasure of Man* (New York: Norton, 1981), 123–43.

11. Ibid., 135–36.

12. Anthony Flint, "IQ Fight Renewed; New Book Links Genes, Intelligence," *Boston Globe*, Aug. 9, 1994, A1.

13. Edward Felsenthal, "Man's Genes Made Him Kill, His Lawyers Claim," *Wall Street Journal*, Nov. 15, 1994, B1.

14. "Transcripts of Acceptance Speeches by Nixon and Agnew to the G.O.P. Convention," *New York Times*, Aug. 9, 1968, 20.

15. President Lyndon Johnson, Feb. 7, 1968, message to Congress on crime, reported in *Congressional Quarterly Weekly Reporter*, Feb. 9, 1968, 257.

16. "Excerpts from Humphrey Text Dealing with Crime," *New York Times*, Sept. 12, 1968, 36.

17. "Learning to Live with Fear," *Newsweek*, March 24, 1969, 62–63.

18. "Are You Afraid of Crime?" *Life*, Jan. 14, 1972, 28A.

19. "A Plan to Cut Crime," *Life*, June 30, 1972, 51.

20. "If Crime Goes Unchecked—What Big Cities Will Be Like," *US News and World Report*, Dec. 8, 1969, 41.

21. Remarks by Dr. William A. Stanmeyer, Associate Professor of Georgetown Law School, to student body of Hillsdale College, Hillsdale, Michigan, Oct. 26, 1972: "Urban Crime: Its Causes and Control," *Vital Speeches*, Oct. 1972, 183.

22. James Q. Wilson, *Thinking About Crime*, 2nd ed. (New York: Vintage Books, 1985).

23. Excerpts of statements on crime and violence made to the Committee on Resolutions, Republican Party Convention, as reported in the *New York Times*, Aug. 1, 1968, A1.

24. Wilson, *Thinking About Crime*, 47.

25. Ibid.

26. John N. Mitchell, address before the Annual Conference of United Press International Editors and Publishers: "Crime Legislation: What Happened Congress?" *Vital Speeches*, Nov. 1, 1969, 39.

27. Wilson, *Thinking About Crime*, 48.

28. Interview with Orrin Hatch, Washington, D.C., Oct. 1994.

29. Sam Howe Verhovek, "Where President's Pitch on Crime Misses Mark," *New York Times*, Aug. 17, 1994, B6.

30. Adam Clymer, "Crime Bill Clears Hurdle, But Senate Is Going Home Without Acting on Health," *New York Times*, Aug. 26, 1994, A1. And see Gerald F. Seib, "Voters Having Changed Congress, Now Want Congress to Change Washington, Poll Indicates," *Wall Street Journal*, Nov. 11, 1994, A16.

31. Remarks made by Sen. Joseph Biden during floor debate of the Violent Crime Control and Law Enforcement Act of 1993, Nov. 9, 1993, Congressional Record, S15384.

32. Remarks made by Sen. Orrin Hatch during floor debate of the Violent Crime Control and Law Enforcement Act of 1993, Nov. 9, 1993, Congressional Record, S15385.

33. Sen. Joseph Biden, Nov. 9, 1993, Congressional Record, S15384.

34. Interview with William Bratton, Boston, Oct. 1993.

35. Interview with Michael Smith, director of the Vera Institute of Justice, Oct. 1993.

36. Ruth Shalit, "The Kids Are Alright," *New Republic*, July 18 and 25, 1994, 23, 24.

37. Interview with Ronald Hampton, Washington, D.C., Oct. 1993.

38. Herman Goldstein, "The New Policing: Confronting Complexity," Conference on Community Policing, National Institute of Justice, Aug. 24, 1993.

39. Ana Puga, "US House Drops Anti-Crime Bill, Puts off Health," *Boston Globe*, Aug. 12, 1994, A1.

40. Interview with Barney Frank, Newton, Mass., Oct. 1993.

41. Fox Butterfield, "Seeds of Murder Epidemic: Teen-Age Boys with Guns," *New York Times*, Oct. 19, 1992, A8; Isabel Wilkerson, "2 Boys, a Debt, a Victim: The Face of Violence," *New York Times*, May 16, 1994, A1; Celia W. Dugger, "Youthful, Impressionable, and Accused of Murder," *New York Times*, May 17, 1994, A1; George James, "5 Young Robbers Took the Cash, Then Killed Anyway, Police Say," *New York Times*, Jan. 3, 1994, A1; Don Terry, "Killed by Her Friends in an All-White Gang," *New York Times*, May 18, 1994, A1.

42. Rose W. Washington, commissioner, New York City Department of Juvenile Justice, Letter to Senate Judiciary Committee, Dec. 2, 1993.

43. "Special Report to the Congress: Mandatory Minimum Penalties in the Federal Criminal Justice System," United States Sentencing Commission, Aug. 1991, 8–9.

44. Stuart Taylor, Jr., "A Test of Reno's Courage," *Legal Times,* Aug. 9, 1993, S36.

45. Barbara S. Meierhoefer, "The General Effect of Mandatory Minimum Prison Terms," Federal Judicial Center, 1992, 3.

46. Testimony of Kathleen M. Hawk, director of Federal Prisons, Subcommittee on Intellectual Property and Judicial Administration, U.S. House of Representatives, May 12, 1993.

47. Dirk Johnson, "For Drug Offenders, How Tough Is Too Tough?" *New York Times,* Nov. 8, 1993, A16.

48. Interview with Orrin Hatch, Oct. 1993.

49. "The Verdict Is In," *American Bar Association Journal,* Oct. 1993, 78.

50. "Special Report," U.S. Sentencing Commission, 107–8.

51. Don J. DeBenedictis, "How Long Is Too Long?" *American Bar Association Journal,* Oct. 1993, 75.

52. Stephen J. Schulhofer, "Rethinking Mandatory Minimums," *Wake Forest Law Review* 28 (1993), 199, 207.

53. Kate Stith and Steve Y. Koh, "The Politics of Sentencing Reform: The Legislative History of the Federal Sentencing Guidelines," *Wake Forest Law Review* 28 (1993), 222.

54. Dirk Johnson, "A Farmer, 70, Saw No Choice; Nor Did the Sentencing Judge," *New York Times,* July 20, 1994, A1.

55. "The Verdict Is In," 78.

56. "Special Report," U.S. Sentencing Commission, Appendix A.

57. Ibid., 10, 51.

58. Ibid., 61–89.

59. Howard Manley, "Harsh Line Drawn on Crack Cocaine," *Boston Globe,* July 24, 1994, A1; Nkechi Taifa, "Unwarranted Disparity in Sentencing Between 'Crack' and Powder Cocaine," Memorandum, *American Civil Liberties Union,* June 25, 1993.

60. Meierhoefer, "The General Effect of Mandatory Minimums," 20.

61. "Special Report," U.S. Sentencing Commission, 76–82.

62. Interview with Barney Frank. And see "Millions Misspent: What Politicians Don't Say About the High Costs of the Death Penalty," Death Penalty Information Center, Washington, D.C., 1992.

63. Interview with Mark Kleiman, Cambridge, Mass., Oct. 1993.

64. Ibid.

65. Albert J. Reiss, Jr., and Jeffrey A. Roth, eds., *Understanding and Preventing Violence* (Washington, D.C.: National Academy Press, 1993), 6.

66. Ibid., 292–95.

67. Interview with Paul McNulty, Washington, D.C., Oct. 1993.

68. Reiss and Roth, *Understanding and Preventing Violence,* 293.

69. "Reducing Crime in America: A Pragmatic Approach," National Council on Crime and Delinquency, Aug. 1, 1993, 24.

70. Reiss and Roth, *Understanding and Preventing Violence,* 5.

71. Adam Nossiter, "As Boot Camps for Criminals Multiply, Skepticism Grows," *New York Times,* Dec. 18, 1993, A1.

72. Ibid.

73. "Murders Across Nation Rise by 3%, But Overall Violent Crime Is Down," *New York Times,* May 2, 1994, A13; Arlene Levinson, "Public Perception of Soaring Crime Skewed, Experts Say," *Los Angeles Times,* May 29, 1994, A9.

74. Special to the *New York Times,* "Violent Crimes with Pistols Rise 21% in Year," *New York Times,* May 16, 1994, A10.

75. Joseph B. Treaster, "16 Days in California and a Fateful Purchase," *New York Times,* Dec. 9, 1993, B10.

76. Reiss and Roth, *Understanding and Preventing Violence,* 255, 270.

77. Barbara Vobejda, "Homicide Risk Found to Outweigh Benefit of Gun for Home Protection," *Washington Post,* Oct. 7, 1993, A4.

78. Steve Yarosh, "A Place for Safe Housing in the Fourth Amendment," *Responsive Community,* Summer 1994, 29.

79. Ira Glasser, "First, Protect the Tenants," *New York Times,* May 7, 1994, 23.

80. Yarosh, "A Place for Safe Housing in the Fourth Amendment," 39.

81. Ellen Neuborne, "Cashing in on Fear: The NRA Targets Women," *Ms.,* May/June 1994, 46; Sally Chew, "Shotgun Wedding," *Lear's,* Jan. 1994, 30; Joy Horowitz, "Arms and the Woman," *Harper's Bazaar,* Feb. 1994, 166.

82. Osha Gray Davidson, *Under Fire: The NRA and the Battle for Gun Control* (New York: Holt, 1993), 46, 156.

83. Jay Simkin, "The War on Gun Ownership Still Goes On," *Guns & Ammo,* March 1994, 25.

84. Ibid.

85. Jeffrey Snyder, "A Nation of Cowards," *Public Interest,* Fall 1993, 40.

86. David M. Kennedy, "Can We Keep Guns Away from Kids?," *American Prospect,* no. 18 (Summer 1994), 74.

87. Joseph F. Sheley and James D. Wright, "Gun Acquisition and Possession in Selected Juvenile Samples," National Institute of Justice, Washington, D.C., Dec. 1993.

88. David M. Kennedy, "Can We Keep Guns Away from Kids?".

89. Interview with John Silva, Cambridge, Mass., Dec. 1993.

Chapter 8: Virtue Talk

1. Joe Klein, "The Out-of-Wedlock Question," *Newsweek,* Dec. 13, 1993, 37.

2. Interview with Nancy Rosenblum, Boston, Aug. 1994.

3. James Q. Wilson, "The Rediscovery of Character: Private Virtue and Public Policy," *Public Interest,* Fall 1985, 3, 15.

4. Kathleen Kennedy Townsend, "A Rebirth of Virtue: Religion and Liberal Renewal," *Washington Monthly,* Feb. 1989, 36. Reprint of an article that first appeared in 1982.

5. Amitai Etzioni, "The Responsive Communitarian Platform: Rights and Responsibilities," Nov. 1991; Walter Shapiro, "A Whole Greater Than Its Parts?" *Time,* Feb. 25, 1991, 71.

6. Kenneth L. Woodward, "What Is Virtue?" *Newsweek,* June 13, 1994, 38.

7. Interview with Nancy Rosenblum, Aug. 1994.

8. Wilson, "The Rediscovery of Character: Private Virtue and Public Policy," 3, 16.

9. Interview with Nancy Rosenblum, Aug. 1994.

10. William A. Galston, "Liberal Virtues," *American Political Science Review,* Dec. 1988, 1279–89.

11. Christopher Jencks, *Rethinking Social Policy: Race, Poverty, and the Underclass* (Cambridge: Harvard University Press, 1992), 79–85.

12. Barbara DeFoe Whitehead, "Dan Quayle Was Right," *Atlantic Monthly,* April 1993.

13. See generally Judith Stacey, "The New Family Values Crusaders," *Nation,* July 25/Aug. 1, 1994, 119.

14. Sara McLanahan, "The Consequences of Single Motherhood," *American Prospect,* Summer 1994, 48, 49.

15. John Howard, "Making Virtue Respectable Again," *Vital Speeches,* March 1991, 484.

16. Wilson, *Thinking About Crime,* 238.

17. Etzioni, "The Responsive Communitarian Platform: Rights and Responsibilities," 1.

18. Judith Shklar, *Ordinary Vices* (Cambridge: Belknap Press, 1984), 5.

19. Wilson, "The Rediscovery of Virtue: Private Virtue and Public Policy," 3, 15.

20. Daniel Patrick Moynihan, "Defining Deviancy Down," *American Scholar,* Winter 1993, 17–30.

21. Weinberg, *Attorney for the Damned,* 38–41.

22. Snyder, "A Nation of Cowards," 24.

23. Testimony of John Hanna before the Joint Committee on Criminal Justice, Massachusetts State Legislature, July 1, 1994. (John Hanna is the son of George Hanna, whose testimony is cited in Chapter 3.)

Index